AEROMORPHOSIS

AEROMORPHOSIS

A Memoir,
The Evolution of American Aviation

By
Samuel Don Smith

Copyright © 2021 by Samuel Don Smith

Library of Congress Control Number: 2021912772

ISBN: Hardcover 978-1-7377386-0-2
ISBN: Softcover 978-1-7377386-1-9
ISBN: e-book 978-1-7377386-2-6

All rights reserved. No part of this book may be reproduced or transmitted in any form or by any means, electronic or mechanical, including photocopying, recording, or by any information storage and retrieval system, without permission in writing from the copyright owner.

This book was printed in the United States of America.

"Science, freedom, beauty, adventure. What more could you ask of life? Aviation combined all the elements I loved."

Charles Lindbergh

Dedication

The Covid-19 pandemic and the isolation that it imposed on all of us provided me with a perfect opportunity to commit my thoughts on aviation safety to paper. This book is dedicated to the many who have been lost to the disease and to those brave individuals who cared for us during the crisis.

Table Of Contents

1. The Early Days 13
2. Jets! 29
3. Intermediate Training 45
4. Advanced Training 55
5. The 48th Fighter Interceptor Squadron 61
6. Welcome to Keflavik, Iceland 84
7. Make Yourself Useful 91
8. Face-to-Face with Ivan 102
9. Not Today 109
10. The East Wind 117
11. Combat Pike 127
12. Fireball 139
13. Summer Idyll 151
14. William Tell 154
15. The Bottom of Reykjanes Bay 176
16. Test Pilot 181
17. Raggedy-Ass Militia 197
18. Airline New Hire 205
19. Early Retirement 216
20. Rotorhead 226
21. Fluff 229
22. Soaring 236
23. TriStar 244
24. Crash 252
25. Holding Hands in a Hot Tub 261
26. In Command 265
27. A Book Review 283

28. World Record Flight	286
29. Get Out of Jail Free	289
30. Moose	297
31. The Mighty Dog	300
32. Bottom of the Barrel	313
33. ICAO, IFALPA, and HUPER	322
34. Big Dog on the Big Dog	334
35. T-Bird	351
36. 777	361
37. Fido	375
38. MRO	380
39. Jet Set	383
40. Flunt	388
41. ERISA	400
42. AirVenture	403
43. Go Late, Leave Early	406
44. Childhood's End	409
45. The Year 2053	412
Epilogue	415
INDEX	421
Photography Credits	441
Author's Notes	442
A Final Thought	443

Foreword

Don Smith is not a Bob Hoover, but they clearly came from the same bolt of cloth. Both were smitten with a vision of aviation at an early age and an almost fanatical drive to be pillars of their respective professions. From his early years growing up in southwest Texas, coming full circle back to flying light airplanes after retirement, Don brilliantly walks the reader through a half century of American aviation with his unique perspective. Stories of USAF undergraduate pilot training, flying supersonic fighters, operational USAF assignments around the world, and Texas Air National Guard service provide page-turning entertainment. Following that, his candid, sometimes critical, sometimes humorous look into airline flying is riveting. During his most successful career with Delta Airlines, he was also an industry leader in the areas of *Crew Resource Management* and Flight Safety. *Aeromorphosis* is an easy read filled with interesting and revealing examples of an era of spectacular advances in aviation across the board. He is an interesting exception to the perception that fighter pilots have big watches and a small brain. His PhD and literary style dash that notion.

General Eugene Habiger
USAF (Ret.)
Former CINC STRATCOM

1. The Early Days

As a typical airplane-loving kid in the early 1950s, I wanted an excuse to hang out at the airport. The Ground Observer Corps satisfied that need nicely. The Ground Observer Corps, organized in the early 1950s, was intended to supplement the poor radar coverage around our borders. Observations were telephoned to Filter Centers which were then sent to Air Defense Command Ground Control Intercept (GCI) sites. The program was eventually expanded to a cadre of 750,000 volunteers aged seven to eighty-six years old working at over 16,000 posts.

That seven-year-old mentioned above might have been referring to me. My hometown, Uvalde, Texas, was a former WWII training base. As such, it had an abandoned tower from which we would dutifully scan the skies for the approaching Russian bombers. Of course, everything from Piper J-3 cubs to B-36s would be reported to the Filter Center in San Antonio. The completed form pictured below was used to report activity.

I was quite proud of my "wings." Upon sighting an aircraft, I would do exactly as outlined in the form, except our base was Fox Quebec 11 Black. Sightings were frequent. A refueling track passed directly overhead, providing action reporting KC-97s refueling B-47s. T-29 Navigator training aircraft droned overhead daily. My mother never seemed to mind driving me to the airport and back. She probably regarded the whole thing as a great babysitting service.

Aeromorphosis

I once toured the Filter Center which was located at the intersection of Broadway and Hildebrand streets in San Antonio. There was a big glass screen on which an Air Force sergeant plotted all the reported aircraft from the back side of the screen. Numerous consoles operated by officers sported arrays of lights, buttons, and telephone dials. That building was demolished to make way for the USAA building there. USAA later moved to their sprawling fortress on Fredericksburg Road. Little did I know that the elaborate Semi-Automatic Ground Environment (SAGE)* system coming online to replace the Ground Observer Corps would figure prominently in my Air Force career.

*The Semi-Automatic Ground Environment was a system of powerful (at the time) computers that aggregated information from many radar sites and produced a single picture of the entire US airspace. Associated with that process, the direction of ground and air defenses emanated from the system to respond to potential attack.

1. The Early Days

After receiving my driver's license at age fourteen (it was a Texas thing), I returned to the airport as a line service technician (gas boy). Aside from just being around airplanes, I learned quite a bit about the machines and their pilots. Some pilots were nice, and some were condescending cheapskates. Lessons learned there served me well later. That is, be nice to your line service guy; he can make your life miserable in ways that you can never know. That same adage applies to airline captains and their first officers. After I graduated to "student pilot" status, I would work all day and then fly off my earnings in the evening. Wages were low, but aircraft rental was cheap. I remember standing on the ramp looking sad as a local entrepreneur taxied out. He stopped and waved me toward his Bonanza.

"Do you want to go with me to San Antonio for a short trip?"

Yessssss. Pete Knowles had a very successful business in the steel pipe business, and he was a nice guy.

I fell in love with the looks of the F-106. After ordering an official USAF photo of it, I placed the framed photo above my bed for the years I attended high school. That photo pictured below, wrinkled from being folded in storage, featured F-106 S/N 570241. What are the odds that I would someday fly that very aircraft?

Official USAF photo of the F-106

1. The Early Days

Solo at sixteen, private pilot license at seventeen, commercial pilot license at eighteen, flight instructor at nineteen: I thought I knew something, a very dangerous situation. Body hauls proved to be good money and flying time. Frequently a military veteran would pass in a faraway place and need to be moved to their final resting place. Paying me a couple of hundred bucks (including airplane) to do that proved to be a good deal for everyone. That and flight instruction was the only pay to be had. Surprisingly to me at the time, no one wanted to hire a 300-hour commercial pilot to do anything important.

To move a body, I removed the right and rear seats from a Piper PA-28-180 Cherokee and flew to the pickup point. It seemed as though the same person always delivered the body to the airport. He would drive up to my airplane in a big black hearse and step out wearing the same black suit with tie. He would stand there with his hands together in front of him and say, "We have done a really nice job of preparing Mr. _____. You don't want to put him in a bag, do you? That would ruin everything."

It happened exactly that way nearly every time. I would always allow them to place the body next to me, uncovered. On the delivery flight, I would frequently have conversations with them. I never received a single complaint. They were some of the best passengers I ever had.

There is an apocryphal story about a fellow body haul pilot who experienced an engine failure and subsequent emergency landing in a field. When the authorities arrived, they accused him of having a fatal accident.

During the summer before my senior year of high school, four of us airport kids started an airplane refurbish project. We pooled $400 borrowed money and purchased a neglected Piper J-4, N26196. Chester Nielsen, the local airport operator, and I put a new propeller in the back of a Cessna 172 and flew to Foster Field near San Antonio. He put that prop on the J-4 and flew that wreck back to Uvalde. Gutsy move. Soon there were only two of us working on the project under Chester's supervision. We stripped the fabric, sanded and painted the structure, recovered with new fabric, and ran out of money. To fly, we needed to accept the fact that the engine was poor. It only had one really good cylinder. To start it, we would turn the prop through until we felt a little resistance (the good cylinder), and give the prop a whirl. Takeoffs were long and exciting with little power to be had. It was certified as airworthy, and I flew locally for thirty-seven hours in it.

Stripping Fabric from J-4.

1. The Early Days

Down to the Metal

Original J-4 Spec Sheet

I had quite a few valuable "learning experiences" during that period: there is a time when one must assume control of the airplane, no matter how humiliating it may be to the student or copilot. I learned the sinking feeling that comes when one may not have enough fuel to get to a place to land. I realized that flying can be fun, although sometimes solitary and occasionally terrifying. The joy always exceeds the pain.

A popular practice among non-instrument-rated pilots, which continued until very recently, was scud-running. This usually happened on a cloudy day with low ceilings. One usually chose to conduct such flights by continuing toward the destination when confronted with decreasing cloud heights and visibility. Aborting the flight and returning to the takeoff point is usually the preferred choice, but youth, inexperience, and arrogance prompts one to continue. The few radio towers were avoided visually, and box canyons did not exist in the flatlands. This practice has become rare today due to the spate of cell phone towers and the tracking ability of the air traffic control system (more on that subject in later chapters).

At Texas A&M University, I became a member of the Flying Kadets. That organization had a budget from the student council which allowed us to compete at the National Intercollegiate Flying Association (NIFA) meets. We would overload two Cessna 172s and fly off to places such as Carbondale, Illinois; Boulder, Colorado; Athens, Ohio; and Lafayette, Indiana. At the meets, we competed in various flying contests, but never won any of them. Surprisingly, we survived with no incidents or accidents. Close, but none to record. I learned about flying at high density-altitude in an underpowered, overloaded airplane on one of those trips to Colorado. The lesson: when you are in a downdraft and full power will not keep you from sinking, the downdraft will go horizontal close to the ground and you will probably not crash. On that same trip, I flew from Boulder

1. The Early Days

to Denver Stapleton to load up for the trip home. After waiting for most of an hour for airliners to take off, an ominous cloud appeared and light rain began. The tower advised that at a nearby airport the rain was heavy and the wind was gusting to 70 knots.

"What are your intentions?" he asked.

Tough call: taxiing back to the chocks and getting hit by such a gust would surely flip the airplane. If I took off, I might be overtaken by the front. With heavy rain beginning, I took off and quickly turned south away from the advancing weather. Denver soon was reporting large hail, wind gusts, and low ceilings.

On another occasion, I delivered an airplane to Houston from College Station without checking the weather. An hour after takeoff found me groping through low visibility in a high-traffic area. Those experiences suggested truth to the old adage, "To survive, one must gain experience faster that he uses up his luck."

In the summer before my sophomore year at A&M, a local mega farmer, the late Howard Collins, invited me to accompany him to his farm in Mexico. I met him at a crop duster landing strip in Batesville, TX, and helped him load his Mooney Super 21. We filled it completely, leaving no space unoccupied. Inside, we carried some fairly heavy tractor parts. Thus loaded, we assumed that the aircraft was at its maximum gross weight! We cleared the wire at the departure end of the runway by inches. Lesson learned: a real weight and balance calculation is not just for sissies.

Landing in Brownsville, we cleared customs and performed another strange operation: we unloaded the tractor parts. This was my first clue that this trip was going to be exciting. After takeoff, we landed after a short trip to Matamoros. The customs agent there demanded that we unload all the contents of the aircraft, food, camping gear, clothes. Fifty dollars persuaded him otherwise. Happily on our way, Howard asked me to circle (at low altitude) back to Brownsville, where we landed and reloaded the tractor parts. Taking off to the north, we let down and circled back to the south for the remainder of the trip.

"Did you know that the Mexicans want one hundred percent tax on tractor parts? That's not fair. I'm opening up undeveloped land, and that does them good," explained Howard. OK, I'm a smuggler, but the statute of limitations must have run out.

The next leg was down the east coast to Tampico. The beautiful scenery relaxed me after the stress of becoming a smuggler. At Tampico, I contacted the tower (in English), trying my best to sound professional.

"Tampico tower, this is Mooney N1304W, five miles north, landing."

"Roger Mooney, land on any damn runway you like."

That was a surprise. They were very casual about aviation in Mexico in those days.

After refueling and lunch, we took off for Howard's farm, near Monte. Due to the frequent rains, the landing strip was "a little soft," as reported by Howard's manager on the ground. When I landed, it was more like a "splat." We quickly came to a stop, sinking in the mud up to the landing gear doors. No worries, though, we were planning to stay for a week anyway. I made my bed under the wing of the airplane that night. The weather was mild, and I was very comfortable—until sometime in the night, I heard an extremely loud

1. The Early Days

(and close) scream. Later, I learned that it was a frequent occurrence, due to many black panthers in the area. I slept in the airplane for the rest of the trip.

On the second night, early in the evening, we were finishing our dinner near a big campfire when the Agrarian Land Reform (Reforma) rode in. Land reform programs in Mexico date from 1910. These believed in the redistribution of little-used agrarian land from the wealthy landowners to the poor, the underlying logic being that fallow land owned by the wealthy would be given to the poor and put to good use.

About a dozen men on horseback rode in, and from their mounts in the flickering firelight announced, "We claim this land for the people of Mexico." It could have been Pancho Villa. They each wore large sombreros, pistols on each hip, crisscrossed bandoliers across their chest, and a rifle saddle gun. It appeared to me that they intended to kill us.

Fortunately, Howard spoke fluent Spanish and became very persuasive.

He argued, "The land was unusable and I am clearing it and bringing it into cultivation. For that, I should be allowed to farm it for a while before returning it to the Reforma."

After a long discourse, they finally moved on. I'll never know if there was any real danger, but it was terrifying.

The runway dried out and we were able to return with little trouble.

During this period, I became friends with an "old guy." Wrather Holmgreen must have been at least sixty. His father had founded

Alamo Iron Works in San Antonio, and in his younger days had been the "genius bad boy." A certifiable mechanical genius, he had designed and built much of the machinery in his father's company. As a retired engineer, he became a very wealthy rancher who loved to fly. When we first met, he owned an Ercoupe. At my urging, he upgraded to a Cessna 182.

"Hey, Don, how about flying out to the ranch and flying with me in the 182?"

I would fly to his ranch, buzz his house, and plan for him to pick me up in his truck. The house was only a short distance from the strip, and of all the times I did this, he was always waiting for me when I shut down the engine. We would then ride to his house and drink coffee with him and his wife, Wilba, before flying. The house was originally built in the 1850s. Wilba had dozens of pet deer, quail, and turkey that she would feed for our amusement.

At times he hangared his airplane in Uvalde and would ask me to bring it to the ranch for a little flying. On one such occasion when I was returning to Uvalde in the Ercoupe, a strong crosswind prevailed. Fred Weick created the Ercoupe with the amateur pilot in mind. Although later modified with rudder pedals, this one had only a single brake pedal on the floor. Its manual advised pilots to land it in a crab in such situations, since the wing-low technique is impossible without independent rudder control. As the pilot turns the yoke to one side, the flight controls coordinate the turn with both aileron and rudder. The nosewheel also turned as the yoke was turned. The wing and landing gear are extremely strong, permitting crabbing touchdowns. All went well until a few seconds after touchdown. The airplane began drifting toward the downwind side of the runway. Trying to no avail everything I knew from more conventional aircraft to prevent the impending off-runway

1. The Early Days

excursion, the crash seemed inevitable. At this point, I remembered a much-maligned statement in the manual: "When confronted with (such a situation), release the controls." What did I have to lose? I released the controls and the airplane miraculously snapped straight ahead on the runway! Thanks, Fred.

An endorsement for aircraft spins was required for obtaining a flight-instructor rating. Although I had successfully performed the maneuver solo, an instructor's certification was required. I contacted the local airport manager at the time, Art McKinley, for the checkout.

"Sure, no problem, let's jump in the Super Cub (PA-18) and do it," he said.

With scrawny me in the front seat and 300-pound Art in the rear seat, we taxied out and took off. Experienced readers will see this coming, but not caring about weight and balance at the time, I cheerfully began the maneuver. What a surprise, with the weight so far to the rear of the aircraft, it immediately rolled inverted and began an inverted spin! Not having seen that before, I flailed a bit and finally recovered. Lesson learned: always consider weight and balance. Also, consider wearing brown pants if an exciting flight is in the offing.

My friend, Ernest (E.W.) King, arranged for me to rent an old Piper Apache 150 pursuant to a multi-engine rating. Oscar Vickery, another aspiring pilot, and I alternated flying and observing the other from the rear seat. The PA-23-150 is very underpowered. Legend has it that the purpose of the second engine is to take one to the scene of the crash. Lightweight, it will generate a slight climb on one engine, if the pilot performs correctly. Also critical is maintaining airspeed above VMCA, or critical single-engine control speed, airborne.

Speeds below VMCA on one engine render the aircraft uncontrollable, since the rudder is inadequate to control the asymmetrical thrust from the remaining engine. The most difficult maneuver is climbing out from an engine failure just after takeoff, known as a V1 cut in the airlines. In the Apache, this is especially challenging due to the low power and ineffective rudder.

I still remember the drill: gear up, flaps up, mixture up, prop up, throttle up, identify dead engine, confirm dead engine by reducing the dead engine throttle to idle, dead engine prop feather, dead engine mixture cutoff. I remember coming very close to the hangars at Castroville Airport during this maneuver. Forty years later, it was easy in a B-777 with lots of power, a big rudder, and automatic engine out rudder compensation. After my successful rating flight with an examiner, I flew the Apache from San Antonio to Uvalde with my sweetheart as my first passenger. She must have been favorably impressed; we were married the following year.

I also earned an instrument rating in 1967. The examiner for the check ride was C.R. (Pinky) Nelson. Only after the flight, I learned that his nickname derived from all the pink (failing) slips that he awarded applicants. As a contrast to modern concepts of workload and automation, I remember that flight as being very busy. With no autopilot, I was asked to demonstrate holding at an intersection with a single VOR navigation radio. To do that, one first aligns on the inbound course, then quickly changes frequency and radial to determine if you had arrived at the holding point. If not, go back to the inbound station and course to remain aligned (in the event of a crosswind). Back and forth, back and forth, until arriving at the holding fix, then turn outbound for a minute, turn back, and intercept the inbound radial. In airline parlance, that would be called an unacceptable cognitive workload. In the 1960s, pilots were expected to be able to do all that, plus fight a fire, plus calm the passengers.

1. The Early Days

Measuring up to that expectation proved to be impossible in the long run. More to come on that subject in the chapters on workload, automation, error trapping, and error mitigation.

Later that year, I attended Air Force Summer Camp at Holloman AFB, NM. I recall it to be an attempt to inflict a level of suffering to ROTC cadets similar to that of the Officer Candidate School. As a person who had lived in a rather harsh environment at A&M's ROTC program for three years, it was little challenge. Riding in a jet aircraft proved to be the highlight of the program. Every cadet, pilot candidate or not, got strapped into the rear seat of a T-33 and subjected to high speed, tight turns, and steep climbs. The non-pilot cadets were mostly terrified. Most of the rest experienced nausea and vomiting. When my turn came, a very weary-looking Captain Cochran asked me if I had ever flown an airplane before. My answer in the affirmative seemed to relieve him somewhat. Once airborne, he performed some maneuvers and gave me the stick. I could hardly move it at all! After I struggled a bit, he chuckled and said he was playing a trick on me and would turn the aileron boost back on. With that, I did a creditable job of imitating some of his maneuvers.

I had experienced "Gs," or the force of multiple gravities, before in light airplanes. For those who have never had that experience, it can cause some discomfort. If you think that it might be fun to zoom and roll like Maverick and Goose in *Top Gun*, you are correct. However, the price to pay is the suffering that high G flight inflicts on the body. To the uninitiated, three Gs usually causes tunnel vision, graying of colors, and mental confusion. The force of the multiple gravities causes the blood to drain from the brain and pool in the lower body. More can cause loss of consciousness. Pilots who routinely participate in Air Combat Tactics (ACT), develop a higher tolerance, enhanced by using the M1 maneuver, which is deliberately tightening the leg and abdominal muscles. G-suits, or anti-gravity suits, contain pneumatically-filled bladders that squeeze the legs and abdomen in proportion to the Gs encountered. G suits usually add about one G to one's tolerance and extend the time available there. Third-generation fighters such as the F-106 were structurally limited to 7.33 Gs. Fourth- and fifth-generation fighters such as the F-16 (4th) and the F-35 (5th) are limited to nine Gs.

"How did you like that four-G loop?" asked Captain Cochran.

"I got a little dizzy," I replied.

"Are you game to see six?" he asked.

"Sure."

I woke up a little later, just in time to hear Capt. Cochran say, "You *wanna* see how we egressed in Vietnam?"

Of course I did. He maneuvered the aircraft over Cloudcroft and dove into the canyon leading to base. We flew down the center of the canyon at 350 knots, not more than a few hundred feet from the walls. It was easily the most exciting thing that had ever happened to me. I think Capt. Cochran finally had a flight that day that made his day slightly enjoyable. I always wondered what he had done to deserve such punishment.

From that moment, my focus was to be accepted into Air Force Undergraduate Pilot Training (UPT). I worried about failing a course in my senior year; I worried about a body part betraying me and failing the physical; I worried about being denied my Air Force Commission. In retrospect, the military needed bodies for Vietnam in the summer of 1968. The bar was low. People my age were getting blown out of the sky daily. They needed me as badly as I needed them.

2. JETS!

In August of 1968, I received the orders from the Air Force that made my dreams come true.

Aeromorphosis

After only one more physical, I was in. Not only had I succeeded in persuading the government to hand me millions of dollars' worth of training, they were going to do it only one hundred miles from home. Of course, the catch looming in the future was the prospect of flying dangerous missions over Vietnam. Like one's future old-age demise, the prospect of a violent death in a faraway place seemed insignificant at the time. My classmates showed an equal amount of enthusiasm. It was the beginning of a bond that endures today.

```
                    DEPARTMENT OF THE AIR FORCE
                HEADQUARTERS 3510TH FLYING TRAINING WING (ATC)
                   RANDOLPH AIR FORCE BASE, TEXAS 78148

AERONAUTICAL ORDER                                      16 October 1968
124

The following officers, 3517 Stu Sq, ATC, this stn, Class 70-03, who are
assigned to course of instruction for qualification as Pilot, are required
to participate frequently and regularly in aerial flights as crew members
per sec 102, EO 11157, 22 Jan 64, and para 4-4a, AFM 35-13. This order is
effective for the period 17 Oct 68 until completion of training, unless
sooner relieved or suspended therefrom by competent authority. FSC 7Y.
Officers will comply with para 2-10, AFM 35-13. Authority: Para 4-8a,
AFM 35-13.
```

1ST LT JOHN F PERRY, 095730 (USMC)	2D LT EDWARD C LAFON, FV3226833
2D LT JOE M ALEXANDER, FV3226450	2D LT DAVID G LAW, FV3226494
2D LT RODNEY L ALLISON, FV3234322	2D LT WILLIAM K MCDAVID, JR, FV3226903
2D LT REGINALD C AMELE, FV3226310	2D LT RONNIE L MCPHERSON, FV3226677
2D LT RONALD L ANDREA, FV3226731	2D LT FARREL W MEDEIROS, FV3226952
2D LT ROBERT E BARNETT, FV3226445	2D LT JOHN R MEEK, FV3230992
2D LT DAVID N BASSETT, FV3226924	2D LT WILLIAM T MINOR, FV3234484
2D LT WILLIAM G BRANDON, JR, FV3230597	2D LT TOMMY N NEELEY, FV3226192
2E LT ORMIN E BROWN, FV3226354	2D LT KERMIT R POPE, JR, FV3232212
2E LT TERRY L CHILDERS, FV3226349	2D LT HENRY D ROGERS, JR, FV3233594
2D LT ROBERT W CONNERS, FV3233990	2D LT ROBERT K SAWYER, FV3234526
2D LT ROBERT J COURTER, JR, FV3232981	2D LT ROBERT L SCHOENSTHEINER, FV322642:
2D LT DAVID M CRONK, FG3235302 (ANG)	2D LT MICHAEL D SCOTT, FV3226601
2D LT JAMES H CUMMINGS, FV3226635	2D LT KENT H SHERROD, FV3226491
2D LT DAVID H DOBSON, JR, FV3226730	2D LT PAUL A SKOPAL, FV3212071
2D LT GREGORY A DOTEN, FV3226797	2D LT SAMUEL D SMITH, FV3215561
2D LT JAMES E EASTERLING, III, FV3234778	2D LT ALLEN T SNYDER, FV3215604
2D LT WILLIAM M FISCHER, FV3226502	2D LT STEVE F STRICKER, FV3234280
2D LT LARRY E FLETCHER, FV3226874	2D LT CLAUDE T SULLIVAN, FV3209682
2D LT MICHAEL J FORD, FV3234312	2D LT GARY A SWINDLEHURST, FV3226578
2D LT PAT C FRAGILE, FV3215294	2D LT RONALD P TORONI, FV3226593
2D LT ANTHONY C FREDERICKSON, FV3226927	2D LT DENNIS E TRUSTY, FV3226425
2D LT DUNCAN S GREGG, FV3230863	2D LT JOHN F TURNBULL, FV3215901
2D LT NORMAN L HAMMAR, FV3226509	2D LT WILLIAM C TURNBULL, FV3233048
2D LT DAVID W H HOPEWELL, FV3226568	2D LT RONALD J VOGT, FG3235256 (ANG)
2D LT JAMES P HUST, FV3231678	2D LT GARY W WEBB, FV3215577
2D LT ALAN C JAECKLE, FV3215524	2D LT DONALD R WILLIAMS, FV3232745
2D LT CLIVE G JEFFS, FV3226894	2D LT PAUL V WILLIAMS, FV3232012
2D LT ROBERT J JOHNSON, 0108347 (USMC)	2D LT JOSEPH R WOLOZYN, FV3211332
2D LT STEPHEN D KELLIAN, FV3232708	2D LT RANDALL E WOOTEN, FV3215701
2D LT DAVID A KNITT, FV3214256	2D LT RANDOLPH L WRIGHT, FV3231902

2. Jets!

The order above lists the entire Randolph AFB Class 70-03. We were divided into two sections. After a year, 26 members of my "A" section graduated. I had little contact with the members of the "B" section then, and have not kept contact with any of them. The expected attrition certainly happened. However, the wash-out rate remained low because of the demand for bodies in the war. *The New Tigers-USAF Pilot Training in the 1960s*, by Herbert Molloy Mason, describes the year very well. I Zoom monthly with the surviving members of my section.

After four years of studying aerodynamics, propulsion, and aircraft structures at A&M, the academics at UPT struck me as very straightforward. My impression of military training, in general, is very practical, efficient, and informative. To produce a pilot capable of flying a supersonic aircraft in a single year commands respect for their methods. Present-day UPT has evolved much. The aircraft are more sophisticated and reliable, the equipment (GPS) has matured, and the way we humans interact with our machines is different.

The Attrition Machine

The T-41 is a slightly modified Cessna 172. Our class was bussed to Stinson Airport on the south side of San Antonio to suffer through a course of thirty hours to see if we would get airsick. Some of the students, many of whom had never flown at all, proved to be incompatible with aviation. This process was much easier and cheaper in the T-41 than it would have been in jets. Hallmark Aviation held the contract to train us in the basics. My instructor, A. M. (Mitch) Phillips, wore an airline-looking shirt with captain's epaulets and company wings. He needed to be a versatile instructor. He didn't have much trouble getting me through the course, but he worked very hard to get some of the zero-timers through. Mitch was an aspiring airline pilot, but lacked an instrument rating. After a typical flight, he would secretly ask me to sign his logbook indicating that I had given him instrument instruction.

T-41 Mescalero aka "The Attrition Machine"

The previous class had a loudmouthed guy with several flying ratings who washed out of the T-41. Allegedly, he asserted that he was smarter that the instructors and that the program needed improvement. I vowed to keep my experience a secret. One day during our morning briefing, the scrawny, mean-spirited chief instructor said, "Lt. Smith, stand up." He asked, "Do you have a private pilot license?"

"Yes, sir."

"Well, do you have a *commercial* license?"

"Yes, sir."

2. Jets!

I could see where this was going. It was a battle of experience and ratings. He was going to run through the ratings that he had and humiliate me with his superiority. I was OK with that, I just wanted to survive.

"Instrument?

"Yes, sir."

"Multi-engine?"

"Yes, sir."

"Instructor?"

"Yes, sir."

"Instrument Instructor?"

"Yes, sir."

"Very good, be seated."

Whatever was going on in his mind, he had decided to fold on the confrontation. That was the last I heard about the subject. I never knew how he found out about me.

In spite of losing a few of our classmates to the attrition machine and in spite of the overly officious demeanor of the instructors, it was a happy time. We gathered at the bar and celebrated our successes and lamented the unfairness of our failures. They say that soldiers in mortal combat develop friendships and loyalties unmatched in the human experience. Perhaps there is a continuum of the levels of such threats/friendships. Even though the threat was minor, we shared it and became closer.

Young, Strong, and Skinny

2. Jets!

The TWEET (6,600-pound dog whistle)

The T-37, otherwise known as the Tweet or the 6,600-pound dog whistle, is/was a jet! The puny J-69 engines were most efficient at converting jet fuel to noise. Since replaced by the T-6 turboprop, tandem trainer, it served us well in the basic training role. Loud, inefficient, short-ranged, and underpowered, it had little else to recommend it. A variant of the T-37 was later equipped with more powerful engines and weapons and was employed in Vietnam. Having side-by-side seating allowed the instructor to closely observe the student. That also allowed him to grab the student's oxygen hose and shake it when more focus was required. Spin training to proficiency terrified many of the students as well as some of the instructors. Most aircraft will recover from a spin on their own if left alone. Not the Tweet. Once begun, a rapid push on the stick was required, lest it continue into the ground. Few aircraft in the Air Force inventory could be spun; it was more a test of courage than a needed skill.

Jet engines accelerate much more slowly than reciprocating engines. The Tweet taught us that jet engines accelerate very slowly, especially from idle power—a lesson the pilots of the Asiana B-777 that recently landed short at San Francisco apparently never learned. Jet trainers are equipped with ejection seats. The ejection simulator gave us a 15 G kick in the rear. That was enough to instill a great deal of respect for the devices in the aircraft. Forgetting to pull out or replace the safety pin for the seat caused major repercussions. Woe be unto the student who discovered a seat pin in his flight suit after retiring from the flight line. In those days, the firing of the ejection seat on the ground meant certain death. Today, they are so sophisticated that a pilot can eject on the ground or at low altitude, inverted, and the seat will fly a safe trajectory.

We learned about parachutes. Rather than sending us to jump school, parasailing filled the bill. We would strap on a harness with the partially inflated canopy stretched out on the ground behind us. A long line connected us to a jeep. After a pull by the jeep and a few steps, the canopy would inflate and up we would go up. At 300 feet, the tow line was jettisoned, and voila, we were in the terminal phase of an ejection. Learning to steer the canopy into the wind and properly execute the parachute landing fall (PLF) served many of us well.

For T-37 training, we were assigned to B-flight, commanded by Maj. Joe Neely. We were also introduced to our training officer, Maj. Duane Sprick. The cadre of instructors in our flight were surprisingly cheerful and motivated, considering the challenge of the job at hand. Maj. Sprick, a former F-100 pilot, chose me as his student. An old-school fighter pilot, he joined/instigated rowdiness among us. Wearing his flight suits unzipped down to his waist infuriated his strait-laced superiors. The T-37 was easy to fly, so Major Sprick and I spent much of our flying time with shenanigans. One of our favorites was to get the airplane nearly vertical and at the last minute the pilot not flying would say "forward" or "back." As the airplane tail slid backwards, to make it fall forward, the stick would necessarily be pulled back and vice versa. The trick was to point the nose a little past vertical or it would always fall forward. Solo day meant flying a few patterns with one's instructor, stopping on the taxiway, letting him out, and flying a few solo patterns. Even with one thousand hours in my log, it was still an exciting day. Fast forward to T-38 solo day; it was much different: get your assigned airplane, go to it alone, fly solo.

My classmate, Gary Webb, a fellow Aggie, had a memorable experience in the Tweet. While in the practice area, his fuel gauge began to indicate an increasing quantity. We had been warned that this might mean imminent dual engine failure. He declared an

2. Jets!

emergency and headed back to base, not knowing if he would make it. Once safely on the ground, and rolling down the runway, the exhaust gas temperature gauge (EGT) popped out of the instrument panel and dangled by its wiring. Few of us could make sense of the two unusual events (they were not related). Discretion being the better part of valor, he stopped the airplane on the runway, shut down the engines, raised the canopy, and exited the airplane. Gary, quite the raconteur, tells the story with a flair, challenging all of us to make a better decision.

Flying the Dog whistle

T-37

While in the T-37, we were all treated to a few formation flights. I think the instructors dreaded the initial instructional flight. That was the students' first feeble attempt to master the art. I was allowed to fly the wingman position for a short while. The lesson had its desired effect: this is going to be really difficult to master.

Meanwhile, academics continued. Weather, navigation, performance, Morse code, hydraulics, aerodynamics, and anything remotely related to flying were taught. On each subject, an instructor would present the information, answer questions, and tell us what is important. We knew exactly what was required of us and, done properly, we passed. There were no trick questions to determine whether we had read the footnotes or done additional research.

2. Jets!

The White Rocket

It is impossible to overstate the degree of happy anticipation that all of us felt going into T-38 training. It was fast (supersonic), beautiful, nimble, reliable, and it looked like a fighter. First flown in 1959, the Air Force eventually received more than 1,100 of them. Having hydraulically actuated flight controls and high operating speeds made for a problematic pilot-machine interface. Early models suffered from frequent pilot-induced oscillations (PIO). These happen when the pilot inputs an increasing series of corrections to counteract the aircraft's reaction to his or her previous inputs. When encountered, the aircraft porpoises uncontrollably. The modern term for this phenomenon is "aircraft-pilot coupling."

By the time I flew it, PIOs had mostly been eliminated by the implementation of a heavier "stick feel." That is not to say that PIOs didn't happen, but we were trained for their prevention. Even so, stick forces were light. At high speed, the aircraft could easily be overstressed by too much back stick. Aileron forces were even lighter. The aircraft would roll at 720 degrees per second. If one attempted to hit the stop to one side or the other on the ailerons, the aircraft would perform an uncountable number of rolls before ever hitting that stop. On a cold day, it could reach 30,000 feet in one minute. Ours had primitive instruments. In 2001, the Air Force began receiving the T-38C, which has upgraded avionics and propulsion. Only now is its replacement, the T-7 Red Hawk, arriving. The T-38 has been the standard training aircraft for test pilots, F-15, F-16, F-22, F-35 pilots, and many more. In the 1960s, all Air Force pilots received the same training for their wings. Later, tanker, transport, and bomber pilots were separated from their class and received advanced training in the T-1 Jayhawk (Beechjet business jet). But for us, everyone in the class who made it thus far was going to know the T-38.

My first flight was with our Flight Commander, Maj. Stanley Slater. The major had a gravelly voice and a gruff demeanor. This first flight was called the "dollar ride." It is supposed to be a motivational flight, a time to experience the airplane and the local area without being graded. I was stunned at the performance and the sensitivity of the flight controls. Soon afterwards, I was assigned to my permanent instructor, 1st Lt. Rick Vaile. I believe that happened in order to give the new instructor a student who might be less challenging to train. That couldn't have been more wrong. Rick's instructor skills exceeded those of all the others. Clean-cut, quiet, and knowledgeable, Rick had everyone fooled. He was a crazy man in the airplane. I would frequently ask him questions about maneuvers or aircraft systems that could not be answered in our texts.

Fighter-type Air Force aircraft descend for approach and landing either by en route descent or jet penetration. In the former, the pilot gently descends in a manner similar to larger aircraft. In the latter, the descent is begun close to the destination at a high altitude (usually about 20,000 ft.) and steeply descends until a few miles from the base and the final approach. This technique is advisable in mountainous areas or bad weather.

Jet penetrations are usually conducted at high speed, low power, and high drag. I asked Rick if it would be possible to slow the aircraft (the T-38 would not stall, just develop very high sink rates) for a falling-leaf descent. I slowed the aircraft, and although the nose remained high, the vertical velocity increased to 5,000 feet per minute. Approaching 10,000 ft., I pushed over the nose and increased the power, arriving at the desired fix earlier than would have been the case at high speed.

Rick said, "Wow, that's a data point, I didn't know it would do that."

2. Jets!

On another flight, Rick led a formation with my Class Commander, Capt. Richard McChord, in his aircraft. I flew solo. While in the training area, Rick took control and performed a barrel roll with me in the outside fingertip position. It was not an approved maneuver.

When we debriefed, Richard said, "Your instructor sure is hard on you."

Where Rick Vaile really set his hair on fire was the low-altitude navigation sortie. Due to potential bird strikes, we were prohibited from flying lower than 3,000 ft. Sufficiently far away from base, I asked Rick if I might get a little lower.

"I thought you would never ask," he replied.

There are few thrills available anywhere that exceed the thrill of flying 300 knots or more at 50 ft. or lower. After a few minutes of that, Rick took the controls (from the back seat) and flew even lower. What a hoot, Lieutenant Clean-Cut was out here scaring cattle with a supersonic jet.

Everyone got a boom ride. Except for an occasional mistake when performing an aerobatic maneuver, the only time that the T-38 was taken supersonic was on that flight. A non-event: climb up, go fast, go home. At the debriefing, we completed the "boom log." In that, the time and track of the flight was recorded for everyone to see.

"Why would we do this? I asked.

"In case someone has a broken window or a dead chicken, then everyone will know that you are responsible."

I flew a lot of fast airplanes, but that was the last boom log I ever completed.

Of course, we had check rides. Not only did our grade on such flights determine if we were to receive Air Force wings or not, but also our ranking in the class which determined our choice of available aircraft. One of the maneuvers on the contact check was the cloverleaf. In that maneuver, the aircraft is pulled to the vertical, as in a loop, then rolled 90 degrees to finish in another plane. Four such maneuvers trace a path resembling a leaf of clover. It's easy to accomplish in geometry, but difficult to perform with headings, altitudes, and airspeeds consistent throughout the maneuver. I don't remember what it was, but Rick had the solution. He taught me the exact power settings, Gs to pull, speeds to maintain, and timing. I cheated, but it was perfect. Thanks, Rick.

When it came time for the four-ship formation check ride, I was surprised that the four top students were paired (with two instructors) for the flight. The plan called for a thorough evaluation of maneuvers that were very sophisticated, given that a year before, none of us had flown a jet. Fingertip, echelon, and trail formation; pitchouts; rejoins; cross-unders, trail loops, return to base in fingertip and rearrange to echelon right for landing, all at five miles per minute; it was comprehensive and we aced it, except….

After a nearly perfect flight, Dennis Trusty, solo in the number 4 position, got too close to number 3 during landing approach and executed a missed approach for a later landing. The examiner praised him for his good judgement and safety.

I said, "Dennis, the evaluators were ahead of you, they couldn't see you, so why didn't you just extend your downwind? They would have never known."

"I was just pumped up and got too aggressive."

We all received good grades.

2. Jets!

My last flight at Randolph was with Col. Colin J. N. Chauret, the group commander. He liked to fly with all the graduating students who had received a fighter assignment. He was a P-51 pilot in WWII and an excellent pilot. He demonstrated his command of the T-38, which was considerable, and said, "OK, it's your airplane, do anything you like." (Try to impress me, kid.) I put the airplane in a steep dive, pulled up to the vertical, and started rolling as rapidly as I could. Then I reversed, rolling rapidly in the other direction. The jerk was sudden, and I heard his helmet hit the canopy. He didn't say a word, though. We returned to base and he demonstrated a complete approach without changing the throttle setting, a good trick.

With that flight, I was finished there. We were awarded our wings and set out with a full ration of luck and an empty bag of experience.

Don and the T-38

Aeromorphosis

USAF UPT Class 70-03, Section A

Notice the "Cobra" on the patches and dickies we wore. Since we all expected to be assigned to Vietnam in some capacity, the Asian script and viper seemed appropriate. We call ourselves Cobras to this day. As of 2021, eighteen of the twenty-six in my section survive. Six have passed from natural causes, one in combat, one in training.

Lowe's Hardware generously grants military veterans a 10% discount on purchases in their store. Upon checkout, the cashier frequently says to me, "Thank you for your service."

My reply to her and to all US taxpayers: "Thank you for paying for my pilot training."

3. Intermediate Training

Each graduating class received a list of available assignments. This "block" of assignments came to our class in September of 1969. It contained one fighter, an F-100. With the war raging, bombers, transports, forward air controllers (FAC), and first-assignment instructor pilot (FAIP) billets filled the rest. I was allowed to choose any aircraft, even those not in the block. I requested an F-4 assignment.

The personnel center replied, "No, you would just kill yourself. Choose the F-100 or something else."

Even then, the F-100 was long in tooth and a poor performer. I had always admired the looks of the F-106; it was fast, and based entirely stateside. The photos of the cockpit showed it to be fully tricked out with gadgets. What I didn't know was that its mission was dying. A few short years from then, Aerospace Defense Command would morph into ADTAC (Air Defense Tactical Air Command) and then completely disappear into the Tactical Air Command (TAC). A few quality officers in ADC went on to stellar careers, like Pat Gamble (Aggie, four-star general), but most were regarded as second-class members of TAC. My power to choose aircraft was a great asset, but like some professional athletes, I spent my wealth in the wrong places. I chose the F-106, which, although a great experience, started my Air Force career with an impediment.

Fairchild

Nearly all of us went immediately to survival school at Fairchild AFB, WA. The weather began to get cold there in November. Along with two of my classmates, Bill Minor and Mike Ford, I drove there from San Antonio. We stopped in Phoenix, Las Vegas, San Francisco, and Portland. Along the way we had some fun and saw the first Boeing 747 being tested at Moses Lake, WA.

The course syllabus seemed to outline a good learning experience… not! Either survival school or a kidney stone is the worst thing that has ever happened to me. Little did I know that the prisoner of war portion would be so strenuous. The escape and evade (E&E) portion promised to be just another camping trip, with some harmless folks chasing us. It promised to be challenging to some of the students who had never spent a night out of doors.

I am an Eagle Scout; this will be easy, I thought.

The hiking over mountains, scrounging food, and staying dry wasn't fun, but the concentration camp was as bad as a kidney stone. I knew something was amiss when I applied the anti-interrogation techniques given in class to the situation in camp. They didn't work at all. No positive feedback from performing as I had been instructed. The interrogator just laughed and stuffed me in a 1'x1'x3' box and beat on the outside. Years later I heard a rumor that the survival school had become home for all of the sadists/weirdos in the Air Force. When discovered, a huge house-cleaning happened with rampant firings and even some jail time. We all vowed to resign from the Air Force if we were ordered to return. Traveling to my next assignment, I contracted a severe respiratory infection, probably as a result of being put in an outdoor cage, naked, in freezing weather, and doused with water.

3. Intermediate Training

Preparing for the Trek

Which Way Now?

Perrin

Having barely survived survival school, I checked in at Perrin AFB, TX for pre-interceptor school. The theory was that lieutenants needed thirty hours in the back seat of the T-33, flying ancient non-directional beacon (NDB) approaches, procedure turns, and holding patterns to achieve the instrument proficiency required of an interceptor pilot. After that, a couple of months in the F/TF-102 would teach us how to recognize a radar return, lock on to a target, and fire weapons. Apparently, the F-102 was much cheaper than the F-106 to use for us to learn the basics.

If any of us thought we knew something, the meeting with the Wing Commander, Vermont Garrison, dispelled any such thoughts. Fifty-four at the time, he came across as a silver-haired gentleman who had done it all. One of seven Americans to achieve Ace status in both WWII and Korea, he had seen more combat, won more medals, and done more in airplanes than these scrawny kids would ever think about. I always wondered what he was thinking as he graciously greeted the young wannabe fighter pilots standing before him.

The instructors in the T-33 instrument program were not fast burners. That is, most were looking forward to retiring as majors soon. Their *raison d'etre* seemed to be to show these lieutenants, all graduating at the top of their UPT classes, that they knew very little compared to the instructors. They succeeded. Flying a back-course localizer approach from a procedure turn in heavy icing conditions in a T-33 will humble most of us. They were able to elevate our skills to the bare minimum to proceed into the F/TF-102.

A radar return on an interceptor's scope looks much like the blips of light on an air traffic control screen.

"There he is, there he is, lock on, you idiot," screamed my instructor.

I learned about radar returns, range gates, ECM, antenna elevation angle, chaff, snap-ups, rocket beams, and most of

3. Intermediate Training

the stuff that interceptor pilots are supposed to know. My first impression of the Deuce was that it is big compared to the T-38. At 30,000 lbs. vs 12,000 lbs., it seemed like a monster. The two-seat TF-102, or "tub," as it was known, is almost certainly the ugliest airplane ever to embarrass the Air Force inventory. With side-by-side seating (so the instructor could shake your oxygen hose), it had a wide nose with huge windscreens and canopy. The right (instructor) seat had the throttle on the outboard (right) side, requiring him to fly the stick with his left hand and manage the throttle with his right hand. This proved to be an extremely unnatural situation, and many just flew with the right hand and reached under to manage the throttle.

One of my first rides with Captain Sam Ward found us at 3,000 ft. above the flat Oklahoma terrain.

Sam said, "You want to see a split S?"

That is a maneuver in which the aircraft is rolled 180 degrees and the nose is pulled down through the vertical to level off in the opposite direction, forming a half-loop. I had performed this maneuver many times in the T-38, starting at 20,000 ft. and finishing at 10,000 ft.

I said, "Sure," expecting to see a climb to higher altitude.

Imagine my surprise when he lit the afterburner, opened the speed brakes, rolled inverted, and began to pull the nose down toward Oklahoma. I genuinely thought we would crash. The airplane did a tight reversal and headed in the opposite direction with altitude to spare. Its huge wing made it able to turn very tightly. However, the J-57 with only 16,900 lb. of thrust could not sustain a turn long enough to make it a viable fighter.

Aeromorphosis

TF-102

Solo a Fighter!

3. Intermediate Training

I still wonder about the residents of Pottsboro, TX. The little town sat just off the north end of our runway. Almost daily, F-102s would take off in full afterburner at all hours. The noise is excruciating. Even the deaf would have been shaken as aircraft passed low overhead.

I don't remember my first flight in the F model, the single-seat version. At UPT, we were never trained at formation landings. I anguished greatly over my first formation landing. Looking back, it seems simple: fly formation down to slightly above the runway, land, stay on your side of the runway, and get stopped. Nevertheless, it was a proud day.

The F-102 carried missiles and rockets. The rockets were 2.75" Folding Fin Aerial Rockets (FFAR). They were carried in the doors covering the missile bay. Short ranged and unguided, they were necessarily fired at close range on airborne targets. The tactic used to fire them was called the "rocket beam." All of our intercepts simulated actual firing of weapons which was reserved for ranges, mostly over water. To conduct a rocket beam, the interceptor lined up on a perpendicular path to the target and closed in on it, maintaining a constant line of position. That is, as the intercept progressed, I could see the T-33 target at a stationary position on my windscreen, about 30 degrees from the nose. At the last minute, the radar computer would simulate a rocket firing and display an X on the radar scope. The pilot was required to *immediately* turn to pass behind the target. It was really close. To make matters worse, there was a computer malfunction which had happened in the past called "no F-pole." That meant you would crash into the target even if you followed the guidance. I always imagined a waist gunner on a bomber shooting at me, being perfectly stationary in his sights. Again, an exercise in courage, with little or no practical application.

Aeromorphosis

Perrin lay adjacent to Interstate Highway 35. One evening when I was there, an inebriated citizen of Sherman, Texas turned toward the base instead of IH-35. Arriving at the base, he sped past the gate. Seeing the runway, he assumed it was the highway and turned toward his Dallas. By the time the Air Police caught up with him, he had exited the end of the runway and snagged several fences. He was furious. How could the interstate just quit with no warning!

Late in my stay at Perrin, I was assigned a "very high, very fast" target. Lining up in front of the oncoming aircraft, I began searching as it neared. The Ground-Controlled Intercept (GCI) officer began at one hundred miles.

"You have one target bearing three six zero, angels five zero, range one hundred miles. On a good day, that low-powered radar of mine could see a target at thirty miles. "Target now three six zero for fifty miles." Yes, he was closing fast. "Three six zero for thirty miles." There he was, illuminate the target in azimuth, go to action switch one and move the range gate out to the target, release the action switch, lock-on, attack display shows steering command. Uh-oh, the attack display showed an A for abort, intercept not possible. Flashing high overhead in the opposite direction was a B-58 Hustler. I never had a chance.

Occasionally, we were graced with other unusual targets. The B-57 Canberra is an American-built bomber, manufactured under license from the British Electric Company by the Martin Aircraft Company. It was a challenging target because it could go high and slow. The rules of engagement (ROE) then, as now, required a visual identification of the target as hostile before firing upon it. To accomplish this, the front-stern-reattack was invented. The interceptor approaches from the front to quickly identify the target, then turns and attacks from the rear. This works pretty well when the target sustains its course

3. Intermediate Training

and speed. Not so with the B-57. During the reattack, the interceptor usually loses sight of the target and must reacquire it either visually or with radar. Ordinarily, that target reappears a few miles ahead. The favorite maneuver of the B-57 pilots was to slow and turn as soon as the interceptor passed by. Rolling out for the reattack, the B-57 was nowhere to be seen, because he was at my six o'clock, a fatal mistake in combat. Ever after that day, I always paused a bit before starting the reattack.

B-57 Canberra

My classmate, Malcolm Emerson, while flying a tub (TF-102) with Lt. Col. Tinglestad, a known screamer and highly avoided instructor, experienced a stuck microphone button. The first thing I heard on the radio was, "F---ing radio. The cheap son of a b--- has never worked right. God--- useless piece of s---."

"But sir, I think we have a stuck mike button."

"Hell, no, that's not the problem, it's just f---ed up."

"Really, sir, if you'll just switch to intercom, I think it will be OK."

"No, you idiot, just RTB (return to base)."

"OK, have it your way." I was delighted when this short-tempered old goat was called on the commander's carpet to explain his bad language on the radio.

I was happy to leave that oppressive environment for my introduction to the F-106, the speedy, spacious, needle-nosed sentinel of the sky.

4. Advanced Training

Tyndall AFB, at Panama City, Florida, was the home of all things interceptor. Called Air Defense Weapons Center (ADWC), it was commanded by Brigadier General James Price. The weapons center oversaw squadrons dedicated to training, test, weapons, and targets. I reported to the Combat Crew Training Squadron (CCTS). Malcolm Emerson, Don Thornton, John Maier, and I made up a class. The training atmosphere was greatly elevated from that at Perrin. Young, highly motivated instructors demanded our best in a very compact course.

The F-106 airframe was a Cadillac. It really would go Mach 2, even with the 360-gallon drop tanks. It still holds the official world speed record for single-engine aircraft at 1,525.95 mph.

As I understand the early development of the airplane, the decision to make it a single-pilot airplane came about with the assumption that there would be a lot of automation to help the busy pilot. For some reason, we seldom used it. Either from mistrust, or fear of becoming too dependent on it, most everything was manually flown.

I believe that sometime back in the early 1950s, the generous defense budget permitted Convair (later General Dynamics) to attempt to build an ultimate weapon, where cost was no object. The radar engineers must have been ecstatic. The airplane was to have everything: fast tuning magnetron, multi-mode storage tube, rotating beacons than went flush, vari-ramp intake ducts, internal weapons bays, and a tactical situation display down between your ankles that showed targets and navigation info. What was the catch? All the resources in the world could not implement that design into a reliable machine with analog electronics.

The fuel system was complicated and frequently problematic. Like the Concorde, fuel was (automatically) moved to manage the center of gravity during supersonic flight. I heard that it had 256 valves. It had unusually long legs for a fighter. Many times, I went from Langley in Virginia to Homestead in Florida and had two hours of fuel left for "training" maneuvers. As the late Israeli Gen. Moshe Dayan once said, "The F-106 is a great fighter because the way you win a dogfight is to keep to enemy from killing you until he runs low on gas and turns for home. Then you shoot him down."

With no flaps, it landed a little fast. We were supposed to fly final at 170 knots plus a little more if we were heavy with fuel. Most of us did not get much slower. At altitude, we didn't get slow there, either. It was anxious to spin if you accidently put in a little aileron when pulling Gs. I think that was because of the shape of the fuselage: small at the top, fat at the bottom. There is a famous (true) story about the farmer in Montana calling the 71st F.I.S. and saying, "You need to send someone out here to shut off the jet that landed in my field. It's scaring my cows." A pilot had gotten into a spin, couldn't recover, and ejected. Probably because of the change in airflow over the absent canopy, or the thrust from the ejecting pilot, the airplane recovered itself and made a perfect landing in a snow-covered field.

4. Advanced Training

71ᵗʰ F.I.S F-106, The "Cornfield Bomber"

The fire-control system and weapons were laughably ineffective by modern standards. The MA-1A radar system was impossible to maintain. The ground-control commands, electronically linked by SAGE (semi-automatic ground environment) and BUIC (backup interceptor control) were as ambitious and unreliable as the MA-1A. In theory, all the pilot had to do other than take off and land was to manage the throttle, lock onto the target, select a weapon, and hold the trigger down. Ground control intercept (GCI) would control the flight path of the aircraft and show a target marker circle (TMC) in the scope. All the flight path commands would show up on the instruments as command bugs, and the target would magically appear in the target marker circle. That magic worked maybe half the time. We had a procedure called Modified Close Control (MCC) in which GCI would send only target data to the airplane, and the on-board computer would control the attack. I was supposed to log six MCC intercepts every six months. I never saw a single one that was successful.

I flew the F-106 before it became upgraded with the bubble canopy, M-61 cannon, hot line gun sight, and boresight infrared lock-on capability. Those modifications were, in my opinion, desperate attempts to extend the lifetime of an obsolete system. The F-15 Eagle, sometimes called the "Hudson*," was already coming on line, and the funds would have been better spent there. Capable of firing the Genie, a big nuclear-tipped unguided rocket, the F-106 would have been formidable in a real war, except that no one is going to fire a nuclear weapon unless WW III happened. On the more practical side, we had AIM-4 Cs and Ds. These little guided missiles were so primitive that an Alaska F-106 had a tough time shooting down a huge weather balloon. To exacerbate their unreliability and short range, they were very complicated to fire on a maneuvering target. The pilot had to activate the missile batteries, which only lasted a short time, then activate the missile hydraulics, which lasted an even shorter time. If you were trying to shoot at another fighter and he was maneuvering, the chances were that you would decide to activate the hydraulics, and then find that your adversary had temporarily escaped, rendering your missile dead.

*A derogatory term comparing Rock Hudson to an F-15 pilot, before the days of enlightened views on sexual preferences.

The F-106, although fairly small by airliner standards, was very complex. Its equipment included a powerful J-75 engine with variable intakes for supersonic flight. The fire-control system was the best we could do at the time, being ambitious but generally unreliable. Multiple powerful generators powered the radar and aircraft systems, and a complex inertial navigation system attempted to compute the aircraft position (my watch does a much better job of that today). Like drinking from a fire hose, the training came fast. However, being summertime, we were allowed to rent ski boats from the base marina. Panama City's TV station is WMBB which,

4. Advanced Training

they say, means World's Most Beautiful Beaches. The sugar-white sand, combined with the turquoise water and warm weather, made for pleasant weekends.

Flying the Six was like the Deuce on steroids. Everything was bigger, faster, newer, and more capable.

Proficiency in missile beams was required. The Six didn't carry FFAR rockets like the Deuce, but a similar tactic was employed with missiles. The big difference: firing took place farther away from the target. I was conducting one of these when I heard heavy breathing from the instructor in the rear seat. It suddenly occurred to me that he was stressing over the apparent collision course we were on. What a sissy, this was nothing compared to a rocket beam in the Deuce.

Our class was ordered to participate in a Project Falcon 1970, whose purpose was to allow Air Force Academy Cadets to experience flight in a fighter aircraft. Our job: strap the cadets in the rear seat while one of the instructors readied the aircraft. To a man, every one of them demonstrated a blasé, condescending, entitled attitude, and they were cadets! The weather was terrible that day. One of the aircraft returned with part of its tail missing after a lightning strike. Maybe that impressed at least one of the cadets.

Although I had flown supersonic a bit, the prospect of traveling at Mach 2, twice the speed of sound, caused some anticipation. After takeoff from Tyndall, my instructor and I flew south in the warning area to abeam Tampa, turned north, and lit the afterburner. Just like the T-38 flight, nothing much happened. The summer cumulus clouds far below drifted past rapidly, while the Mach meter slowly wound up to the big 2.

Aeromorphosis

Mach 2 Pin

Upon reaching Mach 2, my instructor cautioned me to slow down by reducing the throttle to minimum afterburner and zooming to a higher altitude, before disengaging the afterburner. Failure to do that would result in a deceleration so abrupt that my face might slam into the instrument panel. After a few turns, we returned to home base to present me with my m2 pin. We joked that it stood for "married twice." Little did I know how prophetic that would be.

My tac eval (tactical evaluation) went OK and I was off to my first real assignment at Langley AFB at Newport News, Virginia.

Air Defense Weapons Center F-106 formation takeoff

5. The 48th Fighter Interceptor Squadron

I arrived at the 48th a little before my classmate, Malcolm Emerson. For a while, I was the first lieutenant-pilot seen in that outfit in years. Nearly all of the other pilots had seen combat in Vietnam. Some treated me as would a kindly uncle, others not so much. Some savored their cushy, stateside assignment as a reward for surviving perilous combat missions. Whereas I, being inexperienced and somewhat of a burden, did not deserve to be there. An inauspicious start to be sure, it made me anxious to prove my worth.

Langley AFB, like Randolph, was a command headquarters base; Tactical Air Command at Langley, Air Training Command at Randolph. As such, the officers' club at both places sported the finest accoutrements. Generals and colonels were sighted frequently. Everyone necessarily behaved themselves, as the atmosphere was rather strait-laced, at least when we were at or close to base. Our (Air Defense Command) squadron billed itself as "The Protectors of TAC," an irony that reportedly infuriated the 4-star TAC commander, William Momeyer. He didn't want to hear the sound of an F-106 when he boarded or deplaned from his VIP T-39 Sabreliner, and he had the horsepower to make it happen!

Aside from maintaining the aircraft and armament, aircrew training, and aggravating Gen. Momeyer, the primary mission consisted of air defense alert at Langley; Homestead, Florida; and Wilmington, North Carolina. Alert at Langley was either conventional, armed with AIM-4 missiles, or Nuke, armed additionally with the AIR-2A Genie nuclear-armed rocket. When someone high in the Department of Defense chain of command decided that a threat had arisen, we would assume alert. At Langley, we seldom flew from conventional alert and *never* from nuclear alert. It was quite a thrill for me as a twenty-three-year-old lieutenant to check out a top-secret nuclear authenticator, a .38 pistol, and ready an airplane equipped with a nuclear weapon. I'm sure they watched me very carefully.

Bob Western was/is a great guy. He had logged a MiG kill in Vietnam and was the most well-liked guy in the squadron. One day we were on a training mission and he lost his radio. (A common occurrence.) I asked the ground controller to vector me to a front intercept at 5,000 ft. below Bob's altitude. As we closed, something wasn't right about the intercept. By the time I figured it out, we passed head-on, co-altitude, close enough to feel the jolt as he went by. It was as if I was a passenger, it happened so fast. Seeing an F-106 passing in the opposite direction closing at 1000 knots, about 100 feet away is something one doesn't forget. I joined up on Bob, took the lead, and took him home through some heavy weather. I flew a terrible approach. The only thing he said about it was "Thank you."

Being a "Class 2 Detachment," Wilmington was rarely staffed. Occasionally, a few fighters would be dispatched to check its continued capability. We enjoyed getting away from home base to a more relaxed environment. On one occasion, six of us were sent there as an exercise. Being the most junior, I flew in the sixth position in the formation. Approaching Wilmington lead put us in a six-plane echelon for a flight near the crowded beach. As we passed slightly off shore, I could look down the echelon and see all five of my wingmen perfectly aligned. Normally in such a formation, it's a crack-the-whip situation where each aircraft amplifies the corrections of the aircraft between him and lead.

5. The 48th Fighter Interceptor Squadron

However, these pilots were so accomplished in their performance that number five was rock steady. I understand the sunbathers appreciated the show.

Up until 1969, an F-104 Squadron had defended South Florida from potential Cuban attacks. However, due to a snafu in which a defecting MiG pilot landed undetected and parked adjacent to Nixon's Air Force One, they had been replaced with 48th FIS F-106s.

Rumor had it that during the MiG's arrival, Homestead Tower personnel said to one another, "Hey, look at that jet on initial approach, he sure is smoking a lot."

Sometimes we would swap fighters and aircrew by flying an F-106 from Langley to Homestead. On other occasions we would swap aircrews only by flying a T-33 down. The T-33s were pretty old then, and would not pressurize for flight above 31,000 ft. That necessitated a fuel stop. Two of our pilots decided to disregard the 25,000 ft. cabin altitude limitation to make it nonstop. They made it OK, but subsequently were hospitalized for decompression sickness, the bends. On another occasion, two of our guys, after sightseeing over the Dismal Swamp on their way to Wilmington, discovered that they were critically low on fuel. By jettisoning the drop tanks and their associated drag, they barely saved the airplane. Harsh punishment followed.

On one flight, Bill Jones and I were to reposition two airplanes to Homestead. Bill decided to let the kid (me) lead. I planned meticulously, hoping to impress the former F-105 pilot on my wing. The flight went well until we reached the Miami Area. A giant thunderstorm blocked our path. I canceled our instrument flight plan and let down over the Everglades. Knowing that there were no obstacles out there, I soon found myself (and Bill) smoking along in heavy rain at 300 feet, trying to stay visual. I suppose he thought that this was an interesting was to do it, and was not excited at all. Suddenly we passed over what is now Dade-Collier Airport. A guy was standing there with a fedora hat on, holding a shovel. That scared the hell out of me. I decided to pull up into the clouds, admit to using poor judgment, and get an IFR clearance. Shortly after I started the pull, we broke out into the clear, with the initial approach to Homestead directly ahead. We did a little whifferdill maneuver onto a visual approach and landed uneventfully. Bill later asked me how I did that. I always wondered if he knew how lucky I had been.

Richard Nixon frequently visited the Miami area in 1971. That required us (or gave us the excuse) to fly in case of danger to the president.

To the Men of the 48th Fighter Interceptor Squadron
With appreciation and best wishes,

Richard Nixon

5. The 48th Fighter Interceptor Squadron

During those years, several airliners were hijacked and flown to Cuba. The 48th alert F-106s were always scrambled to intercept them. However, our orders were to follow behind, making sure not to allow the hijacker to see us, then turn around before getting to Havana. I always wondered what our purpose was. Perhaps to locate the wreckage if it had been flown into the water.

All the fighters that I flew came equipped with an oxygen system that was considerably different from most. Instead of the more common diluter/demand system, these used a pressure-demand configuration. With a diluter demand, one encountered resistance when inhaling, but exhalation remained normal. With the pressure demand system, 100 percent oxygen was forced into one's lungs simply by allowing it to happen. The exhalation phase met with much resistance, opposite from the more *normal* T-38. It was a reliable system; few problems were encountered. However, after a day of flying and breathing pure oxygen, the middle ear would become saturated with it and the body slowly absorbed it. Frequently, in the middle of the night I would awaken with an earache similar to the ones encountered when descending in an airliner.

The Air Force frequently conducts exercises to test its readiness and intimidate our foes. For some reason we always conducted these in the middle of the night. Either to test our ability to fly the mission at the worst possible body time, or because of the availability of the airspace—no one knew. The usual scenario: dismissed at two o'clock p.m. and told to report for duty at midnight.

"Go home and get some sleep," they said. Not a chance.

The winter weather had begun, and we were obligated to wear bulky rubber dry suits to fly over the cold water. I was assigned "Combat Air Patrol" or CAP, which meant fly in circles until an intruder arrived.

I probably had just dozed off when the aircraft violently snapped into a turn. Having set the automation so that the ground controllers commanded my heading, I had been given a target. It was a T-33, and I was able to intercept it for a simulated kill. That went OK, so I went back on CAP. While circling, my right arm kept getting more and more cold. In response, I kept turning up the heat, but my arm remained cold. I groggily looked at the oxygen control panel and noted that it looked like an ice cube. Since that did not compute, I looked around to find that the oxygen hose had separated from my helmet and was spewing what looked like snow. I might have set a record for getting from 40,000 ft. down to 5,000 ft. and breathable air. When I read about modern military exercises, I understand the necessity of testing our capabilities under the most adverse conditions.

On another flight, I was to reposition a single airplane from Homestead to Langley. We usually flew the Atlantic Routes (far offshore) between Bimini and Wilmington. It was at night, and I was somewhere in the middle when I got a call from Air Traffic Control Center.

"Mike Golf 15 (all of our fighters carried the Mike Golf callsign), say your Mach number and altitude."

I replied, "Point 92 and thirty-seven thousand." That was normal cruise for us.

"Eastern 500, say your Mach number and altitude."

Although we were on different frequencies, the controller relayed, "He says he's doin' point eight five at twenty-seven thousand."

"Mike Golf, your traffic is an Eastern 727 at your twelve o'clock, ten miles, opening."

5. The 48th Fighter Interceptor Squadron

I locked onto him, and sure enough, the break in the overtake circle unwound to a little counterclockwise from 12 o'clock on the display, indicating he was faster than me. If you do the math, it really is true, because of the warmer temperature at the lower altitude. This went on for a few minutes with the Eastern Crew needling me (via ATC) about my big, fast fighter.

As only a twenty-four-year-old smartass can do, I asked, "Jacksonville Center, Mike Golf requests flight level 500 and increase true airspeed to one zero zero zero knots."

I was cleared as requested and soon watched the airliner's lights disappear behind me. Yes, I had plenty of fuel to do that.

I almost had to bail out of a T-33 on a trip to Homestead, due entirely to my own stupidity. As a new member of the Daedalian Society, I wanted to attend a meeting. I couldn't have chosen a worse one than at Bolling AFB in Washington DC. The organization is an honorary one, mostly composed of dedicated aviator patriots and a few new guys. Many of its members are accomplished career military aviation officers. As a newly promoted first lieutenant, I was much in awe of the rank there. There were few there who were not active or retired generals. I eventually achieved the lofty rank of captain before I opted for the airline life. My plan was for Bill Jones, a squadron pilot, to pick me up at Andrews AFB in Washington in a T-33 on his way back from Dover AFB, Delaware, where it had maintenance performed. Bill and I rendezvoused to plan the flight to Homestead, where we were to start F-106 alert the next day.

The weather briefing was daunting. Absolutely no base east of the Mississippi had weather above minima. After a few hours, we decided to detour far west to get around it. Just as we were walking out the door, the weatherman stopped us and said that Shaw AFB in

Aeromorphosis

South Carolina had opened up and Pope AFB would be a legal alternate. We launched into a forecast of possible tornadoes and large hail, but hopeful that the ceiling and visibility would hold. Bill was a gentle giant of a man. Soft-spoken and clean cut, he had survived 100 missions over North Vietnam in the F-105. He was at once the nicest guy you could ever meet and totally fearless.

> Half a league, half a league,
>
> Half a league onward,
>
> All in the valley of Death
>
> Rode the six hundred.
>
> "Forward, the Light Brigade!
>
> Charge for the guns!" he said.
>
> Into the valley of Death
>
> Rode the six hundred.*

*Poem by Alfred, Lord Tennyson about a failed British military action against Russian forces in the Battle of Balaclava during the Crimean War.

That was the two of us. Taking absurd risk in peacetime, without any urgent need for our arrival, and somehow feeling invincible. After begging air traffic control to vector us around the worst weather, we arrived at a lower altitude, perhaps fifty miles from our destination. I was in the rear seat, and looking down, I uttered something that I have never said since.

5. The 48th Fighter Interceptor Squadron

"Bill, I can see the ground, we've got it made now."

Then came the bad news. The weather was heavy rain, with visibility near zero, and the wind at 45 knots right down one runway and perpendicular to another. Our alternate offered exactly the same weather. We chose the nearby runway that favored the wind, even though the visibility was near zero. Bill flew down to the GCA minimum altitude, saw nothing, and conducted a missed approach. Fuel was low, so we inquired about the alternate. Same story: heavy rain, visibility zero. We had fuel for one more approach. The weatherman said the visibility on the crosswind runway was a little better, so we elected to stay at Shaw and try it there. I was chosen to fly the approach from the back seat, and Bill would look forward to pick up the runway. It was the most focused approach I had flown then, or since. The plan was to land, or pull up and eject. When the GCA controller said, "Minimums, take over visually," I asked Bill, "Do you see anything?"

He said, "No, just level off and hold your heading."

Tick tock, tick tock.

"Hey, I see it off to the right, I have the airplane." He had visually picked up the runway, but we were already halfway down it. He cobbed the power, and did an aerobatic steep turn right, then left to line up, plopped the airplane on the runway, and had far too much speed for the runway remaining. Halfway to the end of the runway, there was a flock of seagulls. When we passed the area, they flew up and the airplane suddenly veered sideways.

I said, "Hell, Bill, forget the seagulls."

He said, "I didn't see them, I'm just trying to get stopped.

One of the suggested methods to stop the T-33 short is to raise the canopy for additional aerodynamic braking. The T-33 can fly with the canopy fully open.

"Canopy," said Bill, and as it opened, the rain poured in.

We could see the end of the runway coming, and it was a 50/50 chance of stopping before it ran out. We made it with the nose sticking over the grass. We sat there for a few moments with the rain pouring in and the engine whining at idle.

Bill said, "I sure am glad we made it."

I said, "Oh, yeah, that's good."

He said, "No, I mean, we would never have been able to talk our way out of this one."

Flying out of Homestead proved to be mostly enjoyable. Being a TAC F-4 training base, no one there knew what we were permitted to do. A maneuver that required practice and proficiency, the simulated flameout pattern (SFO), completely disrupted the normal traffic pattern. Simulating engine failure by reducing power and extending speed brakes, we would arrive at "high key" overhead the runway at 12,000 ft. Making a gentle 360-degree turn put us in a position to land. It was never meant to be a formation exercise. Nevertheless, we would call, "Red flight of four F-106s high key in thirty seconds."

"This is Homestead tower, all F-4s break out of the pattern, F-106s inbound to high key."

Flown in formation, it was a completely useless maneuver for training, but, witnessed from the ground, was a graceful and

5. The 48th Fighter Interceptor Squadron

impressive maneuver. Never actually landing, we would perform a (very) low approach and depart the pattern, now sufficiently chaotic to our satisfaction.

The simulated flameout pattern, flown by a single fighter, did have a useful purpose. All single-engine fighter-type aircraft have an emergency procedure to possibly save the aircraft if the engine should fail. Altitudes and sink rates vary among different aircraft, but for the F-106, arriving overhead an airport at 12,000 feet meant having a good chance of landing safely (with a sufficiently long runway). The flameout landing procedure called for attempting to restart the engine, followed by the extension of the Ram Air Turbine (RAT). The RAT is a small, propeller-driven hydraulic pump which powers the flight controls (in the absence of the engine-driven hydraulic pumps). Once overhead the airport and sinking rapidly, the landing wheels were extended and the aircraft maneuvered for a landing. The maneuver might have worked if the pilot could stop on the available runway using brakes, drag parachute, and tailhook. I never performed a real flame-out landing. If at any time the maneuver appeared to be unworkable, we were to bail out. We were told that the cost of the aircraft (in 1970 dollars) amounted to about $5,000,000. As a twenty-three-year-old lieutenant who believed himself to be bulletproof, that figure prompted me to believe that great risks were justified in order to save such a valuable commodity.

Twenty-five years later, I visited the 309th Aerospace Maintenance And Regeneration Group (AMARG) near Tucson, Arizona. Also known as the "boneyard," that is where obsolete military aircraft are stored until they can be used in an emergency or scrapped. Of the 240 F-106s built, more than one hundred of them were stored there (perhaps some had already been scrapped). How foolish of me to decide to take great risks to save one when, in the end, there were many left over.

The Cuban invasion never came. The closest I came to a MiG happened on a midday scramble toward Cuba. The latitude 23 deg., 30 minutes north limited our area of operations. I was vectored toward a Cuban fighter that went back and forth just south of the line. Doing the same, north of the line, I could see his condensed vapor trail.

Early one morning, Malcolm and I (the two lieutenants) were scrambled at six thirty a.m. Soon we were behind a Piper Aztec twin-engine civilian aircraft flying over the water at 500 ft, with no lights. Unable to slow to his speed, each of us in turn would pass by him about 50 knots faster and perform the standard intercept signals. With no response from the pilot, and no radio communication, it was time for Plan B. Passing beneath him at high speed, selecting afterburner, and turning rapidly enough to generate some rough air got some results. His lights came on and GCI reported that he had turned on his transponder and called approach control on his radio. We were dismissed after he announced his intention to land at a small airport near Miami. The local police, sheriff, DEA, FBI, and others cleverly surrounded the airport with a few thousand personnel and many vehicles, all with flashing lights. The pharmaceutical entrepreneurs decided rather than landing there, ditching in the swamp would be preferable. GCI asked us to look for him, but we never had contact again. The incident received some media attention, much to the chagrin of the detachment commander. The squadron commander criticized him for choosing to put the two least experienced pilots together on alert. An article published in the local paper follows:

"Two NN Men Down Mysterious Plane

Two Newport News men, one a native, helped down what is believed to have been a flying drug smuggler yesterday in Miami, Fla. First Lt. Malcolm E. Emerson and First Lt. Samuel D. Smith, both F-106

5. The 48th Fighter Interceptor Squadron

pilots of the 48th Fighter Interceptor Squadron, Aerospace Defense Command at Langley Air Force Base, shadowed a small twin-engine plane reported to the ADC detachment at Homestead Air Force Base (Fla.) by the border patrol about six thirty a.m. Sunday. The small aircraft was reported "mysteriously" circling about one hundred feet off the ground in southern Miami. The Langley-based squadron maintains an alert detachment at Homestead, which operates on a weeklong rotation system whereby pilots from here serve a seven-day stint at assigned intervals. According to a 48th FIS spokesman, two F-106s were scrambled at Homestead in response to the border patrol alert. "This is standard procedure," the spokesman said. "Alerts like this come in from the border patrol almost daily. It appears that planes are rented in the States and taken down into Mexico, and on the way back the operators drop their goods around here, planning to come back later to collect. Marijuana has been brought into the country this way on several occasions." He said after the jet pilots had spotted the smaller craft, they stayed with it for a while until the Aztec pilot "contacted Tamiami Airport (a small landing field in Miami) and said he was having some radio trouble but would land." He said the F-106s then returned to Homestead, but that the Tamimi police were waiting at the airport. The smaller plane, however, did not land. Instead, its pilot put down in a field in south west Miami and got away. A helicopter located the abandoned plane four hours after the interceptors left off their surveillance. The spokesman indicated that federal and metropolitan investigators are looking into the matter today. He said there have been drops of marijuana in the Miami area, and border patrol personnel in that area were on the alert. When found, the red Aztec was empty, it was reported. According to reports, the plane was rented from Piedmont Aircraft Corp. in Raleigh, North Carolina. Lieutenant Emerson, one of the newest pilots in the 48th FIS, is a native of Newport News. He attended Virginia Tech prior to entering service. He and his wife Ann presently reside in Newport News. First Lieutenant Smith, and his wife Glenda, also are residents of Newport News. The 48th FIS is commanded by Lt. Col. Daniel H. Parris."

Our duty schedule: a day on thirty-minute alert, a day on five-minute alert, and a day off. The times describing the alert duty meaning the amount of time allowed to become airborne after being given notice. Thirty-minute alert allowed napping at the officers' quarters or playing golf. Five-minute alert meant being close to the cocked aircraft and hurrying. Coming off five-minute alert, the pilots would fly their aircraft on a training mission, thus exercising the aircraft. On one such training flight, I flew an Aerial Combat Tactics (ACT) mission against the Detachment Commander. It was a legal dogfight. The major trounced me on every pairing. I was reminded of the personnel center's refusal to assign me an F-4. I continue to believe that there was a North Vietnamese major with my name ready to be painted on his MiG-21 had I gotten my wish. During such dogfights, we frequently began head-on at supersonic speeds. After the merge, we would sharply turn the aircraft to engage. During that turn, usually at four to six Gs, the aircraft would pass into the subsonic regime as it slowed. At subsonic speeds, the center of lift on the wing moved forward, allowing much more control authority from the elevons. The effect in the cockpit was a rapid G onset. Relaxing back pressure on the control stick prevented overstressing beyond the 7.33 G limit. That seemed natural to me; however, a few pilots, in the heat of the mock battle, overstressed their aircraft.

The ADC formation manual described our procedures in great detail. However, the only limitation on the number of aircraft attempting a formation takeoff was "75 ft. of runway width for each aircraft." On a 300 ft.-wide runway, that computes to four aircraft! Á la the Thunderbirds, we blew out of Homestead in a four-ship formation. The squadron commander said that he interpreted the manual differently, and shortly afterward, the manual was revised.

5. The 48th Fighter Interceptor Squadron

I was, and remain, an inveterate airborne sight-seer. At Homestead, I would frequently be left to my own devices with two hours or more of fuel remaining. Flying low over the clear, turquoise waters on the Florida Keys and the Bahamas never got boring. Andros Island had been reported as an illegal drug-staging area. I wonder if my buzzing the island caused any consternation among their cartel members. I was never reported.

Weapon System Evaluator Missiles (WSEMs, pronounced *wizz-ums*) looked like actual missiles except they were blue and lacked missile hardware. Loaded on the missile rails, they would electronically record the signals sent to them by the aircraft. Each aircraft required a successful simulated missile launch every month or so. Failure to qualify an aircraft rated alongside high treason for the pilot, operations officer, and commander. Finding oneself returning to base without having qualified the WESM, we frequently sought other aircraft to run on. Airliners, being large and easy to lock on, fit the bill. Except for the color of the missile, the attack was identical to a real firing. I understand that the practice was discouraged after I left.

When we flew from alert, we would run practice intercepts with live missiles aboard. "Missiles Radar" or "Missiles IR" would be selected on the armament control panel. The only difference between that and a live firing was that the "arm/safe" switch would remain off and safety-wired closed to remind us. That worked pretty well except for the time in 1961 that a New Mexico Air National Guard F-100 shot down a B-52.

Just to be sure that the Arm/Safe switch functioned properly, after takeoff and pointed in a safe direction, we always performed an "Arm/Safe" check. To do that, with the arm/safe switch checked in the safe mode, the rotary switch was turned to "Trigger Salvo" and the trigger pulled. If all went well, nothing happened. We always checked in with GCI, saying, "Arm/Safe check complete." For a fellow F-106 pilot departing Tyndall for a training mission followed by a trip to home base, this did not go well. With the trigger depressed, the missile bay doors opened, distributing his missile bay cargo of clothes and lots of frozen shrimp across the Florida landscape.

I received my first Operational Effectiveness Report on December 16, 1970. According to Col. Billy Hudson in a paper written at the Air War College:

"The process of identification, selection, training, and appointment of leadership is crucial to modern organizations. The leaders directly affect the future of the organization by setting policy, plans, and guidance. Therefore, it is essential to assure that the process for installing those leaders is correct in all aspects: from evaluation of potential candidates to sustained development of managers in the organization. A key instrument in this process is the ongoing performance appraisal which rates performance and promotion potential. The United States Air Force (USAF) performance appraisal system for officers is the Officer Effectiveness Report (OER). The OER is used for several personnel decisions, including officer promotions. As part of the officers' "selection folder," the OER provides basic data upon which promotion selection boards base decisions. Therefore, the OER should evaluate the factors which will contribute to the officer's success in the higher grade and position of authority."

That definition, at first blush, seems pretty straightforward. However, long before my tenure in the Air Force, inflation happened. The resulting system demanded that promising officers be given not only the highest ratings in the various categories, but additional endorsements from high-ranking commanders, praising the subject officer. The really outstanding officers thus must have appeared

5. The 48th Fighter Interceptor Squadron

identical to the promotion boards. This system not only wasted the valuable time of supervisors, but rendered promotions decided by a "good ol' boy" system of rumor, backstabbing, and innuendo.

My flight commander, Rolland Truitt, called me into his office to review my first OER. He said, "I have given you a 'good' rating on your OER. I didn't give you the highest rating in all categories because it's important for you to show improvement in the future."

Not knowing what that meant, I read the document pictured below.

Wow, that sounds like I walk on water, I thought.

Extremely complimentary of my performance, the document seemed to exaggerate my performance in a good way. Little did I know that my career had just been dealt a fatal blow. The "fast burners," or young officers who are promoted early in their careers, all receive top ratings in all categories on all their OERs. In. subsequent assignments I did show improvement, but I carried that albatross for the duration.

Capt. Truitt's havoc was not limited to my harassment. ADC had a skill level system: depending on one's level of performance, one was entitled to wear a patch declaring him "Qualified," "Skilled," "Expert, or "Master." Major Bill Schwoeble found his rating downgraded from Expert to Skilled, due to an allegedly weak performance on his Tac Eval. I have never heard of that happening before or since.

Although the officer rating system has morphed many times since my experience, it is set to undergo a complete reformation. Here is what the Air Force said in 2021 about this:

"Some negative information that once might have been withheld from Air Force officer promotion boards will now be seen and evaluated, the Air Force announced. The new rules comply with the fiscal 2021 defense policy bill, which mandates more transparency in promotions. The Air Force's top personnel officer, however, said it won't end the careers of those making 'one mistake.'"

I wouldn't want to be the first guy to get a real, uninflated OER.

First OER

5. The 48th Fighter Interceptor Squadron

Toward the end of that assignment, I was curious about the airplane's capabilities. Luck would find me alone in the warning area off the east coast. My mother always said,

"Idleness is the devil's workshop."

True to the adage, I decided to see how high I could get the airplane. Level at 37,000 ft., I accelerated to 1.6 Mach. At that speed, I started climbing. At 65,000 ft., still at 1.6 Mach, I leveled off vertically and rolled into a 15-degree banked turn. Knowing full well that a stall at supersonic speeds would happen with no buffet warning, I decided to roll no further. After turning a little, I went back down. No, I did not have a pressure suit on, so court-martial me. I was there, that's the way I remember it.

A senior captain, Dave Roeder, flew the F-106 in the 48th FIS. Dave had the unusual distinction of having flown the B-52, the F-105, and the F-106. Of course, F-105 pilots who flew in Vietnam had poor odds of survival. Even the best of the best of them were frequently lost on that mission. Dave, a former bomber pilot, survived with distinction. However, a habit from the B-52 betrayed him. Contrary to B-52 procedure, most airplanes demand landing with one's heels on the floor, so as not to apply any braking at touchdown. Suffice it to say that Dave blew tires frequently in the F-106. He later became the Air Attaché in Tehran with incredibly poor timing. He was released after 444 days in captivity. That's Dave with his arms up in the photo.

Hostages Released

There is a widely disseminated photo of the Mercury Astronauts who were photographed beside an F-106B, airplane number 70158. That airplane became one of our two Busses, or two-seat airplanes in our squadron. Since none of the senior guys wanted their name on a bus, I got my name on it for a while.

5. The 48th Fighter Interceptor Squadron

Mercury Astronauts and "Don's" F-106B #158

Don and F-106A of the 48th F.I.S.

Compared to modern fighters, the F-106 was fast, had good endurance, and could turn well, once. However, the engine and electronics technology of the age presented insurmountable obstacles to its effectiveness. The F-16, although eclipsed by the F-35 and F-22, owes some of its success to its heritage at Convair/General Dynamics. They took the F-106, put a tail on it so it could go slow, a big engine so it could sustain a turn, and created a reliable fire-control system and weapons. They didn't have to start from scratch.

On a cold December day, my flight commander excitedly approached me.

"Hey, Don, I just got notice of your next assignment," he said.

Great, I'm finally going to get to fly that F-4 that I wanted when I graduated from pilot training, I thought.

"It's an F-102 to Keflavik, Iceland," he shouted.

I was devastated. Not only did this assignment send me to a God-forsaken, arctic wasteland, but it also condemned me to a lesser airplane. The orders stipulated that I would be temporarily assigned to the 111th Fighter Interceptor Squadron at Ellington AFB, near Houston, Texas, for requalification training in the F-102. After that, I would be subjected to a Permanent Change of Station (PCS) to Keflavik Naval Air Station, Iceland.

The requalification course at Ellington only lasted two weeks. Flying the Deuce struck me as much easier than I remembered.

George Bush was there, driving the squadron commander, Jerry Killian, crazy just because he wouldn't wear his hat. I never flew with him because I was a student, and only flew a few flights with an

5. The 48th Fighter Interceptor Squadron

instructor, Rich Mayo. Being an Air National Guard Squadron, the 111 FIS employed both full-time (technician) pilots, and part-time (downtowners) ones. I enjoyed the experience; the notion of being a part-time fighter pilot appealed to me.

6. Welcome to Keflavik, Iceland

Overcast clouds, strong winds, low temperature, and an odor of rotten fish greeted me upon arrival. Every newly assigned pilot at the 57th Fighter Interceptor Squadron had gone through that rude sensory awakening. That ritual: introductions, followed by a nap, more introductions, a party, a night's sleep, and work the next day. Energetic and friendly, Lt. Col. Tom Sawyer commanded the squadron. He later became a major general (two star) in the then newly formed Space Command. Large, loud, and intimidating, Lt. Col. Howard H. (Mac) McWhirter handled squadron operations. He has since been enshrined in the Georgia Aviation Hall of Fame. Major John Cronin, a tall, solemn man, kept us trained, and boyish-looking and friendly Maj. Dan Fullerton was the standardization/evaluation officer. Even through the fog, I could feel the unique attitude there. That was one of independence, competence, and a little mischievousness.

As I emerged from the squadron building, I began to see the local scenery for the first time. I could see some wisps of smoke coming from the north. In that town, Njardvik, a fish-processing plant gave the area its famous aroma. I remember the odor as being extremely unpleasant. The landscape consisted almost entirely of rocks. As Carl Sagan might have said, there were "billlions and billlions" of them. The whole island is a volcanic rock, with a few glaciers here and there. There was an old saying among the G.I.s that if everyone who left the island took one rock, then eventually it would disappear and no one would need to come there anymore. Trees exist elsewhere.

6. Welcome to Keflavik, Iceland

The 57th F.I.S. was a tenant unit on a Navy base. The Air Force has neat, clean bases, The Navy has neat, clean boats. Anything that is too valuable to dump overboard, but not needed immediately, the Navy places in a pile at a base. What can I say? The place was a dump. Every Navy base I ever saw looked as though some huge explosion had happened. Adjacent to the Air Force Bachelor Officer Quarters (BOQ), I could see a sidewalk with a handrail stretching across a vacant lot to the Officers' Club. That handrail became important during snowstorms. My room lay on the second floor of the L-shaped building, near its apex. Nearby, the Whiff, the 57th's bar and center of most social activities, was within crawling distance.

Without unpacking, I slept about five hours, probably spread-eagle, facedown. Rudely awakened at five o'clock, I was to be the guest of honor at a drinkathon, a tactic to acclimatize me quickly to the time change. It was there that I had the pleasure of meeting nearly every officer in the squadron and a few wives. Yes, wives. When one was assigned to Iceland, the choices were offered to go "accompanied" or "unaccompanied." The catch: if one chose accompanied, then he was obligated to stay two years, rather than one year. Every Air Force officer was also obligated to serve a remote tour about every six years. If one chose to serve in Iceland unaccompanied, then you filled the "remote" square. Tom Sawyer had just returned from flying F-100s as a "Misty" in Vietnam. He had little use for another remote tour. His wife, Faith, was appropriately cast as social director. The two lieutenants flying the T-33, Mark Shaw and Bob Hervatine, both had their wives with them. They were always gracious hostesses and, although pleasant to behold, often made us feel more homesick.

A new pilot at the Whiff was an event. Everyone turned out to meet him and get to know their new squadron mate. I had just recently been promoted to captain. In the 48th, I had been the "kid," entitled to passes for poor behavior. I properly saw this as my chance to change my act. I pretended to be a longtime captain. From that first night, the camaraderie was palpable. Everyone realized that even with all the survival equipment, if one were to experience an engine failure more than a hundred miles or so from shore, you became (very frozen) dead meat. A symbolic initiation rite called "Whiffing" happened later, but the real one was your first scramble on the Russian TU-95 bombers that frequently passed nearby. Being slightly dehydrated from the long airline trip, I was quick to accommodate my hosts in their plan to encourage me to drink too much free beer. I awoke the next morning with a wide-awake headache and began my check-in.

It took until Feb. 15 to get in-processed at CBPO (Consolidated Base Personnel Office), briefed on a couple of hundred things, fitted with an anti-exposure suit, and get scheduled in one of the two Tubs (TF-102) for my local checkout.

Bart Lynn, a major, was to be my flight commander and my checkout instructor. Bart is a very soft-spoken Mormon, short on words and long on skill and patience. He showed me a few very important differences about flying in the arctic, one of which is to make very sure that the chocks are touching the tires. That is, not a hair away from them but touching. When the ground is slick, the tires often slide on the ice after engine start, even with the brakes locked. If the chocks are carefully wedged under the tires, you stay. If not, you push your chocks into the rocks with your brakes locked. It was easy to give Bart my undivided attention on such matters.

The Tub was a strange-looking and strange-acting bird. The instructor, sitting on the right (yes, it was side-by-side) had to fly the stick with his left hand and the throttle with his right. This was apparently a difficult trick for some. The glare shield, that piece of plastic

6. Welcome to Keflavik, Iceland

extending from the base of the windscreen practically to the tip of your nose, was always in the way. That and the radar scope seemed to be right up in my face, all the time. The canopy was a huge affair that was supported pneumatically and reminded me of a Klingon Battle Cruiser when open. The windscreen was composed of three very large panels of multi-layer NESA glass. NESA is an acronym for Neo-Electric Sensing Agent and is made by PPG. It is a layer of liquid electrolyte sandwiched between layers of glass. Alternating current electrical power is applied to this liquid and it stays warm to the touch and thus fog free. The most uncomfortable thing about this first flight here, however, was the anti-exposure suit I was wearing. This "poopie suit" was filched from the US Navy. Unlike the one-size-fits-all Air Force suit, this one fit well. A dry suit, one first pulled the suit feet on by stepping through the opening in the front that stretched from just left of the pubic area to the right shoulder. Then, standing up, one did a sort of dance from the hip to get first one arm, then the head and other arm in place. The plastic zipper was pulled up to the shoulder and you were ready to put on your boots, gloves, jacket, survival vest, parachute, helmet, knee board, and checklist.

Pitiful me. I don't want to be here. It is a cold, ugly place. I am wearing far too much stuff to be comfortable. The jet is old and strange. The engine compressor stalls when taxiing in a cross wind. It is snowing and there is a gusty cross wind.

"Hey, Bart, this is really great," I lie. I couldn't have been more uncomfortable.

"Right." He's seen this act before.

We're going to take it easy on this first one. We'll run some medium-altitude front-stern reattacks. I feel much better after we get going on the simulated attacks. The Deuce is still the sweetest flying jet I have ever flown. The roll response isn't the dizzying 720 degrees per second of the T-38, but it is enough. The pitch isn't too sensitive. It's just right. It's solid in formation. The afterburner lights with an explosion that kicks you in the back. You *know* when it lights off. I can fly this thing. In fact, I'm sorta having fun.

Bompf. The windscreen on my side is now a white frosty opaque with spider webs on it. OK, I've seen a broken windscreen before on the F-106. No big deal, but on my first flight here, is it an omen? I scrunch down in my seat even though it serves no purpose. Bart takes control of the jet and returns to base (RTB). The guys really yuk it up over my having one of these on my first flight here. I only half-jokingly say that I thought I didn't like it here, and now I'm sure.

Two days later, we try it again. That same day I fly the F-model (single seat) in the afternoon. I fly a little formation and make an instrument approach. I feel pretty good. Flying solo is a very special thing. You can take lessons until your instructor says that you are capable of flying alone. But until you have done it alone, you haven't done it. Of course, you say, but the instructor would be there to take over. It's more subtle. Suppose you have ten thousand hours of flying time and you are taking seaplane lessons. Insurance won't allow you to solo. If you walk away with a rating and no solo time, that little voice says, "You could do it, but you haven't." And you always wonder a little.

Later, I had two TF rides with the Squadron Training Officer, Maj. John Cronin. I didn't like John at first. He was a tall, serious, seemingly humorless man with very short hair. He was the antithesis of Dan Fullerton. Maybe they were a Mutt and Jeff team who were that way intentionally.

6. Welcome to Keflavik, Iceland

John took me out to humiliate me. He succeeded. With 230-gallon drop tanks that we carried on nearly every mission, the Deuce was limited to 435 knots indicated air speed (KIAS). We were to do high-speed, low-altitude (500 ft) intercepts and I was to wear an instrument hood. Picture me in a 60-degree banked turn at 500 feet and 400 KIAS under the hood, trying to find the target in the scope in the few seconds I have before the (simulated) missiles use up their (simulated) electrical power. I was using a lot of concentration just staying right side up.

John was a graduate of Interceptor Weapons School (IWS, pronounced *eyewash*) where they do this sort of stuff for fun. He successfully showed me that he could do it and I needed some practice.

Five days later, I repeat the TF in the morning and F in the afternoon with Maj. Dan Fullerton. Dan is the squadron Standardization/Evaluation (Stan/Eval) Officer. He is a boyish-looking fellow with an easy smile. Stan/Eval guys are supposed to be mean and serious. Why is this man smiling? Later I will realize that it's because we all either do our job right or it will kill us. We are highly motivated and his job, enviable among Stan/Eval types, consists of giving check rides to guys who do well every time. I guess I'm a little nervous about flying with him. I have a terrible ride. I can't find the target; I overshoot the reattack; my instrument approach is wild; I make a lousy landing. I'm embarrassed. Dan is still smiling. His wife is gorgeous; maybe that is why he smiles all the time.

Years later, I cooked a meal for Dan. I asked him if it tasted OK. He replied that he couldn't really tell, since he had his taste buds shot off in the war. I don't know what that has to do with Iceland, but I get a kick out of that every time I think about it.

That afternoon, I flew an F out of the alert facility. They needed to change the aircraft for routine maintenance, and I enjoyed the experience of seeing the area. The flight ended in a weather recall. We were a little jumpy about the weather there. The alternate at that time was (British) RAF Lossiemouth, Scotland. No short trip. A trip there was not an option when low on fuel. Luckily, the really heavy snow showers never lasted very long. The fog and low ceilings could outlast you, though. No big problem that day. It was starting to get bad, so we all landed.

After a night checkout (aren't they all in February?) and a whiffing, I was ready to pull alert.

Whiffed? That is your initiation to the Bar-Club at the Bachelor Officer Quarters, the Whiff. We had the Whiff, and the Navy P-3 Squadron had the Brass Nut. When you are the Whiffee, you star in a drinkathon and allow everyone to see you looking very foolish. There is an old ejection seat for a throne, and I really felt more a part of the squadron when it was over. My Whiffing was fairly benign, since it was before the return of Chuck M. More on him later. Fortunately, my room was nearest to the Whiff, and they didn't have to carry me far.

7. Make Yourself Useful

Major George Caulkins and I sat on the front row in the briefing that morning. On the wall behind the podium, a grid showed who was assigned to what duty. Each duty had appropriate squares, and each square had two hooks to accommodate a plastic name tag. Everyone had a name tag with the first four letters of his last name on it. For alert that day, two plastic rectangles with "CALK" and "SMIT" declared that George and Don would be the ones to fly a scramble.

George was a rather smallish man with a lot of character. He had flown in Vietnam and, like me, had recently flown the F-106. George, being senior, was lead pilot, and I was wing, or "two." In a somewhat surprising circumstance, neither of us had actually been on alert before at Kef. After what seemed like hours of briefing the same things that we had all heard a thousand times, we were dismissed to go to our duties.

I went to the personal equipment room and grabbed my helmet, parachute, and anti-exposure or poopie suit. This would all become drudgery after I got used to it, but this first time was making my adrenaline flow a little. The off-going crew was glad to see their replacements arrive and lost no time removing their equipment from the fighters. The auxiliary power units were always started at changeover time so that the ongoing crews could check out the electronics in the aircraft. What with the noise and the mechanics, security police, pilots, and cooks scurrying around, it looked as if war was imminent. The fighters were to be "cocked"—that means, ready for a scramble, or able to become airborne within five minutes. No one but the pilots would be allowed in the cockpit after the aircraft were cocked. That was a sound policy, since each pilot had a different way of building his "nest." In order to make a quick takeoff, it was important to find your cockpit and your equipment the way you expected.

An hour later, the place looked like a ghost town. Everyone was settled into a routine. Some reading, some cooking, some watching AFRTS (Armed Forces Radio and Television Service, affectionately known as "A-Farts"). I read. Only later in graduate school did I ever read so much as I did that year. We also had a pool table and a dining room. The food was acceptable, and its price was right.

The Russians came through our airspace about once each week. We knew the schedule for their Cuba run, but the ELINT, or electronics intelligence missions, were irregular. The majority of our business was simply showing ourselves to the Tupelov-95 bombers as they passed through the Icelandic Air Defense Identification Zone (ADIZ). The game they played was to take off from their base in Murmansk on Kola Bay, an inlet of the Barents Sea, fly around the north end of Norway, pass through the Icelandic ADIZ, stir up the American surface fleet in the North Atlantic, and return. They could have just as easily and economically passed outside our ADIZ, but that wouldn't have checked our response. Neither did they file an international flight plan for the same reason. That was fine with us; it was good for our job security.

The Tupelov-95 remains the world's fastest propeller-equipped bomber. Like the American B-52, they are extremely long-lived, and expected to remain in service until 2040. The NATO designation, "Bear," stemmed from the custom of naming Russian bombers with words beginning with the letter B. Further, NATO uses single-syllable words for propeller-driven aircraft, and two-syllable words for jet-propelled aircraft. We called them "Bears" and the intelligence people called them "Zombies."

7. Make Yourself Useful

On a clear day, planes departing from Murmansk are visible from Norway. The types of bombers and tankers taking off revealed their mission and flight path. When we received a phone call that evening advising us of approaching "Zombies," it wasn't because Icelandic radar could reach great distances. Several hours later we could expect to fly. After rehashing our plans and getting our equipment "really ready," all we had left to do was go to sleep for a few hours and then wake to one of the most exciting events of a lifetime. Of course, neither of us could sleep.

Expecting a four o'clock a.m. takeoff, I tossed and turned sleeplessly in bed until three. George was already up. We went down to the kitchen for an early breakfast, then suited up. That meant waffle-weave underwear, both tops and bottoms, quilted underwear, rubber dry suit pulled up to the waist, and combat boots over the rubber footies of the dry suit. The rubber gloves associated with the dry suit were already in our cockpits, as were our helmets and parachutes. Rather than putting the suit completely on, we always tied the sleeves of the rubber suit around our waist so as to prevent getting too hot.

When the yellow light in the aircraft area, illuminated and the klaxon in our quarters sounded, we were officially on battle stations. That meant that we should be in the cockpit, strapped in and as ready as we could get without starting the engine. Soon I was strapped in, eyes fixed on the green/yellow/red set of lights whose yellow member glowed brilliantly. Anxiously we waited for the green light that meant that we would be allowed to fly and do what you have trained so long to do.

I began wondering how I was supposed to feel. Was I afraid? Without a doubt. Could I do it? Probably. Would I admit my doubts? Not a chance. At that point, the inevitability of flying over the Arctic Ocean on one engine in a few minutes sort of detached from me. I never again worried about how I felt about it, that night or on any other mission.

The klaxons are ten inches square and capable of making an unpleasant high-pitched, loud buzzing sound that would make a baby's cry seem soothing. All eyes were fixed on the trio of lights as the appointed time arrived.

The yellow light went out, and for what seemed like an eternity, nothing happened. Maybe it had all been canceled. *I am going to be very disappointed if that is the case.* Then, to my great relief, the green light illuminated, and the klaxon sounded steady. I am really ready. Both hands on the throttle; start button depress with left thumb; throttle outboard to arm starter; throttle back inboard. There was an explosion behind me. That was normal, of course, for the starter to make so much noise. At 10 percent RPM, I moved the throttle to the idle detent and the J-57 came to life. Shiny switches forward and guarded switches closed, radar on, ejection seat pin out, canopy closed and locked, I was ready to go. I saw George pulling out of the adjacent stall.

"Sloe Gin zero one flight check-in," he calls.

"Two," is my only reply.

"Kef tower, Sloe Gin zero one flight, scramble." George sounds determined.

"Roger Sloe Gin zero one flight, you are cleared for takeoff, MARSA, climb gate to angels three seven, heading zero six zero, contact Drainage Control on channel four."

That meant that we are to climb in afterburner (gate) to 37,000 ft. and that the Military Assumes Responsibility for Separation of Aircraft (MARSA).

7. Make Yourself Useful

"Roger, cleared for takeoff, let's go button four."

"Two." I change the radio to preset channel four.

"Sloe Gin zero one flight check-in."

"Two."

"Take twenty seconds, two." Which is, of course, the plan that we briefed until we could puke.

George does not stop rolling to make his takeoff. The taxiway from the barn makes a delicate fillet with the runway and he simply accelerates through it. The lights of his aircraft are soon obliterated in the bright plume of his afterburner. It makes a loud, deep explosion more felt than heard as it begins. I look away in an attempt to save my night vision. Twenty seconds later, with the throttle already full forward, I move my wrist outboard an inch and an additional 15,000 horsepower is unleashed. The response is delayed only a second, a loud thump, much more acceleration, and the Engine Pressure Ratio (EPR) gauge dips, then recovers to where it was before, indicating proper exhaust nozzle operation.

I see George begin to rotate and then he is lost in a plume of snow that the afterburner and wing tip vortices blast into the air. I wonder if I will be able to see far enough to keep my aircraft on the runway when I enter the cloud of snow. Never mind, though, at 135 knots, it's time to fly. I'm off, gear up, yaw dampers on, drop tanks on. Wake up down there.

The radar is already searching where I knew George would appear. Sure enough, after a few sweeps filled with ground clutter, a single bit of video separates itself from the rest. George is now two miles ahead of me. True to the plan, I maneuver to keep him at that distance.

Later we contact military GCI control. "Drainage, Sloe Gin zero one flight with you, scramble."

"Roger, Sloe Gin flight, Drainage Control, you have two targets bearing zero six zero for two hundred and eighty, angels three one, climb gate (in afterburner) to angels three seven."

It is a very dark night; there is no moon. But that is the very best condition for seeing the aurora. Tonight, it is spectacular. To my left is a shimmering curtain about 30 degrees up from the horizon. It reminds me of a curly candy from my childhood. There are reds, yellows, and, rarest of all, greens. I can see George's rotating beacon far ahead. I look down at the attitude indicator and I am in a 30-degree right bank. Quickly rolling level on instruments, I swear to be more cautious about letting the illusion of the aurora fool me into thinking of it as a horizon.

I refer to George's aircraft as "George" and to my aircraft as "me." We are powerful birds roaring through the night. Rather than a delicate, neurotic human sitting at the controls of a 35,000-pound, supersonic weapons system, we are one. George is one too. We see in the night and through clouds. We can unleash missiles that follow and kill. We can go very fast. Pretty cool, huh?

"Sloe Gin zero one flight, contact Polestar on 364.2."

"Zero one flight, roger, let's go button six."

"Two."

7. Make Yourself Useful

"Zero one flight check in."

"Two."

F-102 with aurora

"Polestar, Sloe Gin zero one flight."

"Roger Sloe Gin flight (British accent), you have two targets in trail, angels three one and three two, bearing zero six zero for eighty, fly heading zero seven five, descend to angels two-niner.

The concept is very simple. First, you tune up your radar and locate the target. Next, designate what video the computer is to track (lock on). Follow the steering dot in the radar display and look outside when the computer tells you.

I select the 80-mile range and the "Vis Ident" mode. In the Russian bomber, the Electronics Warfare Officer far ahead is aware from my radiation pattern that I have not selected any weapons to become active. I begin to work the hardest part, the antenna elevation. The B sweep is going left to right and back once each second. The radar beam is very narrow in order to concentrate power into it. This is done in order to be able to burn through enemy jamming. Tonight, with no jamming, it serves only to make it difficult to find the target in elevation.

"Target zero six zero for sixty."

The target is 3,000 ft. higher than I am. Take off two zeros, that's thirty, and divide by tens of miles, that's six, and I set the antenna at six degrees up. If this were a movie, a harp chord would sound as the b-sweep reveals a bit of video, one-quarter inch across and one-eighth inch deep. I move the thumbwheel a fraction of a turn down and the next sweep reveals two targets. I'll have to wait until they are at forty miles before the computer can lock on. Meanwhile, I must tweak the antenna elevation up a bit every few seconds to keep the returns on the scope.

"Sloe Gin zero one has contact zero six zero for forty-seven," George announces.

"Contact is target."

"Sloe Gin zero one flight, uh, we'll take a judy (our own control of the intercept) now."

"Roger Sloe Gin zero one flight, judy is target.

As the returns pass inside the forty-mile mark on the scope, I squeeze the switch beneath my left index finger and the b-sweep goes into super search, rapidly going back and forth across only an inch hori-

7. Make Yourself Useful

zontally on the scope. At that same time the movable part of the stick in my left hand begins to control the position of the b-sweep on the scope by positioning the handle left or right. I super search the rear target for a moment, tweaking the antenna elevation for the brightest return, and then pull the action switch (the trigger-like switch under my left index finger) to the fully depressed position. This freezes the b-sweep over the target and causes the range gate to appear. This a one-fourth-inch-deep bit of video within the b-sweep that designates a range at which I want the computer to lock on if it sees any targets. I move the range gate to superimpose it over the target by moving the same handle forward and aft. When it is superimposed, I release the action switch. I am instantly rewarded with a lock-on display. A three-inch-diameter circle appears with a break in it extending from the eight to the nine o'clock positions. This indicates that I am approaching the target at 800 nautical miles per hour. Also appearing are a smaller circle and a dot near the center of the scope, indicating that I am on course for a near collision. Not to worry, George swings the formation wide to the left. We roll out a couple of miles behind the trailing Bear.

"I'll take the leader, you take the other one," George orders.

We are a little low on fuel. This is probably his reason for deviating from our original plan. We would ordinarily remain in formation and the lead fighter would pull in close, while his wingman remained in a position to protect him. I lock on to the trailing aircraft and follow the steering commands. Presently I can feel the bomber's engines. Soon, a red VI flashes in the scope, indicating that I am two hundred ft right, two hundred feet below, and five hundred ft behind the target. I look up, and sure enough, there it is. It looks like a brilliantly lit Christmas tree. I pull up alongside. In the dim ambient light, I can see the configuration well enough to determine that it is an ordinary D-model.

Aeromorphosis

"You ready?" George is already ready.

"Affirmative."

Going home suddenly sounds appealing. Although great fun, this is still very unfamiliar and unfriendly territory.

Far ahead, I see a pair of red rotating beacon lights swing sharply to the right, diverging from what appears to be a small city. I roll in behind.

"Two's tied," I indicate that I am able to follow.

The aurora is spectacular. I am mesmerized by the myriad shapes and colors. A dark night at the Arctic Circle at 37,000 feet is one of the best places to observe. Ahead, the curtain of red and green fades and in an instant brightly reappears in exactly the same shape at my right side, still upwards at a 30-degree angle. It hangs there for a few seconds fluttering gently, much like a heavy concert hall curtain that has been closed rapidly. Now it darts back to what appears to be a collision course for George. It grows rounder. It now changes into an evil-looking face. I wouldn't lie about this. It looks exactly like a face with an open mouth that George is flying into. Sort of like imagining that puffy clouds were ships or rockets many years ago.

I drift in mindless diversions, easily following George toward home.

"Wind is one-six-zero at forty, call initial to runway one seven," Kef tower says with some trepidation. All runways are named for their orientation. They are numbered according to the points of the compass, reflecting the magnetic compass reading to the nearest ten degrees and dropping the last digit. Runway one seven is oriented

7. Make Yourself Useful

along a one-hundred-seventy-degree heading. The reported wind is nearly aligned with that runway.

The bad news was that runway one seven is short and lacking in approach lighting or electronic glide slope. The good news is that we have 40 knots of headwind to help us stop. I tuck in tight and George says that I should take ten seconds. In good weather, fighters usually fly down the runway centerline at seventeen hundred feet above the ground, called initial approach, then turn abruptly, which is called a pitchout, make an elongated three hundred sixty-degree descending turn, and land. Until I rolled out on final approach, I had never thought about how to land with absolutely no visual cues other than the white runway lights and three green ones on the near end. There was no instrument landing system, no GCA, no visual approach slope indicators, no trees, no other lights, or any of the things that I was used to. This was an illusion called a "black hole approach." Too flat an approach and you scrape yourself off on the rocks. Too steep and you crash-land. This must be what a carrier landing looks like, only this is a longer boat with no glide slope indicator.

In a moment of divine inspiration, it occurred to me that if I was descending at more than the customary seven hundred fifty feet per minute, then I must be too steep. Likewise, less than the magic number would mean that the approach was too flat. I was aimed at the runway threshold and the vertical velocity indicated three hundred feet per minute. *I am way low. Add power and pull up*, is the message. I can hear my heart thumping. *I'm really going to look stupid, dying on my first scramble.* I ease the nose over, now at two hundred feet above the rocks. Vertical speed eight hundred, fly down to the runway, roll it on. No sweat, I had it wired the whole time.

8. Face-to-Face with Ivan

Colonel Budd Butcher became the commander of Air Forces Iceland (AFI) long before my arrival. He was the sort of officer that the taxpayers get at bargain price. He's twice the man at a thirtieth the salary of the pretender who ran Delta Air Lines in my later days. Because of him, the system worked so smoothly that one hardly noticed its function. He was a personable man, and I looked forward to an alert tour with him. His wife, Inger, was from Norway. They were married when he was on an exchange tour several years earlier. Theirs was one of only a very few of such marriages which survived for more than two or three years. Many Scandinavian women, and especially Icelanders, found it perfectly reasonable to marry an American soldier, move to the United States, see America, have a child, and return home with or without a husband within three years.

He immediately put me at ease with his modest manner and informed conversation. The weather was great, and when we were advised of an airborne order (a scramble at a known time), we were both happy to hear it.

As we climbed into the clear, cold air, with me in tight formation on the right wing, a sense of belonging occurred to me for the first time. Remembering my first flight at Kef, the contrast was dramatic. On that day I had been flying in that intolerable rubber suit, over this barren land of wind and fog, thinking that I could never get used to this hell. Now I felt comfortable with the country, its weather, the F-102, and my role.

8. Face-to-Face with Ivan

Col. Butcher yaws the nose of his aircraft; it is my signal to loosen up to route formation, a relaxed hundred feet out from him. I can see the whole island. The day is spectacular. Not a cloud to be seen. In the southwest, which is behind us, lies the Reykjanes Peninsula. To the north along the west coast is a string of mountains, glaciers, and active volcanoes. To our right are the Vestmannayer Islands, including Heimay and Surtsey, recently born volcanic islands. Ahead is Hofnafoðer, and its US radar site. Along the south coast, a fine black line accentuates the margin between the tall cliffs and the surf, a beach composed of coarse black sand. Below is a flat meadow area that extends to the southeast coast and then beyond in a natural bridge at the coast line. It's large enough to fly a B-52 through it. The top is so flat and large that the effect is more of a tunnel than a bridge.

Iceland is about three hundred miles wide by two hundred miles tall. The name for the country in Icelandic is "Iśland." I wonder if this is the etymology of the English word for land surrounded by water. This would be the only time I could see the whole island at once.

As we go "feet wet" (over water), our GCI controller vectors us toward the Bears. Closing to one hundred eighty miles, nearly head on, I can see two tiny white icicle-like condensed vapor trails far ahead. Their returns soon appear on my radar scope.

The time to close on them passes quickly, and when within a few miles of them, Col. Butcher turns to position us more abeam than head-on to the targets. We split our formation to close in on them one on one. I begin a slow right turn to roll out, heading the same direction and beside the trailing bomber. Even if I misjudge the closure rate, I am well below him and will be safe. I reduce power slightly to join on him. I glance into the scope and notice that it has broken lock in the maneuvering. No matter, I approach visually.

I arrive at the scene with way too much overtake. Feeling the need to slow down to match his speed, I pull the throttle all the way to idle. Our training officer has previously given me good advice on this issue. It goes something like this: "When you're far out over the Arctic Ocean, if you use afterburner or speed brakes and they happen to get stuck in the on position, you're dead." This is because either way, you will run out of fuel before you get even close to land. You will probably jump out, hit the water, and freeze to death within eighteen minutes if you are able to get into your life raft. Three minutes if you don't. Remembering this, without using the speed brakes, I pull the throttle back to idle and zoom up above the big ship a little. As I ease down to its altitude, I bring the power back up.

KABOOM, KAAAABOOMMMM. Fire belches out of my intakes to a spot well forward of my aircraft. My feet literally dance on the rudder pedals with each report. I receive a large jolt of adrenaline. According to those in the know, the compressor stall and the adrenaline are quite predictable and perfectly harmless. It is an "off idle compressor stall." The F-102, with its long intake ducts, is subject to interrupted airflow under such conditions. The only danger is if the engine temperature rises to very high levels. I check the EGT and find it very low, a good sign. I believe that a compressor stall may be the biggest irony in aviation. How can something so loud and spectacular be so harmless? Ivan is probably laughing at the new guy. I won't make this mistake again.

8. Face-to-Face with Ivan

The author catching up to a TU-95

I have gotten a little behind during this episode and find myself within the pointing arc of the tail gunner. His guns remain caged, pointing straight back and 60 degrees up. I have been told that there is a tradition here. Within the bomber resides an Electronics Warfare Officer (EWO) who commands various gadgets which tell him what I am doing. If I were to be so aggressive as to reach down and select "missiles all" in preparation for actually shooting at these guys, my radar would kick into high gear, increasing its pulse repetition frequency. This would immediately be obvious to the Russian EWO and would likely cause him to pee in his pants. Likewise, four very powerful and accurate 23 MM cannons would be uncaged and track me from the tail of the bomber. We both tacitly agree to the tradition of no hot weapons.

Presently, I catch up. It is an enormous ship, shining in the daylight. I pull up alongside its right wingtip. It has four huge turboprop engines, each connecting two counter-rotating propellers to the swept wing. They emit a gut-shaking deep vibration, quite noticeable even in my cocoon. I can see the pilot in the right seat of the cockpit. He is looking at me but does not gesture. This model is a Bear Delta. It has no refueling probe on its nose as do some models.

I follow the sleek lines back along the fuselage to a window just behind the wing. There, a face smiles and a hand waves to me. I momentarily consider whether I should wave or make a rude gesture. I select the former, fearing fame from a photo of such. Further back, I am absolutely stunned at the drama of the huge red star on the tail. The ship is pulling a mile-long con trail in the smooth air.

I have an extra one thousand pounds of fuel before "bingo." I can afford to wax poetic for a moment. I can remember that my second-grade teacher, Mrs. Corbin, told me in 1953 that Russians are really bad people. After all of this hate propaganda for the last twenty years, I am struck by my similarity to these people fifty feet away from me. We would attempt to blast each other out of the sky if ordered to, but for this hanging moment, we're more allies against the harsh environment than enemies. I begin a feeling of closeness to them that has remained with me since. It strikes me as ludicrous that so many people have told me to hate them. Behind my helmet and tinted visor, I am secretly embarrassed that a moment ago I considered making a rude gesture.

Later, when asked about my year in Iceland, I think of this moment. Props whirling, engines humming, the big red star on the tail. I wish you could have been there.

"Lead's off," I hear Col. Butcher. I hastily grab the camera from the glare shield. It is a 35 MM Nikon with a motor drive and a 135 MM lens. I aim it at the nose of the Bear. Unable to see through the viewfinder with my visor down, I hold down the trigger and sweep along the fuselage, neatly finishing the roll of film at the tail. Now

8. Face-to-Face with Ivan

I slip under their nose to see its number which is on the nose gear door. It is 53, and this maneuver must make them really nervous, since none of them can see me. Some years after my exit from the Air Force, pilots were prohibited from carrying cameras in single-seat fighters, for safety reasons.

"Two's off."

"Drainage, Sloe Gin zero one flight, RTB (return to base)," is Col. Butcher's immediate reply. He had been waiting for me.

"Your pigeons are two six zero for two eighty-five." We are nearly three hundred miles east of "home."

Later, I see the runway from one hundred miles out. Although slightly low on fuel, the approach feels comfortable. Some flights are just better than others.

On May 25, 1972, I received a scramble order for a midday flight. Contrary to the usual easterly vector for Soviet bombers passing through the Iceland-Faroe Gap, today we headed north. The only types of Soviet aircraft ever seen during the year I flew there were varying models of the TU-95, Bear. Except that day. In the bright summer sunshine, we were surprised to approach two TU-114 Badgers, twin jet bombers. I closed in and got a nice photo, and being so close to home, shadowed them for a while. As they passed westbound just north of Iceland, I was fully prepared for them to turn north, away from the land. They turned left toward Iceland and flew directly over the city of Akureyri! Flight Control advised us to keep an eye on them and not to do anything aggressive. At the time, I thought that it was extremely considerate of us not to shoot them down for that, remembering the dirty tricks they used to lure Allied aircraft out of the Berlin Corridor for a shoot-down in previous years.

Aeromorphosis

TU-114 photo by Don

9. Not Today

The pilots at Keflavik rarely received orders to scramble with no warning. November 22, 1972 would prove to be exceptional for me in many ways. The usual sequence: spies inform the intelligence network that a flight of Soviet aircraft was taking off at Murmansk; intelligence computes the estimated time of arrival (ETA) of the Russians at the Air Defense Identification Zone (ADIZ); pilots are warned to be ready to fly in a few hours.

I had been polishing my billiards technique alone while Major Bart Lynn read. Bart is my flight commander, my immediate supervisor, and the officer who writes my effectiveness reports. He is of the Mormon persuasion and never indulges in alcohol, caffeine, or rude language. He has served a tour as an F-8 pilot in an exchange program with the US Navy. That, while being very enjoyable, is usually the kiss of death for a career. Gentle to a fault, he speaks so softly that oftentimes his formation mates must ask him to repeat what he says on the radio.

"*Braaaaaaaaaaaaaaaaaaa*"

The klaxon sounded steadily, indicating a scramble without prior warning. The lack of forewarning suggested that someone had screwed up and let a bad guy get very close, or, more likely, the scramble was called mistakenly on a US Navy P-3 submarine patrol plane returning home.

Whatever the reason, the two pilots have five minutes to get airborne or everyone from here up to the Air Division Commander would be in serious trouble. Now, it's not easy to get dressed for this occasion. First, one must put on his custom-fitted body prophylactic. Legs go in first, followed simultaneously by the left arm and head. The really hard part is to do the little hip gyration and place the right arm in the proper place. With that done, all that remains is to zip up the front diagonal zipper, step into winter flying boots, zip them up, descend on the firepole down to the first level, and make your way to the jet. Once comfortably seated, the idea is to start the engine, and while it winds up, get strapped in with the assistance of your crew chief. If you forget to put your helmet on before doing this, you will discover that the noise of the claxon is nothing compared to the J-57 starter.

Bart's engine starts, just a few seconds after my own. The barn doors are open, I'm strapped in, the canopy is closed, the engine is nearly at idle RPM, the radar is coming up, the scramble light is green, I'm really ready.

"Sloe Gin zero one flight check in," whispers Bart.

"Two."

"Kef tower, Sloe Gin one flight, scramble," says Bart.

"Rrrrrrrroger, Slogan (sic), cleared vector zero six zero, climb gate (afterburner) to three seven zero, cleared for takeoff." Those native Icelanders always talk funny.

Bart instructs me to wait twenty seconds after he lights his afterburner.

9. Not Today

The exhaust nozzle opens on Bart's engine, followed immediately by a fifty-foot tongue of flame and a loud *"POM"* which shakes my insides. As usual, the runway has a few inches of powdery snow on it. The cold air and snow perfectly outline the plume of hot exhaust air blasting from the tailpipe ahead.

"POM" is the incredibly gentle sound in the cockpit as the engine wreaks its sonic havoc on the world outside.

As he rolls down the runway, approaching 125 knots, Bart rotates to takeoff attitude. As he does, the wingtip vortices fan the snow into a huge cloud which completely obscures his jet.

That is not a really big deal, since I couldn't stop even if I wanted to. After takeoff, I tie on behind him. In the cold air, the planes climb well. We level off at 37,000 feet in less than four minutes. Switching to Air Force Ground Controlled Intercept (GCI) frequency.

"Snork, zeeble, splut."

"Sloe Gin zero one, Is that you?" I ask.

"Buzzzz, nork."

"I can't copy you at all, lead."

Bart is now making motions with his hand. He holds up two fingers and then points ahead. This means that number two (me) is to become lead and that Bart will become two.

I nod in a big affirmative child nod and look ahead.

"Two (Bart), rock your wings if you can read me."

His wings rock.

"Two, rock your wings if you are OK and want to continue the intercept."

Again, his wings rock.

"Polestar, Sloe Gin zero one flight with you, arm-safe check complete, with Alpha, Bravo, Charlie. Two has radio receiver only."

Both aircraft are, of course, armed. Both have a salvo of radar missiles, infrared missiles, and ballistic rockets, each weapon corresponding to the "Alpha, Bravo, Charlie," in the check-in. The *Brevity Code** is a huge vocabulary of secret words which enables the job to be done efficiently. It is not really secret, and the Russians knew it better than most.

*See *Authors Notes* for link to the NATO Brevity Code.

"Roger Sloe Gin zero one, you have one target, zero five eight for two hundred twelve. Adolla is controlling."

"Just great, that explains the whole deal."

Adolla is an ancient EC-121 radar picket aircraft. It is a military version of the venerable Lockheed Constellation.

"The controllers never know where they were or what they are looking at with that thing. They probably scrambled us on a boat or an iceberg," I silently say to myself.

"Contact Adolla on 364.2."

9. Not Today

"Roger, Sloe Gin zero one flight, go button 6." (Bart's wings rock) I change my radio.

"Sloe Gin zero one flight check in." (Bart's wings rock)

"Adolla, Sloe Gin zero one flight with you, arm safe, alpha, bravo, charlie."

"Hello, zero one flight, we've got a popup target for you today zero six two for eighty." The voice belongs to a lieutenant who frequents the fighter squadron bar. It has a thick, melodious Georgia twang.

"It's very low and slow moving."

"Sounds like a boat to me," I reply.

"Well, maybe so, but we figured you'd like to go flying today anyway."

"I guess you're right, I have contact zero six zero for six five, very low."

"Contact is target."

"Zero one has a judy (I have a visual or radar lock-on and am taking over the intercept) 060 at 35."

"Judy is target."

The steering dot indicates the direction to the intercept point in three dimensions. Now it plummets. The overtake circle has a break in, and the counterclockwise edge of that break indicates the overtake speed by its clock position. It says 3:30. This is bad news because three hundred thirty is about the fighter's ground speed, and this almost certainly means that the target is stationary. I push over and start down in a half-hearted effort to center the dot in the steering circle. Allowing it to stay low, I level off and pass *high over the target*. The radar breaks its lock-on.

"I really appreciate you guys getting us some flying time, but I'm sorry to say that it must be a boat. I'll make another pass to confirm."

The two fighters (Bart is flying a loose formation) swing wide, turn back, and I lock on again. I start down and allow the radar to break lock again.

"Unless this is a really important boat, we'll just RTB (return to base)."

"We'd sorta like to know what it is, if it's not too much trouble." Potentially being a Russian electronics-gathering trawler, that made some sense.

There was a cloud deck below, and there was little wisdom in asking Bart to have to tuck in tight to follow me down through it. If I left him on top and went down for a peek, I could always find him again with my radar.

"Okay, two, you stay up here and lead will try to get a visual."

"Adolla roger."

Bart rocks his wings.

As the wisps of cloud gently swished past the canopy, I recalled some advice that I had read when I was a student pilot.

9. Not Today

"Never split-S into an undercast," some old P-47 jock had said. A split-S is a maneuver in which one rolls to inverted and pulls down, which from the side would resemble the bottom half of the letter S. That seemed like decent advice for this situation, so I merely eased the aircraft over into a shallow dive.

There was 10,000 ft. to lose, I thought, so why was I being so cautious? Intuition, perhaps. As the clouds enveloped the aircraft, it began to grow a little darker.

Suddenly, a huge dark form appeared ahead of the aircraft, and very close! All joking aside about "lightning-fast fighter pilot reflexes," I pulled the stick as far back as fast as it would go. The wing immediately went into a high-speed stall buffet—a sound not unlike driving down a rocky road. Simultaneously, I instinctively shoved the throttle full forward. For what seemed like an eternity, the aircraft was pointed up and going down. The water loomed very close. I suddenly realized that I had lost track of 10,000 feet during those diving passes by the target, somehow believing to be at 10,000 when I was actually at zero feet. How could this be done? The altimeter arrow which indicates each 10,000 ft is only 1/4 inch long and is rarely noticed.

I usually keep track in my head of each 10,000 ft. I had flown over the boat twice and made a half-hearted attempt to follow the computer solution to the intercept. As I did this, I must have computed the tens wrong. I had been skimming along only a few feet above it, thinking I was at 10,000. Imagine the surprise of the guys on the boat, locked in sea fog, when a big jet passes nearby with condensed vapor streaming off the semi-stalled wing.

As I came roaring out of the fog, I could see Bart exactly where he had been a few seconds before, and incidentally, the mountains of

Northeast Iceland in the distance. Bart is in a gentle bank, watching a spot where he expects me to emerge. To his surprise, I emerge at a very steep angle.

My first thought after such a close call: *What can I say to convince Bart that I didn't screw up?*

"I guess that sea fog is thicker than I thought, let's join up and RTB, two."

Bart rocks his wings.

I had probably been subconsciously aware of the situation, since there are no 10,000 ft. mountains in Iceland.

Climbing out toward the mountains in the distance, I felt strangely fine for someone so narrowly missing his demise. My knees didn't shake, and my voice sounded the usual way. I was breathing a little fast—an adrenaline rush to be sure. It was the most alive I had ever felt. Aside from being a little worried that Bart would figure it out, I felt good all over.

Bart never whispered a word to me or anyone else about it.

10. The East Wind

In 1982, the USAF precision-flying demonstration team suffered a tragic loss. The Thunderbirds, while practicing near Las Vegas, Nevada, crashed four aircraft in perfect formation. The leader had been unable to pull out from a steep dive, due to a jammed stabilizer. The three wingmen obediently followed him to their precisely aligned deaths. Most earthbound persons who heard that story probably marveled at the ridiculous irony of such highly skilled pilots doing such a thing. Every fighter pilot who heard that story silently nodded in understanding.

"Don't get lost on the radio channel changes, be there in formation, and if I crash, there should be two smoking holes in perfect formation." That was the standard formation briefing at the time. Did I believe it? Not exactly, but the message was clear.

Capt. Charles M. really believed it. He had served in the 57th earlier, witnessing the arrival of the F-102 when the F-89s were replaced. I had been at Kef for six months when Charlie arrived for his second tour. His reputation for being a "fighter pilot's fighter pilot" preceded him. Three inches shorter than me at five nine and twenty pounds heavier, he did not stand out as a lunatic. He had short, dark hair, a roundish head, and a narrow pencil of a mustache perched atop of a pleasant smile. His classic pose was standing at the squadron bar, the Whiff, turned toward the door, dressed in a green flight suit, its sleeves rolled up to the elbows, combat boots, no hat, and with a beer in his hand. A likable fellow, always ready with a good story, he

Aeromorphosis

was quick to buy anyone a 25-cent Heineken if you would listen. He soon became the commander of the Whiff. Each officer who came to the 57th squadron was whiffed. This had been a playful initiation that involved drinking and recitations. Charlie made it a near-death experience. It got much tougher under his supervision. I was happy to have been whiffed before Charlie's reign.

On one occasion when flying his wing, Charlie said, "Tuck it in a little, two." He then proceeded to lead us into a very narrow valley which is just east of Reykjavik. I could see the rocks whizzing by his left wingtip and could only guess how close they were to my right wingtip. Returning solo to the area another day, I could see three valleys in that vicinity. I dropped down to slightly above the easternmost one. As I skimmed over the rocks without actually dropping down in it, I decided that this could not have been the valley that we flew into, since it was much too narrow. I maneuvered over to the next one. Same thing. Well, that settled it, it must have been the third valley. It was too narrow for me even as a single plane! But that was just the way Chuck operated, suffering sissies poorly.

I had mixed feelings when the alert board said "M*****" and "SMIT." If I had been hoping for an interesting day, I was not to be disappointed.

It was snowing hard. Only those crazy LofthleÐir Airline pilots were flying in it, practicing approaches; the weather being too bad for us to negotiate. The red telephone rang ominously. It had that bad news–sounding ring.

"Get your shaving kit, a clean flight suit, and stuff them into your cockpit. We're launching you guys in a few minutes on a pair of Zombies. You will recover at Leuchars until the weather clears here."

10. The East Wind

RAF Leuchars lies six hundred forty nautical miles southeast of Iceland on the Channel side of Scotland. Four Squadron, flying the Lightning fighter, made its home there. I had never been there, but the flight sounded like fun, and I looked forward to it.

The plan called for taking off about midnight and conserving fuel the best we could. With the tailwinds calculated at 100 knots, we would be able to make a quick pass on the Zombies and land at Leuchars with over two thousand pounds of fuel. The bingo fuel, or fuel to leave the target, was fifty-six hundred pounds. A few hours later, we departed Kef with Chuck in the lead and me in radar trail. It was still snowing, and the only place to land was six hundred forty miles away.

As we Uvalde, Texas, boys (Matthew McConaughey and I) often say, "Allriiiiiiiight." *I'm finally getting off the rock.*

I had applied for an exchange assignment flying Lightnings at Leuchars when flying at the 48th at Langley AFB. After countless applications and interviews, I had been accepted. Only after getting my hopes up, I was informed that the officer occupying that billet, a Captain Michael Lanning, would be allowed to extend for an additional three years. I was out. The Lightning was one of the hottest and most interesting fighters in the world. It was powered by two huge engines stacked one over the other. Its highly swept wings appeared to be chopped off on a line along the lateral axis. The pilots from Four Squadron frequently intercepted the Bears alongside the 57th pilots, but with one big difference: they usually brought along a tanker. That meant that they could do things such as "hot nosing" and other dramatic maneuvers while far from shore. I had seen these pilots in action and was anxious to meet them. They were our sister squadron and would refuel our F-102s upon arrival.

"Sloe Gin zero one flight, you have two targets, zero seven zero for one hundred fifty," Chuck called for the formation to split up and check out the Bears individually, to save fuel. Even so, it would have to be quick, as I was down to six thousand pounds, only four hundred above bingo.

As I closed in on the trailing bomber, its lights went out! I could still see its silhouette and glow from the engines. Moving away a bit, I followed suit and also turned my lights off. Being the less maneuverable of the two, the bomber pilot prudently decided to turn his back on. As I slipped in closer, I could see that it was an ordinary Delta model. It was going to be too dark to see the numbers on the nose wheel door.

"Two's off, one Bear Delta, one alpha, one bravo, one charlie, five thousand six hundred." My carefully practiced calm voice belied my urge to turn toward Scotland, about forty degrees left.

"OK hang high, two, I'll be off in a minute."

"Two is bingo minus five hundred."

"Lead's off, Pigeons to home plate (what direction and how far to destination), Drainage."

"Sloe Gin flight, your pigeons are one four seven for three eighty."

No sweat, I planned to use about seven hundred pounds for a hundred miles. If we had no tailwind, we would arrive with two thousand pounds. The tailwind would only add to the margin. The first hundred miles used nine hundred pounds of fuel. The 100-knot tailwind had turned into a headwind.

10. The East Wind

"Say state, two." Chuck wanted to know my fuel.

"Three point eight." If the winds held constant, we would arrive with only a thousand pounds plus a little made up in the descent. Emergency fuel was eight hundred pounds.

That five hundred pounds that Chuck farted away would be very nice to have now, I thought.

As we made landfall at the northern end of Scotland, the lights outlining the runway of Royal Navy Kinloss twinkled below. I had a strong urge to suggest diverting into that base.

"Let's balance 'em up real close, two." Chuck was suggesting that since we were low on fuel, it would be good to have an equal amount of fuel in each of the two wing tanks that contained fuel. This would prevent one side from sucking air and possibly inducing a flameout. The gauge selector switch was spring-loaded to total. The gauge now indicated seventeen hundred pounds, not much to go 120 miles and land. As I turned the gauge selector to "3 left," the gauge winds down to eight hundred, the 3 right tank showed 900. Ordinarily an acceptable imbalance. In an attempt to be more precise, I turned off the left boost pumps and began feeding the engine from the right side. Momentarily I checked the right side and it was down to eight hundred. Back on with the left boost pumps and it was finished.

Maybe I'll just check it one more time. Now the right is down to six hundred and the left is still at eight hundred. Oh shit, oh shit. I have eight hundred pounds trapped in the left wing. I've only got six hundred pounds useable and I'm not going to make the runway. I began to visualize performing a night ejection. The problem was later diagnosed as frozen valve in the fuel system, although no one ever knew for sure.

The best scenario would have me parachute to the ground and the airplane hit the English Channel. Fat chance, the way my luck was going.

"Lead, two, I've trapped some fuel. I only have six hundred pounds useable."

"Roger."

Roger? Hell, you'd think he'd show a little sympathy.

"Tuck it in, two. Approach control, Sloe Gin zero one flight requests landing clearance on runway two seven."

"Cleared to land, flight of two," is the instant reply.

We are now thirty miles northwest of the field, throttles at idle, at speed. The only thing I can see is lead's dark silhouette and rotating beacon. I expected that, being very low on fuel, Chuck would maneuver so as to keep the bank very gentle and thereby not risk disturbing the fuel flow. Chuck's left wing dips abruptly. This is the "cross under" signal. It means that I should cross under his aircraft and position myself on the left side. Obediently I begin the maneuver, although for a gentle straight-in approach this side would have been just as good. We are at idle power; the only way I can keep from overrunning Chuck is to crack the speed brakes a little. As I pass under lead, the Gs seem to build. All the strain of the flight must have just gotten to me. No one, even Chuck, would pull a tight turn in this situation. Chuck's fighter abruptly pulls away. In a flash, he is gone. For a moment I considered just rolling wings level and ejecting. Looking right (down), I realized that Chuck had positioned us for a fighter break and I had no clue it was happening. All I really have to do now is extend the landing gear, continue the turn, and land. That is, if the engine keeps running.

10. The East Wind

Chuck had come in fast from the north and entered "initial approach." When I crossed under, I was being positioned for a fighter break. What a dumb stunt.

"Zero two, would you like to have the barrier raised?" came the thick Scottish accent.

A barrier meant to me a wire to catch with the tailhook.

"Affirmative," I reply.

I touch down and rolled out to the end, not using the drag chute. As I turn off, I notice a huge net, much taller than his airplane and as wide as the runway, I had never seen anything like it. I was later enlightened over the subtleties of barriers versus "hook wires." I slowly taxi to the parking area and shut down the engine, which surprisingly is still running.

"Yep, eight hundred left side, zero right. It never fed."

I opened the canopy and took off my helmet. The cool air felt good on my sweaty hair. The engine wound down slowly, and as it nearly stopped, the compressor blades began their characteristic muffled clanking, a moment to remember.

A person hooked a ladder to the canopy sill and scampered up.

"Hi, welcome to Leuchars, I'm Mike Lanning."

For a moment I thought about saying, "You son of a bitch. You screwed me out of an exchange assignment. I'm going to kick your ass." Being a guest in need of help, I decided against that.

Later, I awoke with the phone ringing its goofy British ring. It was Mike, strongly suggesting that we go to the "club" for a round of drinks. Being well aware that their club is different from the USAF clubs, I knew that dress uniforms with tie would be required. Few women and absolutely no smelly flight suits are allowed. The orange flight suit that I had stuffed behind the ejection seat, while not smelly, certainly wasn't very dressy.

"Of course, you can come there in your flying suit, you've earned it," Mike assured me. It was true. No one so much as raised an eyebrow over my appearance. I never bought a drink either. It was among the warmest receptions I had ever had. As we talked about airplanes and whiskey and good cigars, I soon forgot about my rage at Chuck and my imagined injustice at the hands of Mike Lanning. Fortunately, the weather remained below minimums at Kef, so no one deemed it necessary to stay even remotely sober.

On the second day there, I began to get a little restless. Sensing this, one of the pilots asked if I "Mightn't be a golfer." Replying in the affirmative, he then asked if I had heard of St. Andrews. Well, of course, it is the most famous golf course in the world.

"Here's the keys to my car, you'd better go and check it out. It really is only a ten-minute drive." I went straight to the clubhouse at the old course. Very conspicuous, in my orange flying suit and flying boots, I roamed around the huge hall, gawking unabashedly. A leprechaun approached me. He wasn't really a leprechaun, but he was a smallish fellow with an impressive burr in his speech.

"Visiting St. Andrews, are ye?"

"Well, yeah, I'm honored to be here. It's like a church for golf here."

10. The East Wind

"Aren't ye going to play the course before you go back home?"

"You mean guys like me can play here?"

"Cerrrrrrrtainly, anyone can play here."

"Well, I really don't have the proper attire, and it's getting late."

"Nonsense, I'll have none of that. You take my clubs and get yourself out there and tee off, before it gets too dark."

I played the old course out to the water and ran out of daylight coming in. On your scorecard at your favorite course, you probably have "out" for the front nine and "in" for the back nine. That tradition started at the St. Andrews old course, where there are only nine huge greens each with two flags and cups. One for play out to the water, and one for in to the clubhouse. There were some looooong putts. The only thing that the little guy would let me pay for was some souvenir wood covers. The hospitality there was warm. That is ironic, considering how many times I've encountered rude or arrogant people at lesser courses elsewhere.

The next day, the weather had cleared at Kef but was beginning to hang low at Leuchars. As they prepared to leave, Mike promised to send the 57th a bill for our expenses. He never did. Chuck briefed an exciting departure in which we would turn sharply and buzz the squadron operations building.

The weather was low, and as we began a turn after takeoff, the tower admonished us to depart straight out. To his credit, Chuck complied. There was a hill with its top in the fog at the departure end of the runway.

Aeromorphosis

I never did figure out what made Chuck tick. Chuck survived that year at Kef and returned a few years later as the commander. He was fired halfway through that tour.

11. Combat Pike

Combat Pike is a program in which operational squadrons take their own aircraft and pilots to Tyndall AFB and fire live weapons at airborne drones. This program produces good results. The pilots practice their job in a realistic environment and maintenance must produce aircraft and weapons that actually work. Everyone involved happily accepted the opportunity to leave Iceland for a few weeks.

John Maier and I were classmates in F-106 school at Tyndall AFB, Florida. There were four in that four-month program. He garnered the best assignment, Hamilton AFB at San Francisco. Sometime during that period, he married Kitty, a wonderful woman who kept him from taking himself too seriously.

I heard that he had been assigned to the 57th at Kef after I had been there for a few months. I had a premonition of John standing there in the doorway to the bathroom that two suites shared. Shortly, there he was, just as I had imagined, my suitemate.

John and I were among the pilots to accompany the operations officer, Howard H. "Mac" McWhirter to Tyndall for Combat Pike. We launched in several two-ship formations leaving Kef for Sondestromfjord, Greenland. Initially, I flew Mac's wing on the first leg.

As an aside here: Air Force has ships in formations, the Navy has planes. Their ships ply the seas. When I mention a two-ship formation in the company of Navy pilots, I always receive surprised looks.

Aeromorphosis

"How could an Air Force pilot participate in a formation of ships?" they ask.

Flying over eight hundred miles of 32-degree water makes anyone a little jumpy. I wanted to put on my best flying performance for someone as important as the ops officer. Mac was a big, loudmouthed guy who flew the Deuce very well and apparently feared nothing. After takeoff, I found it somehow comforting to remain in very close formation. This was very aggravating for Mac because the airflow deflected by my aircraft constantly pushed up Mac's wing. Finally, he came over the radio,

"Would you give it up and spread it out, practice some other time."

Halfway across the Iceland-Greenland gap, I began to pick up the coastline on radar. It was closer than my flight plan predicted.

"Looks like we're five minutes ahead of the plan."

"That's ice," came the curt reply.

I had mistaken the ice surrounding the coastline for what was to come forty miles later.

Flying thirty thousand feet above the Greenland ice cap is void of visual cues. Looking down through a few clouds, the ice, clouds, and rocks combine to form an image with no depth.

Ernest Gann, in *Fate Is the Hunter*, tells a story of this strange effect. The pilots of a PBY aircraft gently flew onto the icecap without realizing it. The airplane came to a complete stop with the engines at full cruising power. This hazard is exaggerated by the large magnetic variation there. That is, to go northwest, one must steer southwest on

11. Combat Pike

a magnetic compass. Soon we spotted an Air Force "Dye" site, part of a radar early-warning network. This gives considerable definition to the landscape. It is a huge platform on long stilts, much like an ocean-borne drilling rig. We requested a radar fix and found that we were right on course. The poor devils were anxious to talk to us. The chitchat was still going when we finally flew out of range.

Sondestromfjord, or Sonde, lies at the end of a twenty-five-mile long fjord. With steep sides and a six-thousand-foot icecap at the east end of the runway, the approach is formidable. The airport has a flat-topped mountain on the south side, 1300 feet above the runway level. On the north side lies a much taller mountain. Always the showman, Mac elected to reject the usual straight-in approach and fly a fighter-type overhead approach.

A clear day happens rarely in the Arctic, and this was one of them.

"Sonde tower, Sloe Gin Zero One Flight is turning a five-mile initial with two of the finest."

I imagined what fishermen in the fjord saw overhead. Approaching the runway along its extended centerline, 1700 ft. above the runway, and with wingman tightly tucked in, two fighters appear silently from downwind. The pair passes over the end of the runway, with the jet engine noise in tow. Lead crisply breaks into a 60-degree banked turn to the right. Three seconds later, number two does the same. As they proceed abound the turn, the mountain comes up to meet them. While they momentarily fly downwind, away from the runway, they are a scant 500 feet above the rocks and shrubs. They sprout wheels and begin a tight turn and roll out over the runway threshold, first one then the other. Drag chutes billow immediately after touchdown. They join in formation as they clear the runway. Drag chutes pop off the planes simultaneously and they taxi together. Sporting checkerboard rudders, bright red tail and wingtips, canopies open, they disappear below the hump in the runway. A sunny day in Greenland was not wasted.

When I taxied up to the parking area and shut down, I had only one thought on my mind: to pee. I had been carrying several cups of coffee for three and a half hours, and there is no relief tube in the Deuce. A Danish mechanic met me with a stepladder, rather than the fancy custom one used at home. I painfully climbed down, walked behind the wing, and disrobed sufficiently to accomplish the mission. As I was standing there, relieving myself, I looked to my right toward the far end of the ramp. As far as I could see, perhaps a half mile, there were little dark circular stains on the concrete. Only then did I realize that I had become a part of a tradition in aviation there. Nearly every fighter pilot passing here likely had done much the same as I.

The next day we flew to Goose Bay, Labrador. Arriving there with extra fuel, we flew in spread formation up the Northwest River, at low altitude. We probably weren't the first humans to do that, but there was no evidence to the contrary. The scenery passing below looked like a wilderness painting. Steep cliffs rose from the river and tapered off into craggy hillsides. Sometimes, a startled elk or caribou would dash away.

Tiring of that, we landed and joined up with John Maier. The following day, we made the short trip to Griffiss AFB at Rome, New York.

Stormy weather lashed the base that night. When I arrived at the jet the next morning, three inches of water sloshed around the cockpit floor. Transient maintenance had serviced all three aircraft and closed the canopies of two. I remembered that the F-102 was equipped with a cockpit drain plug which opened a path from the

11. Combat Pike

cockpit to the nose wheel well. I pulled the drain plug, started the engine, closed the canopy, and pressurized the cockpit. Water squirted vigorously out the drain, and soon it was gone. However, none of the electronics worked. I requested and connected an auxiliary electrical power unit to the aircraft and turned everything on, in hopes of making the flight to Langley with Mac and John. When Mac gave me the start signal, I still didn't have a radio, but much of the fire control system was functional—a good sign. As we taxied out, the old ARC-34 radio could be heard trying to channelize to the tower frequency. These radios contained a motor that moved crystals inside the radio to tune frequencies, a foolishly unreliable approach as viewed from the digital age. I was faced with a dilemma: I could take off on the wing and "fake it" without a radio. If I lost sight of lead in the weather with no radio, the situation would be desperate. Rain pounded on the tops of our wings as we waited. The clouds were low and thick.

I had been gone from the 48th for only a few months. One of the T-33 pilots was having a bachelor party to celebrate his upcoming marriage. It would most certainly be a party to remember.

Just as I gripped the throttle to taxi back to the cocks, the radio channelized to Griffiss Tower frequency.

"Kerchunk."

"Three's ready." I tried to sound as if I had known all along that the radio would work.

Mac, surprised, snapped his helmeted head around so quickly that his dangling oxygen mask flapped twice. I gave him a thumbs up. Mac, having waited for me for almost fifteen minutes, immediately called the tower, ready.

We taxied onto the runway as the rain pounded even harder. Mac took the center, John on the right and I on the left, which I viewed with additional trepidation. Most fighter pilots are most comfortable on the right wing because of the location of the throttle on the left side. In heavy weather, one can turn a bit toward the left, making it seem to be easier. On the right wing, one must turn away, and it sometimes feels that your hands are behind you.

The "dash one," which is the pilots' bible on how to properly operate an Air Force aircraft, called for the pilot to do two things immediately after takeoff. First was to reach down between your knees and turn on the yaw dampers. This augmented the stability of the aircraft and was highly desirable to have. Allegedly, sometime in the past, some unlucky soul had a runway excursion attributed to a damper failure during takeoff. Foreseeing that I would likely be very busy after takeoff, I turned on the yaw dampers. Also a violation, I turned on the drop tank switch. We were supposed to wait until airborne to turn on the drop tanks.

Mac looked first at John then at me, giving us the runup signal, index finger up, circling. I nodded and pushed the throttle full forward—no need to do it slowly, as the fuel control took care of that. The Engine Pressure Ratio (EPR) needle climbed up and settled into the notch that indicated full power. All the lesser dials being in an eye-pleasing position, I took one last long look at them, knowing that I would not have time to steal a glance for a long while. Mac was impatiently looking at me when I turned my head. I looked at him and nodded affirmatively. He returned the nod and tapped his helmet, indicating that the next signal would be a nod. I had positioned myself forward of the proper formation position. This was intentional, for I planned to slowly slip back into the proper place during the roll. You could slip back, but catching up was nearly impossible.

11. Combat Pike

I felt that my throttle hand was behind my back and that I was turned around to the right. His head went back and tilted up, then, in a fashion with which I was well familiar, snapped forward. I leaped off the toe brake pedals. A good start, we rolled in perfect unison. His head went back again and snapped forward.

I pushed the throttle outboard for afterburner. As the engine nozzle opened, I could feel a sudden loss of thrust, which was normal. The exhaust nozzle opened fully, the afterburner fuel control dumped a quart of fuel into the engine hot section, sending a hot streak of flame through the turbine, which ignited the fuel now streaming from the afterburner spray bars. "*Pom*," then "*pom-pom*," I could hear all three afterburners light. I knew that my engine was OK because I was keeping up with lead. In fact, I was now slightly farther ahead, since I was a fraction of a second early with the burner.

I pulled the throttle back a quarter of an inch, still in afterburner. This caused a pleasing drift back into the position I sought. We all have little gouges, or indications, of proper position: wingtip lined up with the star on the intake, and others, all predicated on being able to see the fuselage. After one acquires experience, it's more a feeling of being in position than a single gouge. I felt good as the nosewheels of three fighters lifted off. My hand was already on the gear handle, and I pulled it up immediately, without looking away from lead. We were tucked in tightly when we entered the low clouds.

"Once you were there, then phhhht, you was gone," goes the C&W song, and so disappeared lead. In a second, my eyes adjust to the darkness and I began to see lead's wingtip. This was by far the thickest weather I had ever seen. I moved in a little closer. My eyeballs were now about five feet from his wingtip; It seemed like three. I could now see about five feet past the wingtip and barely make out the first stall fence, a strip that goes over the top of the wing. A sudden turn by lead now would either lose me or kill me. Not to worry, though, as Mac is as smooth as they come.

"Sloe Gin Zero One Flight, turn left to a heading of one five zero, climb and maintain seven thousand," Mac replies, and banks so smoothly that I do not know. I try to breathe normally, but it doesn't come easily.

I began to creep forward and pull the power way back. We must be leveling off at seven thousand.

"Sloe Gin Zero One Flight (SG01) is level at seven thousand, request higher, immediately."

"Stand by."

I desperately wanted us to climb out of this misery. *Ticktock, ticktock*, we auger on through the rain and clouds.

"Chick-booooom." I head thunder as lightning flashed behind us. Of course, we have no business flying in weather like this, but, after all, parties are important.

"New York Center, Sloe Gin Zero One."

"Go ahead."

"I'm sure you don't understand how important it is for us to climb or you would have already cleared us. What we have here is a flight of three fighters flying formation in weather that you can't drive in. If you don't get us higher right now, I'm personally going to have your ass."

11. Combat Pike

"Yes, sir, climb to Flight Level two zero zero."

Oh, bless you, Mac, I knew that tough-guy act would come in handy someday. We broke out into the bright morning sunlight at 16,000 ft., and John and I loosened up to tactical position to relax. At that very moment, my radio broke channelization and started a raspy "*cha cha cha, cha cha cha.*" I reached down on the right side and tuned the data link receiver to the New York Center frequency. Then I tightened it up to close formation again. Mac was looking down and didn't see me.

"Sloe Gin Zero One Flight contact Washington Center on three eighty-three point one."

"Roger, let's go three eighty-three point one."

"Two," John called.

Mac's helmet snapped to look my way. I waved my hand up and down in front of my mouth, indicating no transmitter. He nodded in understanding and waved his hand up and down beside his ear to ask if I had lost my receiver too. I give him a big thumbs up.

"Sloe Gin Zero One flight, let's go three eighty-three point one."

"Sloe Gin Zero One flight check in."

"Two."

I just nod.

Soon, the old home base was ahead and we did our best to impress the 48th with our landing. A challenging flight to be sure, but a man has to know his priorities.

Aeromorphosis

The big guys were happy to see that their boy had survived the Arctic, apparently unscathed. After a successful party, I retired early.

Late the next day, we made our way into Tyndall AFB at Panama City, FL. We settled into a routine for a week. Rising early, I would eat a big breakfast at the club and report to the test squadron briefing. There I would be informed whether or not I would fly, be an alternate, or take the day off. If flying or alternating, we were then subjected to an excruciating briefing. Regulations specified what information should be covered. For an hour we would listen to things that we had long before memorized. The missile shot would be an infrared heat-seeking AIM-4B. AIM stands for "airborne intercept missile."

The F-102 was the first of a short line of fighters with no gun. The logic held that missiles were so effective that guns were not needed. Against a lethargic bomber-type target, this logic might have worked, but against a rapidly maneuvering fighter, it failed. The AIM-4B and its radar-guided sister, the AIM-4A, drove maintenance personnel and pilots crazy trying to get them to work properly. The intelligence within them received electrical power from the fighter until B-time, when the missile internal batteries were irreversibly activated. These batteries lasted for three minutes. The fins on the outside of the missile were driven hydraulically. At D-time, tiny hydraulic motors were activated. These lasted only a minute. Fortunately, Combat Pike shots were against bomber-type targets, and the threat of a dead missile was low.

We launched in pairs, then split up for the shot. Today's target would be a TDU-25. This is a kerosene lamp with wings, towed behind an F-101 on three miles of wire. The trick, of course, was to pick out the target rather than the tractor. GCI directed the tractor, target, and fighter close enough for me to see them on my radar.

11. Combat Pike

"Red one (me), contact three one zero at six miles and three one zero at three."

"Contact is target and tractor, arm hot."

I had previously selected "Missiles IR" on the rotary selection knob, and now I pulled hard on the safety wired red cover on the arming switch. It popped open, exposing a toggle switch beneath. I pressed it upward with my index finger. "Red One armed hot."

I gently rotate the antenna elevation thumbwheel to make the radar target as bright as possible. Next, I press the Radar-Infrared cross mode button below the thumbwheel. Now there is a new display superimposed on the radar. It is a white dot of video and a tone to hear. The radar dish is now slaved to the IR seeker head. When they sweep past the target, the dot jumps up an inch or so then back down, indicating a strong IR source. I squeeze the action switch, direct the dot to the source, and release it. Now the tone is steady in my ears. The IR lock-on display appears, looking like a big triangle flanked by two smaller ones. Down in the armament bay, the missile goes to internal power. The timing circle shrinks to one-inch diameter. The radar return from the tractor appears at five miles and the target at two.

"Red one, Judy three one zero at two."

"Judy is target, cleared to fire."

I squeeze the trigger full down; the launch will be automatic. The timing circle collapses to a quarter of an inch in diameter and I steer the aircraft to keep the dot inside it. The big pneumatically actuated armament bay doors open with a jolt, and the missile is lowered on its rails. The firing X appears on the scope, and a tiny little rocket appears under the nose and pulls away at a not-too-impressive pace. The doors close.

An IR missile is autonomous. All it does is find the IR source. A radar missile must be illuminated by the fighter until it strikes. In real life, I would break away and leave. However, in the controlled situation, it's OK to pull over a little and watch the missile work. It covers a little less than a mile in less than ten seconds.

I see the target glowing a bright red and the white from the missile rocket motor closing in. The target has a scoring device on it, and I will get full credit for a 5-foot miss. The ancient missile does better than that. They collide in a splash of kerosene, rocket fuel, and metal. Even without a warhead the collision is spectacular. The fireball grows to thirty feet in diameter and quickly subsides.

"MA (mission accomplished), splash (hit the target)," I say excitedly.

"Roger, report arm-safe," the controller replies, not impressed.

I push the arm switch down and move the rotary switch back to Vis-Ident. "Arm-safe check complete, RTB (return to base)."

"Roger, pigeons (direction to home base) are zero two zero for five five, fly heading three six zero for initial approach."

Sometimes the magic works.

12. Fireball

One for one was to be my marksmanship record with the F-102 for a while. Two days later, I drew a lucky lot. One of our pilots was chosen to shoot a combat round at a Mace, a combat round being a live warhead on a missile like I had fired. The Mace was a 1950s version of a cruise missile. It was a big aircraft, about 70 ft. long with shoulder-mounted swept wings and a T-tail. Its purpose: carry a nuclear weapon a few hundred miles. It was contemporaneous with the Regulus and the B-61 Matador. Its only use in 1972 amounted to being a full-scale target on which to test our weapons.

I was selected to be *Shotgun*. I would fly in the vicinity of the test, armed with a full complement of three AIM-4As, three AIM-4Bs, and 24 FFARs, the latter being 3.5 in unguided rockets. If the Mace were to become uncontrollable and threatening, I would receive clearance to shoot it down. I would also chase it off the launch pad. This is a bit tricky, because it accelerates from 0 to 250 knots in a few seconds as it is fired with RATO rocket bottles. It then climbs out on its jet engine. I was told to come across, perpendicular to the line of flight as the countdown proceeded. Close to launch time, I should turn parallel to the expected line of flight and join up.

I could see the Mace pad a couple of miles ahead. Countdown in my ears.

"Ten, nine, eight." The water was on my left. I began a gentle turn in that direction.

Aeromorphosis

"Seven, six, five." Coming up abeam the pad, I dove so as to bottom out at about 300 feet. Speed 300 knots—better too much than too little.

"Four, three, two." I passed the launch pad, hoping for success.

"One, zero, fire." Looking back, I can see the smoke and fire from the RATO bottles. It catches up to me in a heartbeat. The spent bottles drop, and we are flying formation. I'm abeam and a hundred feet to its right. The Mace pulls away a bit, so I light the afterburner and pull in closer. It climbs rapidly, but not so much as to require me to stay in afterburner.

As we climb to the briefed altitude of 15,000 feet, I tell them that their target looks OK. It is the first one I have ever seen; I have no idea what it is supposed to look like. We level off as planned. But the 290-knot cruise speed is quickly exceeded. Maximum speed for the Mace is 400 knots.

"Better pull the power back, it's accelerating through three hundred knots."

No answer.

"Approaching limit speed, *over*" (meaning answer me).

No answer.

"You guys better start a climb or something, we just passed four hundred knots."

(GCI) "OK it's out of control, just let us work."

12. Fireball

"Request permission to destroy the Mace."

"Negative, negative, it's headed for safe water and we may regain control."

Damn, an airplane full of weapons and they won't let me shoot. Flight at speeds above Red line is unpredictable territory, especially for an old machine like the Mace. I ease out 200 feet and pull forward of the abeam. If it explodes, it can't get me here.

Speed 460, 480—this is going to be good if it doesn't run out of gas. My airspeed says 495. I'm going to keep my eyes glued to it now.

The wing on the opposite side breaks at the root and folds back along the fuselage. Losing its balancing force from the left, the whole aircraft rolls violently to the left. But with every lift there is an associated drag, and the nose yaws hard to the right before the wing can roll 90 degrees. As the relative wind strikes the side of the fuselage, it breaks at the trailing edge of the wing. It is nearly sideways now and the tail and nose fold, back leaving the break in front. It explodes into a bright yellow, red, and black fireball about two wingspans in diameter. It seems to spit fire and metal out the front as the edges curl back. Pieces of the tail and wings fall back in a cone behind it, no danger to me. I pull up and turn back to see. It has stopped forward movement now and is raining fire and metal downward.

"Splash one Mace, do you get the kill or do I?"

"Very funny. Get us a location on the wreckage, please."

"OK. I'm going to give it a few minutes to clear first."

Aeromorphosis

I circle there for a full ten minutes, watching the big pieces hit the water, far below.

"I'm going down for a look, prepare to mark on my call."

I push over and fly close to the water, 50 feet. I have oriented this pass where I know the fuselage hit. It's a calm day, and I will likely see anything still floating. Out of the corner of my eye, I see a flash. Only a few feet to my right something huge passes and hits the water with a splash. I instinctively dodge left. It misses me, but not by much.

"There's still stuff falling out here. I'm too low on fuel to get your mark, RTB." I suppose that big, flat pieces of metal do a sort of falling leaf trajectory. I would have bet money that all debris would have settled in 10 minutes. This is a classic case of using up some luck to acquire experience.

I tried to say I shot it down, but no one bought it. It was an exciting mission, and a good one to quit on before returning to KEF.

John took some leave, so it was just Mac and I on the flights back. We found ourselves at Goose Bay, Labrador a few days later. To cross the water to Greenland, we needed a "Duckbutt"—an HC-130 rescue plane that waits in the middle of the track for us to pass. If we were to jump out, they would drop a big thirty-man raft with lots of survival equipment. We would theoretically survive, even in 32-degree water. This had to be coordinated by the Air Force Officer at Goose called the "Ferry Squadron Commander." Imagine that on your resume. Mac and I took off on a beautiful spring day and headed for the track. We had passed the coastline when the Duckbutt came up on the frequency.

12. Fireball

"What is your position, Sloe Gin Flight, we have secured our number three engine."

"Fifty miles past Hopedale," said Mac.

"Looks like a mission abort."

"Can't you guys stay for a few minutes more? We'll be past the ETP (equal time point) in twenty minutes." (The equal time point is the equal distance point compensated for winds.)

"Negative, negative, we have a serious emergency, aborting mission."

"OK, you're the judge of that. Be safe."

We swung back toward Goose and had another sightseeing tour of Labrador. After landing, we gathered on the ramp to watch the HC-130 land with their emergency. Imagine our surprise when it flew overhead and kept going toward Pease AFB, 700 miles away.

"What a pisser, they couldn't stay on track for twenty minutes, but can make it all the way to Pease. Some emergency," Mac groused.

That afternoon, we retired to the Officers Club. A sign posted at the entrance declared "Only Strategic Air Command combat pilots allowed in this building in flight suits." Of course, we had to challenge that rule by conspicuously entering in our flight suits. No one challenged us. While there, we were introduced to a local custom of drinking a glass of gin with a guppy in it. After dropping the fish into the glass, if one could drink the gin before the guppy died, the drink was free. That seemed to be a reasonable bet, but unbeknownst to us, the guppy, once dropped into the glass, perishes instantly and dives straight to the bottom. The bomber pilots had extracted their pound of flesh from the fighter pilots.

Two days later, we were ready to try again. The winds were favorable, the weather unusually cooperative, and Duckbutt in place. It's always been a little tense flying over long stretches of cold water on one engine, even with a Duckbutt. You hear unusual sounds from your aircraft, and every little bump of turbulence startles you. We were just past the ETP when one of my hydraulic systems failed. This illuminates a very large rectangular red light that says "HYD." It's very serious. The aircraft flight controls are moved by hydraulic power. There are no cables to serve as backup to the controls. Fortunately, the F-102 was equipped with two systems. The primary system, which had failed, supplies power to the flight controls only. The utility system supplies power to the landing gear, other components, and more importantly, an additional set of flight control actuators. As an additional backup, ram air turbine (RAT) could be deployed to supply pressure to the primary system if that pump failed. The primary pump had failed and unbeknownst to me had destroyed all the primary actuators with little pieces of metal. The utility actuators operated in parallel and could provide reduced, but sufficient hydraulic power to fly and land.

"Uh, Mac, I've got a problem."

"What is it?"

"Lost primary hydraulics. I've got good control on utility, though."

"Anything I can do for you?"

"Well, I've got plenty of fuel, how about we turn and head for shore then to Sonde."

12. Fireball

"Good idea, turning now."

Aside from having my stomach tied in a knot and squeezing the stick real hard, the rest of the flight to Sonde was pretty routine. After rounding up a mechanic, we heard the verdict. The hydraulic pump blew and ruined all the seals in the actuators. Mac had a phone in his ear.

The rules are clear: no one may operate a single-engine fighter across the Greenland-Iceland gap unless it is part of a multiple aircraft formation. Also, no one may take off eastbound toward the icecap, which rises to more than 6,000 feet just fifteen miles from the airport. That's exactly what he did. Special dispensation, I suppose, permitted this. I was left to wait for help. The Ferry Squadron Commander was very nice about it and offered me his four-wheel-drive Dodge Power wagon for tourism.

Not a bad deal. Even though the sightseeing was limited and the night life nonexistent, I had no reason to hurry back to Kef.

Up bright and early the next morning, I had a big, cheap Air Force breakfast and began the tour. Choices were limited to the pier and the mountain. I decided to see the pier first. Hardly past the west end of the runway, the pier accommodated local Inuit fishermen rather than giant cargo ships. An interesting bunch, they had an appearance much like the Alaska natives, to my untrained eye. The kids had a ready smile, exposing already decayed teeth. Their equipment consisted of a few nets and ancient casting gear. They spoke no English.

Young Inuit Fishermen

After twenty minutes there, I was beginning to doubt that the week would be very much fun. I spotted a road leading northwest from the base that wasn't in the tour guide. The road began with a smooth stretch, but soon deteriorated to a trail. Nothing the Power wagon couldn't handle, though. It was negotiable, and after a few miles, it got better.

As the trail rose up out of the valley, I began to see signs of wildlife. Several varieties of flowers sprang from among the mosses. A covey of ptarmigan flushed from in front of me. As I rounded a hill, a herd of caribou stood, watching me from fifty yards away. With a snort, the single bull broke from the cows and trotted toward me. Defiantly standing his ground, he finally broke and ran when I drove to within 10 feet of him.

12. Fireball

Greenland Caribou

I bumped along for about twenty minutes, getting to a higher elevation. Ahead, I spotted a huge concrete structure. There, situated on a plateau, stood a tall concrete tower. About twenty feet square at its base, it rose perhaps fifty feet. Flanked by two small concrete huts, it had window-sized holes exposed to the elements. The inside of it was completely lined with copper. I guessed that it was some sort of resonating device for an ancient communication facility. Probably WWII era. Standing there with the wind whistling through the walls gave me the strange sensation that I was seeing not just a bygone time of my own people, but an icon of a completely alien time and place. One I could never understand. Returning to the Arctic Hotel, I planned my trip to the mountain for the next day.

A short drive, the top of the mountain lies just south of the base. Seeing the TACAN station was to be the highlight of the visit. Named for *TACtical Air Navigation*, the building proved to be unremarkable. However, the view from the summit was beautiful in an Arctic sort of way. To the west, the fjord, with its steeply walled sides, stretched for miles before disappearing into the haze. To the east, the icecap rose dramatically. Its size and perspective made it impossible to judge the distance. Nearer, the mountain sloped to the southwest in a gently sloping stone surface that stretched down to the water. Occasionally broken by a few shrubs, the slope appeared to be about a mile long.

I picked up a stone and tossed it over the edge. Picking up speed, it spun and jumped for nearly a minute before reaching the bottom. There were larger rocks available, even some boulders. I heaved one the size of a bowling ball over and to the side. It arced toward one of the clumps of bushes. As it went sailing through the clump, it erupted with foxes. They scampered to different bushes. By putting sufficient side thrust on the rock as I threw it, I could aim it at bushes down the slope.

I spent four hours herding foxes that day. On one of my best shots, I put a two-hundred-pound boulder through the center of a bush harboring a known fox. It boiled out, seemingly jumping straight up. I laughed so hard that tears were streaming down my face. Again, the ferry commander came over for a drink and found me cheerful about my touring. He informed me that KEF was sending an EC-121 with mechanics and parts. I would return as a passenger on it tomorrow.

12. Fireball

Sondrestromfjord

The EC-121, Adolla, usually ran the radar picket out northeast of Iceland. I had ridden on it before and had been impressed with the amount of fuel and number of engines that it carried. We were cruising at 7,000 feet on the relatively short leg to KEF. I had settled in with a paperback, being careful to appear to be bored about riding in this "trash-hauler." Presently, one of the enlisted crewmembers burst out of the cockpit, hurried to a spot near me, pulled open a huge trapdoor, and disappeared within. He emerged and dashed to the cockpit, leaving the trapdoor open. In a few minutes, a different guy came out of the cockpit headed for the trapdoor. I let him know that I'm not the least bit interested in what he is doing and that all this activity is disturbing my reading. After all, with ten hours of fuel on board and four engines, how bad could the trouble be? This went on for about thirty minutes and I noticed that we were doing a lot of turning too. Finally, I could stand it no longer.

"You guys are driving me nuts, what the hell are you doing down there anyway.?"

"We've lost our compass system."

"Well, does your whiskey compass work?" The whiskey or standby compass is the one every aircraft carries as a backup. Although subject to great variation in the Arctic, it could be used in a pinch.

He looked at me, and without saying a word disappeared into the cockpit. We made one more turn and later he came and closed the trapdoor. I never mentioned it, but I think I got to them on that one. They probably had their navigator up there taking star shots so as not to look stupid in front of the fighter pilot.

No one was awake when I arrived back at the Whiff. It would have been a great story.

13. Summer Idyll

After returning from Combat Pike, the Arctic summer season began. Being only slightly south of the Arctic Circle, the daylight became nearly constant. The only twilight to be seen happened about two in the morning. The aurora disappeared and, in its place, came something no less spectacular. On a sunny day, the temperature can soar past the sixty-degree mark. This signal, burned into the Icelander psyche for thousands of years, forces them to take off their clothes and sun themselves in their front yards.

Golf? Sure, how about a three a.m. tee time?

Tired of flying night formation? Lucky you, no darkness till October. The flying couldn't have been better. Headquarters lay two thousand miles west. That meant that our squadron, while conducting its mission, could be as autonomous as any in the Air Force. The primary rules: Bring the airplane back after flying, and don't make the locals so mad that they call the State Department.

Buzzing the radar bubbles was not only fair game, but encouraged because it would brighten the day for the poor souls condemned to work over a scope. One radar site was nestled adjacent to the runways at Keflavik. The large rotating antenna was covered by a radio-transparent rigid protective cover. About 80 feet in diameter, it required periodic painting. Several small, ugly buildings containing the associated electronics, offices, and work stations completed the H1 site.

Aeromorphosis

H3 ran most of the intercepts against the Russians. Located at Hofn at the southeast corner of Iceland, it lay two hundred fifty miles east of Kef. Rides for fighter pilots became popular in the weekly C-47 Gooney Bird resupply plane.

Performing a bubble check consisted mainly of saving enough fuel to go down near the surface and then being able to make it to home base, far away. Requests for such were always approved by the GCI controller. Nearing H3, I requested a bubble check.

"I have a visual on you, ETA three minutes."

As implied, I could see the buildings gleaming in the sun. My radar showed its location also, and at 400 knots I would be there shortly. Well, you can imagine that as dull as life was there, they all piled out to see the fighter go by. This is the sort of stuff that makes squadron commanders edgy. I didn't press in too close. Still, you have to put on a decent show. I came across east to west at 430 knots alongside and a little below the bubble. Lighting the burner precisely as I passed alongside the crowd, I pulled up smartly to the vertical with condensed vapor trails coming from the wings. Laying the stick over to the right, the big Delta made almost four vertical rolls before it began coupling, or wobbling on its longitudinal axis. I slowed the roll to get oriented and then stopped inverted with the nose slightly arched toward the west and Home plate. Now gently pulling the nose down through the horizon, I had peaked out at 25,000 feet.

"Good pass, Sloe Gin 11, thanks, pigeons two eight zero for two forty-five."

"My pleasure." I wasn't kidding.

13. Summer Idyll

A minor incident happened at H1, which began as a bubble check by one of my squadron mates. H1 is so close to Kef that a slightly large traffic pattern would take you directly over it. On the fateful day, an Icelander contract person had raised his scaffolding and was painting the bubble at the 25-foot level. One of our squadron's pilots, seeing this, elected to conduct a check. Dipping low over H1, he selected afterburner as he passed by and did a modest pullup. Surprised by the noise, Mr. Johansson lost his balance and fell backward, paint bucket, brushes, and all to the ground. A large white splotch of paint probably still marks the spot where he broke his arm. Nowadays, this would be an international incident, requiring an accident investigation board, a collateral board (to determine whether the pilot should be grounded), and a squadron commander's firing. But in 1972 at Kef, the situation was different. The only evidence of this was the notice on the bulletin board, a copy of which I kept.

"A serious incident happened on 12 Aug at H1 radar site. An Icelandic national, hired to paint the radar dome, fell from scaffolding and received a broken arm. This was due to the low flight and subsequent afterburner noise from a 57th F.I.S. F-102. This cannot be tolerated. In the future, when performing low level flight checks of the H1 radar site, do not, repeat, do not use afterburner."

14. William Tell

During the summer of 1972, we began to get ready for the William Tell Weapons Meet. The pilots anxiously awaited the selection of the team, whose greatest honor was to get off the rock for a month. Ostensibly awarded to the pilots with the best score on practice intercepts, the team of four emerged, with alternates to be named later. The squadron commander, the training officer, the standardization officer and Capt. Nelson "Dog" DeStaffany comprised the team; all excellent pilots, to be sure. Being the last active duty Air Force F-102 squadron, competing in the F-102 division over the National Guard Squadrons made us the regular Air Force representatives. Tom, the commander, always enjoyed publicity, and this proved to be an excellent opportunity for him.

Somehow, he located a batch of old Delmar targets. The Delmar is a 1950s vintage towed target that F-86s used to shoot at with their 50-caliber machine guns. It comes equipped with a carriage assembly with a wire reel. The whole thing is slung under the fuselage or wing of the tractor aircraft. When the pilot pushes a button in the cockpit, the target is released and slowly unwinds the wire reel as it moves back about a mile. The target itself looks exactly like a toy bomb that I had as a child. I wondered if that toy of long ago might have been a Delmar. It stands about four feet tall, ten inches in diameter, and has four tail fins.

If one had ever been towed behind a T-33, we could not find a published procedure. Maintenance managed to attach it to the wing

14. William Tell

pylon and I was selected to chase it on a test flight. Lt. Mark Shaw was to fly the T-bird with Bob Hervatine in the rear seat operating the Delmar reel. The F-102 and the T-33 never took off in close formation because the speeds and accelerations were incompatible. I asked Mark to take line up on the runway in the lead and go first. When the distance looked about right, I would roll and join up shortly after takeoff after he had a chance to accelerate. He rolled about halfway down the runway before I started. Even if it didn't work, I could just pass him up and no harm would be done.

It worked very well. I was tightly tucked in formation shortly past the departure end of the runway and we headed southwest. After we leveled off, I called for the launch. The target came out of the basket nicely, and to my surprise began spinning smoothly.

"Is it supposed to spin like that?"

"Yeah, you didn't know that? It's got a swivel."

"OK, it's doin' right then. It's comin' back smooth. I'm flying back with it."

I slowed a bit and was able to tuck in quite closely to it.

"Don, there's a cloud deck ahead."

"I'm OK, just keep it smooth and I'll fly formation on the target."

Now, formation flying is a mystical art. I think it is done mostly by the subconscious. That may be why it is so difficult to learn. Suddenly, I realized that I had no idea which way was up. Being in the clouds with the Delmar spinning provided no roll reference. Naturally, I immediately began to feel upside-down, so I sneaked a peek at the fighter's attitude indicator. A slight right bank was showing. OK, looking back at the Delmar, that meant I should pull up and roll left a little. Another peek and, voilà, wings level. What a kick, I was doing it. The controls began to feel a little funny, and another peek revealed, sure enough, a right bank. At that point we popped out of the clouds with me still low and rolled right.

"I think it's all the way out," interrupted Mark.

"I'll break off and position for some radar passes."

We ran some high passes and then some with the target literally skimming the tops of the waves. Finally, low on fuel, Bob pushed the button that severed the wire in the carriage and we returned to Kef. The Delmar proved to be a valuable training aid for the low-target competition at William Tell, not to mention fun.

Dog decided that he would rather be a doctor than a general. That is, he submitted his papers to resign his regular commission and also to leave the active-duty Air Force. If he was surprised to be kicked off the William Tell team, he didn't show it. All this created a vacancy for a junior officer on the team. By default, I was selected.

This golden good deal produced many benefits: nearly a month off the island, a chance to fly the same plane nearly every day, something good to include in my effectiveness rating, and celebrity status. At twenty-five years old, the latter seemed very important. I became the token young guy on the team. As such, my position in all formations was four or slot. A four-ship formation has three main appearances.

Fingertip formation is as the fingertips of one's hand appears when held straight out. There is the leader (it's no accident that he is represented by the middle finger) and number two, his element mate, who is alone on one side represented by the index finger. Three and four comprise an element on the opposite side and are represented by the ring and little fingers, respectively.

Diamond, or show formation, is the same as fingertip except that Four moves to a position behind and slightly below lead. Echelon formation is a line of airplanes, all on the same side of lead, with each successive aircraft having its cockpit alongside its predecessor's wingtip. This is useful when arriving for the break or pitchout, wherein each plane can successively break from the formation without hitting anyone. There are other types of formation such as line abreast and tactical, but these are rarely used for show.

Slot should be behind and slightly below lead. It is considered good form to get high enough to get your tail blackened by lead's exhaust. The proper picture while in the slot is lead's tailpipe about ten feet in front of your cockpit and two feet above. There should be a constant "nibble" on the controls caused by lead's exhaust on your rudder. It is really an easy position to fly because so many more visual cues exist over those available when in fingertip.

Don in the slot

Aeromorphosis

I was assigned aircraft number 56870. Manufactured in 1956, when I was ten years old. It was, arguably, our squadron's best airplane. Its history showed excellent reliability in both airframe and fire-control statistics.

Col. Tom flew with us as often as he could, but that really wasn't very much. Most often we flew with Lionel Boudreaux, the alternate, as Two and John Cronin in the lead. John's nature compelled him to be a bit straitlaced around the squadron. However, in the air, he became Major Hyde.

On an unusually balmy day in August, our formation approached the field from the southeast with John in the lead.

"Four, take the slot."

"Four's in."

"Kef tower, Sloe Gin zero six flight, one five southeast at tree (three should be pronounced tree on the radio) thousand.

"Go ahead, Slogan." (heavy Icelandic accent)

"Request high-speed, low-altitude pass over the runway. We'd like to pass over fighter ops and then diagonally across the runway, exiting northwest."

"Approved as requested, caution P-3 in the area," came the immediate response.

From the slot, I couldn't see any of this happening, because I was always looking up at lead. We all tucked in as tightly as we could and waited for the fun. This was going to be a buzz job that they

14. William Tell

wouldn't soon forget. From the increased wind noise, I could tell that we were going quite fast. On the bottom of John's wings and elevons I could see reflections of objects on the ground zooming past. The G slightly increased for a moment, an indication that we were bottoming out of a shallow dive. At that moment the strangest thing happened. Over the previously silent tower radio frequency there came first a click, then a low roaring sound. The roar increased steadily and just as it peaked, in my periphery, I saw a structure flash past very close to the right side of my aircraft. The roar then diminished and finally cut out altogether. I didn't have time to worry about it, though, for now we were pulling some serious Gs, and I could see the ground up above John's airplane. We were doing a barrel roll.

John was grinning like a Cheshire cat. We were walking into ops with our parachutes slung over one shoulder and each with a helmet bag in hand.

"Do you know what that noise was?" John asked.

"I know exactly which noise you mean, but I have no clue what it was."

"We passed really close and below the tower. When we went by, the guy up there must have keyed his microphone and held it up to the glass."

"I couldn't see a whole lot, but I'm beginning to get the picture."

"It was a thing of beauty, we must've kicked up dust in the fighter ops parking lot, then screamed across the airport and by the tower at 450 knots. Then hard pull up into a diamond barrel roll."

"Your ass is grass, and probably mine too. You'll never get away with this."

"Hide and watch," he said with a wink. "We have some privileges now."

Aside from some vague references to safety and judgement, I never heard any more of it, except from the pilots who were duly impressed. I submit that few pilots have had the chance to fly a high-performance bird with so much of their own discretion as we did. Well, maybe the Air Force demonstration team, the Thunderbirds, but they are gods, not ordinary pilots.

We waxed the contest birds, top and bottom. We had the senior radar guys really tweaking the sets. We had our engines tuned to combat trim. That meant that we could get quite a bit more thrust from them. This was at the expense of shorter engine life only if we used the higher exhaust gas temperatures that were now available. The trick was not to push the throttle up so far as to induce high EGTs unless there was a good reason. With utility trim that we usually had, the EGT wouldn't exceed limits even at full throttle. The purpose was to accelerate quickly on the high-speed, low-altitude intercept at the contest.

On our last flight at Kef with John in the lead, we found ourselves practicing formation over Hekla, the semi-active volcano. The scenery was spectacular, and I wished for another aircraft to photograph us. We leveled off and started toward home plate. John was advised by GCI that planes were landing to the east. At Kef, as with all military fields, the direction of the break or pitchout is specified usually for safety or noise abatement. It was left-hand in this case.

As we maneuvered toward the base, John dipped his left wing slightly, indicating that I should return to the fingertip position. We now looked like a left hand with fingers outstretched. We flew

14. William Tell

west for a long time before turning back toward Kef. When we did, we were lined up with the runway. Ordinarily, we would make several close-in turns to get to initial. Everyone in the formation was expecting John to dip his right wing again to indicate that it was time for three (Dan) and four (me) to cross under into echelon right. Imagine our surprise when his left wing dipped. Dan, flying number three position, moved back, opening up a space between lead and himself. Two (Lionel) crossed under lead (John) into the opening and shortly thereafter, we were echelon left. For a left break.

"Sloe Gin one zero flight, break will be left, 4, 3, 2, lead, go button three (tower)."

"Two."

"Three."

"Four."

"Kef tower, Sloe Gin One Zero Flight, initial, full stop."

"Roger, Slogan, cleared for the break."

Everyone at the base who had watched a flight of fighters land probably looked us that day and said to himself,

"I can't believe that stupid flight leader had his formation stacked the wrong way."

Then, the joke was on them, as first number four, then three began a snappy break to the left. There was nothing in the formation manual that prohibits such a maneuver. An old trick, but always fun.

Aeromorphosis

In those remaining days, I flew 870 more than any other person ever did. I knew her like the back of my hand. I haven't before or since felt that comfortable oneness of purpose and execution with a machine like I did that summer. It was with great remorse that I witnessed her crash two years later.

Col. Tom made it a big deal. We were on AFRTS, and interviews appeared in the base newspaper. He wanted a documentary filmed along the way. Unsurprisingly, on the big day when we left Keflavik for Sondrestromfjord, Greenland, the takeoff of the first flight of two was recorded on video. The camera was then put in the cockpit of the leader of the second flight. This allowed the pilot with the camera to pass it to the (already landed) pilots of lead flight, who filmed the arrival of the third flight of two. That's how I was set up for the video taping of my worst landing in the F-102. Maj Dan Fullerton, the squadron standardization/evaluation officer, led our flight, which was last. The departure and crossing were unremarkable. Sonde is challenging even on a good day. The weather required an instrument approach. I clung to Dan's right wing as we approached down the cloud-infested fjord.

Sondrestromfjord Airport is carved out of scarce real estate. The runway begins shortly after passing over the shore. It has a significant hump in the middle of it. That is, during the first 3,000 feet of its length, it rises. It then falls during the last 6,000 ft. The approach plate says, "Upslope first 3,000 feet of runway 10 causes illusion of short runway." Most pilots make two mistakes when landing there. First is the failure to judge the closure with the ground due to the upslope, resulting in a hard landing. Second, thinking the top of the rise in the runway as the end of the runway. This often results in slamming on the brakes, blowing all the tires, only to barely surmount the rise and see the remaining 6,000 ft. of runway.

14. William Tell

Imagine Lionel on the ground near the end of the runway. He is filming Dan and Don making a formation landing. The formation breaks out of the clouds in tight formation. They continue toward the touchdown point. Dan, leading, is watching the runway getting ready to flare out. Don is watching only Dan. Almost too late, Dan realizes that the runway is coming up to him faster than he had thought. His response is to pull aggressively back on the stick. It works—for him. I see Dan's airplane going above me and begin to pull harder and harder. "*Boing,*" the noise of a hard landing. Dan salvages a good landing. Don bounces 20 ft. into the air. Dan's drag chute deploys while Don attempts to keep his aircraft in one piece. It isn't pretty, but after a couple of more bounces, the airplane is still intact. I was condemned to relive that landing many times amid raucous laughter whenever the film was shown. Of course, no one would believe that I had been set up.

Second alternate was Capt. Steve Rogers. For obvious reasons, we called him Capt. America. He had a very pleasant personality, and a boyish face that drove women crazy. That, combined with good flying skills, made him a junior officer who seemingly had everything. After the flight to Greenland, we all went to the Arctic Hotel bar to unwind. Seated next to Col. Tom, Steve confessed to a generous mood. He ordered a stinger, as did Col. Tom. Well, a stinger is a concoction of creme de menthe and brandy. As the name implies, one is plenty. After ordering and receiving a second round, I spotted Col. Tom pouring his into the pot plant. This went on for hours until Steve was literally slobbering. He was dispatched to bed with the admonition that we were to meet at seven the next morning, ready to fly.

Everyone showed up except Steve. Col. Tom very enthusiastically called to me, "Don, you go check on Capt. America and tell him to catch up with the rest of us at the chow hall."

Knock, knock, knock. Pause. *Knock, knock, knock, knock.* Pause. "Steve, are you in there? Hey, Steve, are you OK?" No answer. I guessed that he had already gone to breakfast and not told us, but I had better get a key and check for sure.

I unlocked the door and peeked in. There had obviously been an attack on Steve. The bed on the opposite wall had been overturned. The sheets, pillows, mattress, springs, and frame were scattered across the room. Steve was lying spread-eagle, face down, naked, on the other bed.

"Yo, Steve, are you hurt?"

"Umgnhh."

"Hey, Steve, wake up. What happened? We're waiting on you. Get goin'."

"Don, you're not going to believe what happened."

"Try me," I said, getting a little exasperated.

"Well, you know I had a few stingers last night."

"Yeah, I remember that."

"I woke up last night and I had puked all over myself and the bed, and the wall and floor."

"I noticed the smell."

"I didn't know what to do, so I spread all the bed stuff out so it would dry."

14. William Tell

I began howling with uncontrollable laughter.

"It's not funny, I feel like shit and now I gotta fly."

"Well, take a shower and catch up with the rest of us. We're going to Goose Bay this morning."

Fortunately for him, the weather wouldn't cooperate. We had conditions that exceeded the critical head wind, the wind being so strong that none of us could make it to Goose Bay without running out of gas. I'm sure it was because of Steve's prayers. The following day, the winds were better, but the clouds were too low. After canceling that day, we began to wonder if we were going to attend the starting ceremonies at William Tell. Col. Tom disappeared and shortly returned, announcing that he had "talked with the general." Our orders were to disregard weather minima to the best of our judgement and "just get there."

The following day, we almost pranced into the briefing room. The resident Air Force officer sadly announced that, again, the weather would not permit our flight.

"I have authorization from Major General Price to proceed with the existing weather," Colonel Tom proudly announced.

And we did. Visualize the next scene. Six F-102s all at full power, lined up on the runway in echelon, pilots checking their engines, waiting for the brakes release signal. Lots of smoke and noise.

"Lead's rolling, everyone take twenty seconds."

Col Tom released his brakes, engaged the afterburner, and began accelerating. Unknown to anyone, the pin which connects his

Aeromorphosis

nose wheel steering to the nosewheel had broken. About 100 miles per hour, the entire front end of the airplane began to shake violently. The instruments a blur, he decided to abort the takeoff. He simultaneously pulled the throttle inboard and back, then pulled the parachute-shaped handle on the instrument panel.

"Abort, abort. Sloe Gin flight pull it back, abort." The smoke and noise from five F-102s slowly subsides.

The nose wheel steering pin was quickly fixed and all the flight plans were still good. Soon we were are all standing in a big circle near his plane. The Ferry Squadron Commander and a couple of SAS (airline) mechanics are looking at Col. Tom.

"I think," he began slowly, a sheepish grin forming, "that we…need to go back to the hotel and think about this weather a little more."

Don and 870 at Sondrestrom, Greenland

14. William Tell

We made it to Goose the next day. From there we hopped down to Navy Jacksonville, Florida, where a National Guard F-106 squadron had invited us to get acclimatized to Florida before making the short journey to Tyndall. Additionally, the upcoming Jacksonville to Tyndall leg offered the prospect of having plenty of fuel for our arrival airshow.

Arriving at Tyndall, the show went extremely well, I was told. From the slot, one doesn't see much. We taxied into the chocks in a smart-looking formation where we were besieged by our maintenance folks who had arrived the previous day in a cargo plane. I became twenty-six years old that day.

Everyone joined in the fun. ABC Wide World of Sports worked up a nice story, complete with cockpit video and shots of missiles being launched. Several governors and other assorted politicians appeared at the big dinners. At one point after one long-winded speech, the speaker turned to us and said, "But now I'd like to introduce the *actual pilots*." I suppose that was the day I became what we all strive to be, namely, a real pilot.

The contest consisted of four parts: a live fire of an infrared-seeking missile on a low-altitude, high-speed target, likely the most challenging; a night, high-altitude, jamming-aircraft target; a live-fire front/stern reattack on a drone target; and finally, a medium-altitude live-fire radar missile to be fired at a drone target.

These missions came in random order so as to facilitate scheduling the range and target resources. I drew the low mission first. Long before takeoff, I attended a briefing to make sure I understood the wisdom of shooting at the towed target, rather than the tractor aircraft. Other information about the speed and altitude was uncharacteristically withheld. Capt. Phil (I have misplaced his last name), our team GCI controller and holder of the coveted Master of Air Defense, wasn't intimidated.

"No sweat, just like we practiced. Turn the corner at min range, lock on, get low, drive in, and splash."

Jittery as I approached 870, I quickly got busy and settled into a businesslike frame of mind. It is absolutely essential that one be sure of the armament on his aircraft. I stood for a long moment with my hand on the missile. It was the proper kind, properly loaded. The safety pins would be pulled just before takeoff and shown to me.

I took off alone and broke the safety wire on the arming switch passing the coastline. Phil's voice reassured me.

"Sloe Gin one five, you have one target three three zero for one five. Descend to five hundred feet, set speed four zero zero."

"Sloe Gin One Five has a target three four zero for one one."

"Contact is tractor." The little towed IR target wasn't going to appear until I got behind and closer.

Turning the corner to get behind the target is a very busy time. Phil is trying to get me rolled out right at the two-mile minimum range. If I get closer than two miles without a lock-on, I must break off the attack. The fighter is very pitch sensitive at this speed. I roll into a steep bank and pull hard on the stick. Condensed vapor stands like little clouds outside the windshield and canopy due to the humidity and Gs I am pulling. As I roll out behind them, sure enough, there they are.

"Sloe Gin One Five has two targets, two four zero for five and two four zero for two."

14. William Tell

"Contacts are target and tractor. Cleared to arm hot."

"Sloe Gin One Five arm hot, judy two four zero for two."

"Judy is target, cleared to fire."

Ordinarily, I would select afterburner and press in for a computer fire. But those sneaky devils have me pointed toward the solar system's best infrared emitter: the sun. The trick is to swing to one side without breaking radar lock-on and get the sun and the sun glint from the water, both out of the picture.

I pull the trigger to the first detent and release it. Below, in the armament bay, the missile battery irreversibly goes to internal electrical power. I can shoot after 20 seconds. I lock on with radar and hear the infrared tone in my headset. The missile seeker head is now slaved to the radar dish. With afterburner, the fighter accelerates rapidly. The computer, now in control of the missile timing, commands D-time. Missile hydraulics are now up.

I dip low over the water to allow the missile to look up from the distractions of the water surface. Holding the trigger down, I feel the familiar shudder as the bay doors open. An X appears on the scope. After what seems like minutes, I see the little rocket emerge from beneath and pull away. Bits of rocket motor rattle against the windshield as it pulls up and crosses my path on its way to the target. Since an IR missile is autonomous, I break away, preferring relief from the intensity of the attack to a possible peek at a splash.

The missile guides, but the score is poor. In this case, a good score proves to be a matter of tweaking the guidance on the missile itself. This is my first indication that winning is more than a matter of just flying.

The next flight was to be the night Electronics Counter Measures target. Chaff and ECM are deceptive measures that threatened aircraft use to possibly escape being shot down. Chaff is little bundles of aluminum foil, cut to the wavelength of the attacker's radar transmissions, which reflect the radar energy and appear as an aircraft on the scope. This WWII technique is still very effective in the hands of a skilled electronics warfare officer.

Electronics counter-measures (ECM) is jamming. The threatened aircraft produces radio frequency emissions at the same frequency as the shooter. This appears as a band or strobe on the fighter scope. The attackers know the azimuth or direction to the target, but are denied knowledge of the range. Of course, we have Electronics Counter-Counter Measures (ECCM) such as fast-tuning our radar frequency so the (spot) jammer can't keep up with our radar transmitter. The really sophisticated offensive systems have counter-counter-countermeasures, and so on ad infinitum.

The briefing for this mission was hosted by the Interceptor Weapons School rather than the usual at the test squadron. My brother had asked me to look up a college friend of his named Henderson. Sure enough, Capt. Henderson briefed us. Afterward, I introduced myself, thinking I would get especially good treatment on this flight. Big mistake.

A couple of hours later, there I was, trying to get a lock-on to a target amid lots of old and new chaff. Every time I would lock on, the B-57 EWO would break it with jamming, my equipment being far outclassed. If one doesn't have a lock-on or judy by six miles on the front, safety regulations require breaking off the intercept. The closure rate on a front attack is usually about 800 knots, and from the time the target first becomes visible on the scope until six miles is only a few seconds. Since the target lay high above me, I started

14. William Tell

a pull up (without yet getting a lock-on) at nine miles. At eight, I finally was allowed to get a lock-on without jamming. *Great, maybe I'll get a hack on this one after all.* Everything was looking good, then, at five miles, the attack display disappeared, a broken lock-on.

"Sloe Gin One Five is missed intercept."

"Roger, breakaway two four zero, angels three zero.

I had him fair and square, then he broke my lock, and I had to break it off. That was no test of skill. Chuck Yeager himself would have had to break it off.

"Capt. Henderson," I later asked, "what does an IWS instructor do in such a case?"

"He breaks off the intercept."

"But how does this make for a contest? No one could have gotten that hack."

"This is true, but we give each squadron the same number of impossible intercepts."

I go up and kiss his ass, and he selects me for the blooper. Live and learn, I suppose.

The mid-altitude radar shot, being mainly a test of our missiles, turned out to be pretty routine. But the last one, the Front/stern reattack, proved to be memorable.

The front/stern reattack (FSRA) tactic came from the need to identify a target visually before firing on it. Few pilots, whether in war or training, have the opportunity to fire a weapon on the front attack, then turn around, chase down the target, and fire again.

But that is exactly what I was to do. The intended victim, a Ryan BQM-34 Firebee, began its turn one hundred miles ahead. We were to meet head on. Once paired, we raced toward each other at 800 knots, me 5,000 feet below its 25,000 ft. altitude.

There will be no jamming or chaff on this mission. I easily spot the target on radar at thirty miles. Locked on, cleared to fire, and armed up by fifteen miles, this is a piece of cake compared to last night. Gently start the pullup, trigger full down, D-time, doors, missile away. Smooth, very smooth.

It's a radar missile speeding its way toward the Firebee. Guiding on reflected radio frequency energy from my aircraft, I continue to illuminate the target for the time of flight for the missile. The missile, locked on to radar return enhanced by a traveling wave tube, barely misses the target, but is scored close enough for a kill. I begin a turn, gentle enough to maintain lock-on, but enough to avoid a collision with the target. Now comes the fun. Light the afterburner, start a hard turn back around.

"Sloe Gin One Five, reattack. Judy zero six zero for two."

"Judy is target, cleared to fire."

Now I slam the red guard down on the arming switch, returning it to safe. The rotary selector goes from Missiles Radar to Missiles IR, and back to Arm with the arming switch. I push the return-to-search button on the stick and wait to hear the IR ping as I come around and point toward the drone. I pick it up in the corner of my eye as I come around the turn. It is a tiny, delicate-looking thing, almost floating along peacefully ahead.

14. William Tell

"Meow, meow," says the IR in my helmet's headset. I take the lock-on and see the timing circles start to work. A mile and a half with 300 knots overtake. Armament bay doors open, missile away. I don't have to illuminate this one, but I turn slowly to savor the moment. Not many people get to shoot two expensive missiles on a profile like this, neither in training nor at war. The missile quickly closes the gap. It is homing, not on the little jet engine, but on a bright red flare near the target's wingtip. The missile hits the flare dead center, snatching off it and its stanchion, scored as a direct hit. Afterburner still cooking, I pull up and treat myself to a little roll.

"MA (mission accomplished), splash (hit the target), ammo zero (missiles gone), RTB (return to base)." The radar technicians and mechanics had already heard about our success. The atmosphere was jubilant as I taxied in. My crew chief shoved a beer into my hands while I still sat in the cockpit. It tasted good. Life was sweet.

Needless to say, I didn't win top gun. The 57th came in a distant second to a National Guard squadron. The results proved prophetic. I soon left the Air Force and joined the National Guard.

Guard squadrons are usually composed of a few technicians who are full-time employees. Most of the members of a squadron are down-towners," or those who have real jobs and also are guardsmen. The disparity in turnover is the key. Guardsmen often have long years of experience, happily doing the same task. Their regular Air Force counterpart transfers to a new location and a different job every few years. Our five-year missile technicians were competing with twenty-year experts.

Back in the 1970s, the Air National Guard was simply a reserve of readily trainable people. I think no one expected them to go and fight the Russians using 1950s vintage aircraft. Now the guard flies the latest aircraft. But with that privilege comes the curse———expect a callup to a hot war at any time.

One of our squadron pilots took "my" 870 home; I took thirty days' leave.

Before leaving for the William Tell Contest, I had submitted my request for a full month's leave. Standing in front of Col. Sawyer's desk, the colonel asked, "Do you know how many people have been granted requests for a full month's leave from here?"

"I'm guessing about as many as requested it, sir," I said.

I was fully aware that the most dedicated officers prided themselves in "losing leave." Leave could not be accrued for over a year, and failure to use it allegedly indicated that an officer had been very busy with his duties and thus indispensable. My request included a travel itinerary which revealed my plans to visit the then-communist Yugoslavia.

"Traveling to a communist country is a bad idea for someone in your line of work," he said.

I tried to explain that my brother, who was based in Italy, had planned the trip that way because of his interest in politics and history. He granted my request, but the incident began a rift between the two of us.

During my absence, Heimay, the volcano, had become active and spouted an ash cloud 30,000 feet into the air and devastated a village with hot lava and ash. This piqued my curiosity, and being a dedicated flightseer, I asked my wingman, Kim, if he would like to fly over the volcano. He said no, he would rather do something else, so I would

14. William Tell

just have to tour alone. I did so with great gusto, darting around the ash plume and the spewing lava, happily snapping pictures. That proved to be a big mistake. Shortly before my return, I had missed an important bulletin which had forbidden such things. I had read the Pilot Information File (PIF) before the flight and found nothing unusual there. That bulletin had explained that the rescue effort might have been jeopardized by my flight. I didn't get the word and Kim didn't tell me. That single event proved to be instrumental in my becoming a civilian again.

Smoke Marking the end of my Air Force Career

15. The Bottom of Reykjanes Bay

Sgt. Joe Friday, of television's "Dragnet" fame, would have said it like this: "I was working five-minute alert out of Fighter Ops. It was a cold, windy, January day, what there was of it."

After the morning briefing, my alert partner and I had adjourned to the barn for twenty-four hours of likely boredom. After cocking our fighters, we had settled in for some serious reading. It wasn't tough duty as long as one wasn't called upon to actually fly.

The squadron had four flights. Each rotated through the four jobs at hand. They were alert, training, duty, and off. Alert and off were jobs that I understood right away. Training meant that you were to fly and practice intercepts. Duty meant to do all the little administrative chores that made the whole thing run smoothly.

John Cronin trained us. As the squadron training officer, he gave us our initial check-out in the fighter and maintained records of how many and what kind of maneuvers we had done. As with most squadrons, he was likely the best pilot among us. He was very old, about thirty. On a long, two-year tour, he was accompanied by his wife, Tabby, a dark-haired beauty. John gave his all to the job. He was usually serious, but suffered our spells of incompetence well. He was very tall, with a short crew cut.

John was scheduled to fly a training flight that day, as was Kimmel O., also a major. The now late Kim O. never fit in. He came into

15. The Bottom of Reykjanes Bay

our squadron as a glad-handed, fast-talking hotshot. My immediate reaction was one of caution. My instincts later proved correct.

John and Kim took off in formation in the darkness about ten that morning. I imagine the flight went something like this: climbing through the clouds into the sunlight which shone over the North Pole, they separated to "bump heads" or practice intercepts against each other. After a few of these, John's radio did a common thing: it stopped working. It happened frequently, so it's not a big deal. Being high above the clouds, a rejoin would be easy. John just headed for home and Kim, using GCI vectors and his airborne radar, was soon pulling up alongside John. They had been separated by several thousand feet vertically, requiring Kim to make some big turns to get his aircraft going the same direction as well as swooping down to his altitude. Using hand signals for this situation, Kim determined that, other than a bum radio, everything was fine with John. They elected to quit the practice and return to base. Flying formation in the clouds requires much focus. John probably would not have noticed that Kim was returning to a jet penetration and instrument approach at 10,000 ft. instead of the usual 20,000 ft. Even if he had noticed, he either failed to communicate his concern, or assumed that Kim had an unusual plan.

Fighters usually fly a jet penetration to make an approach. This is the source of a lot of jokes and provides greater terrain clearance than a shallow descent. It starts with a very steep descent from high altitude to a level off about 1,500 ft. above the ground and then a gentle glide to the runway.

The following is only my theory of the events that took place that night.

John probably thought Kim had a good reason for starting this approach 10,000 feet low, but since he couldn't hear the radio chatter, he couldn't have known that Kim had simply lost track of 10,000 ft. during the rejoin. It happens to the best of us. As the two aircraft arrived at the initial approach fix, and being cleared for the approach, Kim looks at John, only twenty-five feet away, and makes a pinching motion with his fingers indicating that the speed brakes will soon be opening. John nods in receipt and gives an extra thumbs up, indicating that everything is OK. They descend steeply and John tucks in close. You wouldn't want to lose sight of lead without a radio.

Kim is flying his smoothest formation to prevent losing his wingman in the clouds. The next level off is far below at 1,500 feet—lots of time, right? Wrong. If there had been an Icelandic fishing boat twenty miles out on the extended runway centerline, it would have been spectacular. Two fighters in extremely close formation exit the clouds at a very steep angle only 800 feet above the water. Instantly, the elevons of the one slightly ahead go fully up. Lead enters a high-speed stall, condensed vapor stands like a cloud above the wings, the air rumbles as it passes the stalled wing. A long trail of fire erupts from its tailpipe accompanied by a loud booming sound. Its flight path becomes tangent to the surface of the water and it skims along with no perceptible space between. It catches the air, not the water, and suddenly leaps skyward, the afterburner extinguishes, and the aircraft rolls sharply to avoid reentering the clouds.

The second one is not so lucky. As lead claws for altitude, two's flight path is only slightly flattened in a futile attempt to maintain formation. It impacts the choppy water with a metallic thud and does not rise from it. The water, whipped into tall waves by the strong winds, seizes the aircraft into its clutches as its left wing tucks under. As it rolls, the vertical fin is scraped from the fuselage. Inverted, the nose yaws 90 degrees right, while the big pieces continue forward. Finally, the top of the right wing smacks the water, igniting a huge fireball that is elongated along the flight path. Only the smaller

15. The Bottom of Reykjanes Bay

pieces continue with any force. A few small bits are thrown almost to the cloud bases as the explosion roars above the sounds of the sea. The lead plane circles the remains once, turns back toward the base, and disappears in the mist. Reykjanes Bay is more than 500 feet deep there.

I was called to get ready for a scramble to help the search and rescue (SAR) effort. The rescue helicopter flew from late morning until they ran out of flares about midnight, only stopping briefly for fuel. The ceilings were low, and the winds violent, a treacherous combination for a helicopter pilot. They found only a helmet and a life raft.

The weather was so poor that we were released from battle stations. I retired at midnight and, surprisingly, dropped right off to sleep. In my dream, I was getting off alert late the following day and had a terrible sense of loss over John's death. We had a *dining in* scheduled. That is a formal dinner in which a pilot's departure is celebrated at many squadrons. I was surprised that everyone had left the operations building to go to the Officers Club for the event. I had expected that it would have been canceled. I hastily hung my gear, went to my room at the BOQ, and changed into my formal uniform. When I arrived at the club, the party was loud and happy. I was puzzled that my friends could be so callous as to celebrate in the shadow of John's almost certain demise. As I walked through the door, I saw the reason for the celebration. John sat at the head table. I immediately realized that I must be the last to know that he had been rescued. Happily, I hurried up to him. I reached to his outstretched hand.

"John, I'm so glad you made it. No one told me," I was saying as he scowled at me. "Geez, you'd think he would be happy to be alive," I muttered.

At that moment in the dream, the bedlam behind me suddenly became quiet. I whirled around to see the scene completely changed. They were still in their formal uniforms, but it was a wake. A military chaplain was conducting John's funeral. I turned back around and John was gone.

I awoke at that point in the dream drenched in sweat. Even today, I still have that dream.

"I was flying my smoothest and leveled at fifteen hundred feet when I saw a glow through the clouds behind me," reported Kim under sworn testimony at the accident investigation board.

"Everything was going normally in the approach up until that time."

Perhaps correctly, he thought that the truth would only serve to end his career in shame. How can I be so sure about this? Just a feeling, I suppose.

Deuces Arriving at Keflavik by Owen Jensen

16. Test Pilot

Well, not exactly. I wanted to be a test pilot, but it was not to be. Probably due to my flight over the volcano, I was assigned to the 4750th Test Squadron as a non-qualified test pilot, rather than going directly to the Test Pilot School at Edwards. As an 1121F specialty code, I would be allowed to conduct minor tests while awaiting an assignment to the Experimental Test Pilot School. Due to the lack of availability of training assets (or some other reason above my pay grade) I received a T-33 checkout while awaiting one in a fighter. This gave me a chance to get reacquainted with Major George Guss, whom I had met at Perrin.

George was an epic story in himself. A former F-105 Wild Weasel pilot in Vietnam, he had over five thousand hours in the T-33. It was a hoot. George showed me things not in the books. The T-33 was famous for getting a cocked nosewheel. It had a free castering nose wheel. If one turned too sharply while taxiing, it would lock fully to one side. George was one of the few who knew how to fix that without getting out of the airplane. He showed me how to detect a partially open landing gear door by flying low and observing the aircraft's shadow. I didn't fly the T-33 again until I arrived at the 111th F.I.S. in Houston, TX.

When my turn came to check out in the F-101, I received a few rides in the rear seat before my training began in earnest. On one of my early familiarization flights, I got a real eye-opener. I was just an observer in the rear seat while the late Dick Holzer piloted. He was a contemporary who had arrived a few months before me. We were in the warning area about 30,000 ft. and 300 knots when Dick asked if I would like to see a loop. I agreed, and he rolled inverted, lit the burners, and pulled the nose down. At 20,000 feet, he rolled right side up and had about 500 knots. Most of the loops I had seen in jets had started at 10,000 feet, ensuring good ground clearance, and denser air. Imagine my surprise when he laid on four Gs at that altitude! Up we went with the needles on the altimeter spinning wildly.

I correctly predicted, "This is going to be really interesting."

He got it perfectly vertical, zero airspeed, at 42,000 ft. It got very quiet, the out-of-sync engines making beat noises, and surprisingly, without any compressor stalls. It seemed to hang there for a while (maybe tail sliding) until the nose fell forward, overshooting past the vertical, with a few oscillations. He wisely accelerated down to 10,000 ft. and 400 knots before pulling out.

I asked, "Wow, does it do that every time?"

Dick said, "Dunno, that's the first one I've tried."

Don and the Voodoo at Tyndall

16. Test Pilot

Being among the most junior pilots in the squadron, I was assigned to the targets shop. Towing targets, flying chase, and writing reports filled my days. To be sure, some fun was to be had doing this.

The year was 1973, and new missiles, guns, gunsights, and targets were being developed for the F-106. Business was good. One new target that we developed and tested was the FIGAT (fiberglass aerial target). The FIGAT consisted of three roughly triangular sections joined together and equipped with tricycle skids. We towed it behind an F-101. We would take off with the FIGAT 200 feet behind connected by a steel cable. The takeoff went like this: light the afterburners, accelerate to 185 knots, disengage the burners (so as not to burn the cable as the aircraft rotated), rotate to 30 degrees pitch up, count to three (so as to let the cable get in trail), re-engage the burners and climb out. Once in the warning area, the target was reeled out to about five miles and an F-106 would shoot at it. Since it had an acoustic bullet scorer on board (expensive) and was of considerable value itself, it was reeled in to 250 feet and brought back for reuse.

Getting a 500-pound, 30-foot long aircraft back wasn't that easy. It had three skids, each equipped with a 10"X10" piece of cut-up rubber tire. The tractor (me) would fly a sort of GCA given by a squadron mate with a handheld radio standing close to the runway. The trick was to fly down the left edge of the runway, knowing that the target was hanging about 50 ft. below, slightly right, and 250 ft. back. The controller would read target heights, and I was to gently lower it to the runway and then cut the cable. It worked pretty well. I never crashed one, but I did have one land long with its nose extending off the end of the pavement.

Aeromorphosis

FIGAT and F-106B

Our squadron tested the supersonic Ryan Firebee II or BQM-34F. It was a supersonic version of the perennial Firebee subsonic jet-powered missile target. It was ground-launched with a single RATO booster. Management decided we needed some photos. If you have ever tried to catch a RATO launch, well, you can't—even in an F-101, which will really accelerate. I had previously chased a Mace launch, which gave me some idea of a procedure. The Firebee, being lighter, accelerated much faster. After a couple of tries, I developed a technique whereby I let it join up with me. That is, I would try to arrive at a point where the RATO burned out at the same time as the drone. It took afterburners to keep up with the little rascal. Once leveled off at cruising altitude, its external fuel tank was jettisoned, allowing it to immediately attain supersonic speeds. I learned that I couldn't keep up with it when that happened. My technique: accelerate and pull ahead of the Firebee and allow it to catch up with me.

16. Test Pilot

BQM-34F Supersonic Firebee

Many older fighter pilots will remember gunnery practice on the Dart. According to the manual: "TDU-10/B Dart target was developed for the purpose of providing a gunnery target that is compatible with the operating airspeeds and maneuver capabilities of modern fighter aircraft. It was towed behind another aircraft on 1,500 to 2,000 feet of cable and was equipped with a radar reflector to permit the use of radar gunsights. Specifications: 196 inches long and weighing 197 pounds."

Providing an inexpensive target for the new F-106 M-61 Gatling Gun tests had eluded the project until someone found some old darts. However, shooting at it with a 20 MM cannon proved to be impractical. We decided to mount a $10,000 acoustic bullet scorer on it, rendering it not inexpensive anymore. Towing it with the F-101 proved to be problematic too. To prevent scraping its fins on takeoff, the ground clearance was increased by shaving a little off the fins and jacking up the landing gear struts on the F-101. Launching it after becoming airborne wasn't easy either. It tended to flail and bang against the fuselage of the tractor aircraft. After a few damaging attempts, I developed a workable technique involving a zero-G launch.

The expensive bullet scorer required the recovery of the dart after firing missions. To enable that, we had a designated drop zone near Tyndall. The squadron commander asked for photos of the target hitting the ground. Obligingly, I briefed Capt. Bill Sieg, one of the younger test pilots, to fly the mission and drop the target at a specific time and place. I borrowed one of our fancy Millikin high-speed (for the era) cameras for the occasion. I set myself in place for the drop about 300 ft. adjacent to the briefed flight path. I readied the camera as the tractor with the dart behind it rolled onto its approach. As it closed, I realized that the tractor (Bill) had aligned on me instead of the adjacent road! I flung the camera to the ground and began to run away from the approaching aircraft. I only got two steps before the F-101 passed low overhead. About one second after that, the dart hit the ground about 20 feet from me, followed by a whistling sound made by the still-attached cable. The debriefing was intense. I remain undecided as to whether I should hold a grudge against those who, without malice, attempt to kill you.

TDU-10 Dart

16. Test Pilot

Another fun project was testing an improved rocket motor for the Genie. The original idea was a nuclear-armed unguided rocket that was so fast and powerful that, once launched, the target could not escape by jamming or defensive maneuvers. We, of course, never detonated a nuke, but we did fire the Air Training Rocket (ATR) to assure effectiveness of crew training, launching aircraft, and the ballistics of the rocket. The ATR was an 822-pound, nine-foot-long powerhouse that could achieve Mach 3.2 in a 2-second burn. The F-101 could carry two of them. The first time I launched one, the rotary door flipped with a thump, the ejector rod fired with another thump, and because my thoughts were racing, the delay of the light-off made me think I had a dud. Then the train left the station: it was spectacular, lots of smoke, noise, and pieces of burnt motor hitting the windscreen. The combat procedure called for an immediate roll and pull to avoid the blast, but in the test world, the tracking called for the fighter to stay steady for a while. That gave me a chance to watch it. It went very high, very fast, and popped a spotting charge after about five seconds. What fun! The Air Force wanted us to evaluate an improved motor for the Genie. We received about 20 ATRs to fire. I shot a couple, but it was really more spectacular to fly photo chase on the shots. When the rocket fired, it shot out a plume of fire that was twice as long as the F-101, which was 71 ft., itself.

F-101 firing ATR

FACIT MISSIONS

The nature of flight test is dealing with unreliable systems. A hot firing mission to test a new gun or gunsight might involve as many as five aircraft, dozens of people on the ground, firing range scheduling, range safety check for boats, GCI control, towed targets, photographic chase aircraft, and most importantly the test aircraft's systems being ready. With the need for all of the resources for a successful mission to align properly, the likelihood of a mission cancellation was high. When that happened, the prepositioned aircraft, such as photographic chase, were left to their own devices. Thus, the FACIT mission was created. FACIT is an acronym for *fool around and call it test*. When two aircraft were available, formation practice was a reasonable alternate mission. The painting below depicts two F-101s practicing trail formation by maneuvering over the top of a cumulus cloud. The cloud represented a mountain, but was much softer in the event of a miscalculation.

F-101s during a FACIT Mission: painting by Owen Jenson, commissioned by Don

16. Test Pilot

I had some other interesting moments at Tyndall. The maintenance and operations higher-ups were having a squabble and I was told to refuse to fly any airplane that was the slightest bit questionable. That day, when I took off, there was a loud *bang* when the landing gear retracted. Not knowing what that meant, I immediately put the gear lever back down. Another loud *bang* and then three green gear safe lights illuminated. I elected to land, stop on the runway, and get towed into the chocks. I was sitting beside the tug driver with my helmet in my lap when the chief of maintenance screeched up, obviously angry.

"Why did you shut down your aircraft on the runway, Captain?"

"It was making loud noises, sir."

"You should have taxied in."

"Yes, sir."

The answer was that the nose gear hydraulic cylinder had detached at one end and was hanging by the hose. When I extended the gear, the actuator rod had fired up to the corner of the wheel well and flung the nose gear out. I used up some good luck that day.

A few days later, I was flying down initial approach when the whole airplane started shaking. I looked down to see the right engine oil pressure hit zero. I shut it down and turned a wide pattern and landed single engine. Same visual: tug driver with pilot beside him, pulling a F-101 into the chocks having shut down the runway. The Chief of Maintenance screeches up with antennas whipping back and forth. He jumps out and, seeing me, says, "You again."

"Yes, sir, an engine quit."

Aeromorphosis

"Why didn't you taxi into the chocks?"

"I wasn't sure what caused it, sir."

"I'll call your commander about it."

The aft-most bearing had disintegrated and blown all the oil out. My commander seemed pleased that I had caused the maintenance chief some heartache.

For training, we frequently flew formation with dissimilar aircraft. We had a routine in which the F-106 would lead, with an F-101 on the wing. The F-106 would perform increasingly steep turns until the F-101 with its tiny wings could no longer keep up. After that, the F-101 would lead for a while. Once in the lead, I would give the afterburner signal and rapidly pull ahead of the F-106. After a while about 1.5 Mach, he would finally catch up and pass me.

F-101 and F-106 formation

16. Test Pilot

The least desirable mission to be assigned was the 50,000 ft. target. That meant flying an F-101 with two 400-gallon drop tanks for three or four hours while flirting with low-speed stalls. Supersonic would have been much more comfortable, but the shooter required a high, slow target. Flying the assigned subsonic Mach number of .99 M gave an indicated airspeed of 250 knots. At low altitude, the F-101 flew very comfortably at 250 knots—then why, I asked, does the airplane protest so much when flying at the same indicated airspeed at high altitude? The answer, of course, was the lower viscosity of the air.

When I studied aerodynamics as an undergraduate, I computed the obligatory Reynolds Number equations for lift at different viscosities. Until I flew these missions, I had never had an intuitive feel for what that meant. In my mental model of the wing at high angles of attack, the smooth flow of air is tending to break away from the surface. At low altitudes, the streamlines of flow immediately above that breakaway point are dense and discourage that separation. At high altitudes, the streamlines are less dense and offer less resistance to the separation.

The F-101 flap switch had two positions: up and down. Lowering full flaps at that altitude would have produced too much drag to maintain altitude. However, by pulling the flaps' circuit breaker, selecting "down" on the flap switch, and momentarily closing the circuit breaker, small flap extensions could be achieved. By bumping the circuit breaker for about two seconds, the flaps would extend slightly, and the pre-stall buffet completely stopped. I finally understood what Reynolds Number meant.

F-102 Drone

Simulating a full-size aircraft using tiny Firebee drones equipped with radar return augmentation devices left everyone wondering if the missiles would really work. The F-104 became one of the early drones, flown from a T-33 chase aircraft. Many other aircraft were modified over the years for various purposes, such as bombing or reconnaissance. Since I had flown the F-102, the commander chose me to head the PQM-102 project, as it existed for Air Defense Command. Systems Command developed the drone, ADC was to accept and operate it. My job: go to White Sande Missile Range (WSMR), live at Holloman AFB, and monitor its development to ensure that the operating command (ADC) wasn't getting a pig in a poke. Unlike modern drones, it lacked GPS navigation and sophisticated control automation. Operations were insanely complex. Towed to the runway and started in place, takeoff was conducted manually by two pilots sitting atop a van nearby. One controlled pitch and power, the other roll and heading. While watching their data link instruments and visual contact, takeoff and landings required exceptional skills. If you have ever flown a drone while it is coming toward you, flight control is confusingly backward. Contrast this primitive operation with present-day drones controlled in Houston, Texas, dropping bombs in far-away places.

16. Test Pilot

PQM-102 Launch

One mission was to test the programmed maneuver. With the touch of a button, the controller enabled elaborate gyrations, simulating an aircraft in a dogfight. Chasing this test, Lt. Col. "Mac" McCormick flew the front seat of a T-38, with me in the rear. The maneuver called for the PQM-102 drone to rapidly roll 135 degrees right, followed by a six-G turn. As we maneuvered close, prior to the maneuver, I cautioned Mac, "Get really ready, with that low wing loading, it's going to be hard to keep up with."

"Yeah, yeah, I'm ready. (on the radio) Control execute the maneuver."

With that, the drone simply turned and vanished, far away from us.

I couldn't help but laugh. The hotshot fighter pilot had essentially been beaten by a drone.

Aeromorphosis

PQM-102, an empty cockpit

As mentioned above, the Air Force was anxious to know if its air-to-air missiles were as effective on a full-scale target as they were on smaller ones with electronic augmentation. Compatible with my philosophy of *you haven't done it until you have done it*, live fire tests of a new model of the sidewinder missile entered our test program. I always thought it strange that we were ordered to conduct such tests on a target that had not yet achieved operational status. The inevitable day came when "my" F-102 number 56870 from my days at Keflavik was scheduled to be fired upon. The results of that test created mixed emotions in my mind. I was pleased that our country's latest and greatest air-to-air missile could, indeed, destroy a highly maneuverable target. However, to witness my old friend violently perish caused a strange sadness. That aircraft had protected me from many existential threats, including my own stupidity. It was a meaningful death, considering the importance of

16. Test Pilot

the mission. The feeling reminded me of the time I was forced to euthanize a fifteen-year-old hunting dog. One's heart wishes that they could outlive one's self and thus avoid any of our remorse. One's head knows that their usefulness is over and their suffering should end. I never thought of that airplane as being human. That would have been anthropomorphism. However, the beloved hunting dog analogy still occurs to me. Perhaps I invented a concept. I shall call it *caninomorphism*.

I commuted between Tyndall and Holloman in F-101 aircraft, refueling at Ellington AFB in Houston, Texas. Recalling the envy that I had experienced for the part-time fighter pilots when I went through F-102 requalification, I never missed a chance to visit with the squadron commander there.

Things began to go downhill back at Tyndall. As the months and years passed, I continued my quest to attend Test Pilot School. Declining an offer to attend Air Force Institute of Technology (AFIT) in Civil Engineering did not sit well with management. Next, I was offered a slot at Squadron Officers School in residence. Having already completed Squadron Officers School by correspondence, I declined. That was particularly frustrating, since I had also completed the next course, Air Command and Staff College, by correspondence.

One day, my immediate supervisor, Lt. Col. Orvin Ramlo, summoned me to his office.

"Here's the deal, Don, you don't have a combat tour on your record, you are not an academy graduate, and you lack a Master's Degree. If you go to TPS you will be flying chase the rest of your career. You will never test the latest fighter. If you are OK with that, TPS can be a lot of fun."

Aeromorphosis

The Air Force created the Palace Chase Program to facilitate the transfer of active-duty officers into the reserves or national guard with little delay and paperwork. Having decided to apply to the Texas Air National Guard, I was able to convince Jerry Killian, the ANG commander, to accept me. Lacking only the Weapons Center Commander's signature, I was summoned to his office.

"Congratulation, Captain Smith, you have been accepted into Test Pilot School. Do you have any questions?" asked General Peterson.

"Just one, sir. Will you sign this Palace Chase request?"

He actually spit out the cigar stub that he was chewing. "What?"

A few months later, I enrolled in Electrical Engineering at the University of Houston, while flying full-time for the Texas Air National Guard.

Don 1974

17. Raggedy-Ass Militia

The Air Force Reserve and State National Guard squadrons were known as the raggedy-ass militia, denoting a more relaxed attitude than the regular Air Force. Even then, with ancient aircraft, the environment was actually more formal than the regular Air Force that I had known. As a member of the 111 Fighter Interceptor Squadron at Ellington AFB, Texas, I wore my dress uniform much more than before. Monthly drills involved marching, speeches, and inspections. The flying, while held to the same standards as the regular Air Force, became much more intense because of the competition for the jobs. Previously, the 111th had been designated as the Combat Crew Training Squadron (CCTS) for all Air Force training in the F-102 and the F-101, including national guard squadrons.

As the squadrons around the country decreased in number, the CCTS duty was relegated to the individual reserve and national guard squadrons to conduct training and upgrades locally, in-house. The 111th had amassed a huge cadre of personnel to accomplish the CCTS mission for two aircraft types. As that mission vanished, the squadron became a (smaller) fighter squadron with no outside training mission.

When I arrived, fifty pilots wanted my job. Many had been instructors in the now-defunct CCTS. That competition put pilot performance under the microscope. Mistakes were punished swiftly and brutally. Viewed from the outside, it was probably typical of any shrinking organization. That is not to say that it was unpleasant, only a little intense. My job as a full-time alert pilot involved twenty-four hours of Air Defense Alert once or twice each week. The pay sufficed to cover the rent, food, and tuition at the University of Houston. The flexible schedule allowed me to make almost all my classes.

After two years in the F-101 at Tyndall, I felt comfortable flying it. The Voodoo was a hard airplane to love. Most famous for its pitch up characteristic, it was at its best when going fast. It was designed with a T-tail configuration. The advantage to that is that the horizontal empennage is not in the engine blast. Later, the F-4, which was largely derived from the F-101, received starkly down-swept horizontal stabilizers. The big disadvantage of the T configuration is derived from the stall characteristics. In a deep stall, the turbulence from the wing impinges on the tail and renders the elevator ineffective. Without proper response from the pilot, a stalled aircraft was likely to fall in a tail-low attitude. The emergency procedure called for the deployment of the (landing) drag parachute in order to point the nose down. I never had a pitch up, but I heard that the emergency procedure worked well, if there was enough altitude to recover. The T-tail configuration is popular in transport aircraft also. With fuselage-mounted engines such as the Boeing 727 and the McDonnell-Douglas MD-80 series, the cabin is quieter than with wing-mounted engines, and less buffet is felt when using the speed brakes. However, like the F-101, the 727 owns some nasty stall characteristics.

Coupling that with its extreme pitch sensitivity, it took some getting used to. Wikipedia has an informative, and from my perspective, accurate description of the development of the aircraft. The airplane would accelerate on a level with modern fighters. It was so pitch sensitive that flying formation was especially challenging, especially after the great flight controls of the F-102. It was a big airplane, 71 ft. long and over fifty thousand pounds with full

17. Raggedy-Ass Militia

fuel and armament. It arrived fast, too. At 175 knots plus a few knots extra for fuel weight, one didn't have much time to correct mistakes when landing out of a low ceiling. Even worse, if you lost an engine on takeoff, you would soon find yourself on final approach at 210 knots.

Formation takeoffs happened fast. When flying wing, I liked to line up almost line abreast, and once afterburners were lit, slowly drift back into fingertip position. It only took thirteen seconds to get to lift-off at 185 knots. Once airborne, it took a quick hand on the gear handle not to trap the nose gear (which retracted forward). Trapping the nose gear was a sure way to ruin a formation takeoff. If you did, the drill: everybody out of burner, get separated (especially in the clouds), cycle the gear back down and then up, find the other guy, get back together. It was a mess.

Afterburner climbs were spectacular. On a cold day, I clocked from lift-off to 30,000 ft. in ninety-nine seconds, with 10,000 ft. at the departure end of the runway. The deck angle was about 50 degrees at first, but it seemed to be almost vertical.

The Voodoo had great wheel brakes. One night at the bar, some loudmouth was bragging about his T-33. I asserted that I could stop the F-101 quicker than he could a T-33. Everyone knows that the T-33 comes down final 60 knots slower than the F-101. It was a bet. I knew the T-33 had lousy brakes, and I had a really good antiskid system. The next day, with a light airplane, drag chute in the air, firm landing, and standing on the brakes, I won handily.

This was the first crewed airplane that I had flown. We flew lots of practice intercepts to maintain our operationally ready (OR) status. With the weapons system officer (WSO) in the rear seat doing all the hard work, all I had to do was fly, center the steering dot, and hold the trigger down. The instrument that received the most attention was the pitch boundary indicator (PBI), #4 in the diagram below.

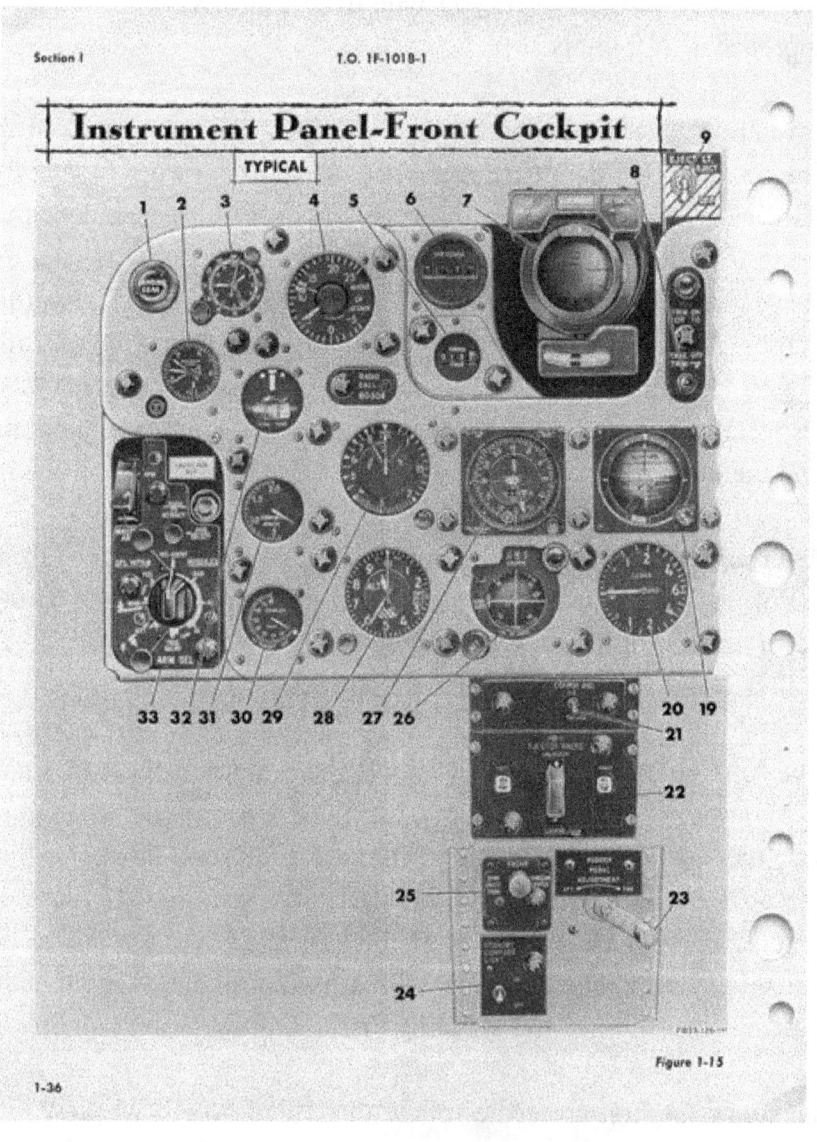

F-101 Instrument Panel

17. Raggedy-Ass Militia

The Alpha wand depicted the instantaneous angle of attack, while the boundary wand indicated the (varying) limit where the redundant limiter system would begin warnings. Fully loaded, the F-101 had a wing loading almost identical to the F-104. Neither turned very well. Most of the pilots were divided into two groups: those who were afraid to turn the airplane for fear of a pitch up, and those who refused to be intimidated by it. If one was in the second group, you could come down initial approach for an overhead pattern at 350 knots, roll into a 60-degree bank, pull the alpha wand to the hatched area of the limit wand, and perform a decent (fairly tight) overhead pattern. If one was in the first group, you had to keep a careful watch on downwind for C-5s, C-141s, and the like.

The F-101 had decent legs. Range was about 900 NM clean, 1200 NM with one 400-gallon drop tank, and 1200+ miles with two 400-gallon drop tanks. Endurance was a little better with two drop tanks, but the drag was so great, all that fuel didn't buy you much range.

Alert, like the regular Air Force counterpart, involved hours of boredom, punctuated by a few real scrambles. I could study in the quiet hours, and always flew the alert aircraft at the end of the shift for crew and aircraft changeover. The invasion never came, but occasionally someone would try to fly across the Aircraft Defense Identification Zone (ADIZ) without proper clearance. Aside from a few lost Cessnas and potential drug runners, I only had one scramble that amounted to anything. A high-flying, fast target being extremely rare, I felt privileged to be among the lucky ones to get called out. After hurrying out to a point about eighty miles south of Galveston, I was feeling lucky to be on the mission. I pulled up beside a big four-engine turbo-prop airplane, and despite my passion for all airplanes, could not identify it. GCI asked me what it was, and I could only describe it—how humiliating. I later found out that it was a Canadair CL-44, a strange aircraft that sported a tail section that swung open for cargo loading. No one else in the formation knew what it was, either.

One evening while the rest of the squadron conducted its quarterly night-flying practice, I was studying on alert, when I hear a loud explosion nearby. I ran from the alert barn to see a huge fireball across the runway. Only 300 yards from the barn, I could barely see the tail of a T-33 protruding from the fire. Otis, a downtowner, and his passenger, Lindell, our flight surgeon, flying a T-33 target mission, had exploded on takeoff. By midnight, the fire-fighting vehicles, ambulances, police, reporters, and various officials had departed, leaving the alert crew for an uneasy night's rest.

The aircraft had come to rest near the departure end of the runway, adjacent to the alert barn. A small stanchion, housing meteorological sensors on the side of the runway, had been sheared by the aircraft's wing. For some unknown reason, the aircraft had taken off, retracted its landing gear, then at low altitude drifted toward the RVR tower and collided with it. The accident investigation board never produced a satisfactory explanation. Contaminated fuel was suspected, although the engine was at full power throughout the takeoff. Lawsuits and insurance denials followed. Five years later, while flying with Lindell's ex-wife's new husband, the cause became obvious. See Chapter 21 for the answer.

The 111th participated in Combat Pike also. In August of 1976, while deployed for missile firing, I looked up my old friend from the test squadron, Clancy Langford. Clancy represented Hughes Aircraft (manufacturer of our missiles) as a technical representative (tec-rep). Being an ancient guy at the time, probably in his fifties, he had flown F-84s while on active duty. One of his squadron mates from his active duty days was John Hume, Vice-President

17. Raggedy-Ass Militia

of Inflight Services at Delta Airlines. Clancy suggested that I look John up and ask him to get me a job. I called his secretary in Atlanta, and although not given an appointment, was advised that he would be in the office the next day. Next, I talked to our detachment commander, Major. Vinny Cerisano, about tomorrow's schedule.

I said, "Vinny, I have something really important to do tomorrow, can I have the day off?" Wink, wink.

From my behavior, he thought I had some romantic rendezvous planned and approved the day off. I believe he never would have done so if he had known the real reason.

The next day, after a short flight in a Southern Airways DC-9, I was sitting in John's office, being as charming as possible to his secretary. After cooling my heels for a few hours, I was ushered into his plush office, complete with F-84 photos. After exchanging pleasantries and reporting on Clancy's stats, there was a very pregnant silence.

John said, "I guess you want me to get you a job flying with Delta."

I probably mumbled something in the affirmative.

He said, "Well, I can't do that. But I can get you an interview."

I was pleased and grateful beyond words. It was what I had hoped for him to say.

The next day, Vinny said, "I can tell from the smile on your face that you had a successful day yesterday."

Sure enough, John came through. Although Delta had not had a new hire class in five years, I was invited for an interview in October of 1976.

"Mr. Smith, this is Mrs. Johnson with Delta Air Lines."

"Yes, ma'am."

"We would like for you to come for an interview tomorrow. Your ticket will be waiting for you at the Houston counter."

Me: "How about the day after tomorrow? I have alert tomorrow."

She: "How about tomorrow?"

Me: "That will be fine."

18. Airline New Hire

Although Delta had a personnel department, they didn't know how to hire a pilot. My interview consisted of a couple of chief pilots asking me questions about my flying experience and a psychologist trying to trip me up. Looking back on the people with whom I flew at Delta, almost anyone who had survived a few thousand hours of jet time can be taught to fly an airliner. More importantly, how many of these would be able to walk a straight-and-narrow lifestyle, given we were to be surrounded by beautiful women and paid lots of money? Later, more than one chief pilot confided in me that 99 percent of their work was dealing with misbehaving pilots. The (non-professional) interviewers should have focused on behavior, rather than aviation. In the end, they hired two classes of fifteen, each with two civilian pilots. If you were a military pilot, you passed. If you were an academy graduate, you were warmly invited.

On January 13, 1977, I began ground school at Delta pursuant to a flight engineer rating. The management at the fighter squadron was very understanding when I requested a transfer to part-time status. At Delta, *everything* revolves around one's date of hire. I would repeat "01-13-77" often during my career and even in retirement when riding as a passenger.

DELTA AIR LINES - PILOT CLASS JANUARY 13, 1977

* 1.	BRADFORD, (DONALD) O.	#256588	C & I
* 2.	ZOCHOWSKI, (FRANK) F.	#363698	FE BASIC & TURBOJET
* 3.	MOSER, ROBERT D. *Bob*	#385402	FE BASIC - C & I
4.	JOHNSON, (JEFFREY) B.	#488983	C & I
5.	BARTLEY, (JOE) M.	#488925	B-727 LIC #461 74 8551
6.	CROFTON, JOHN D. *Jack*	#488959	FE BASIC & TURBOJET
7.	PRICE, (ALAN) W.	#489080	C & I
8.	MCGOWAN, MICHAEL D. *Mike*	#489014	C & I
9.	EGELSTON, (DAVID) P.	#488967	FE BASIC & TURBOJET
10.	SMITH, SAMUEL DON	#489098	C & I
11.	STEINER, (BARRY) H.	#489139	FE BASIC & TURBOJET
12.	LYONS, BOYD K. *Keith*	#489006	FE BASIC & TURBOJET
13.	JOHNSON, (JAMES) B.	#488975	B-727 LIC #350 38 2649
14.	JORDAN, (BRADFORD) D.	#488991	C & I
15.	WILLIAMS, (CHARLES) M. *Mike*	#489147	FE BASIC & TURBOJET

Some readers may ask, "What is a flight engineer?" Before modern cockpit automation and two-pilot cockpits, flight engineers, also known as second officers, flew in a third seat, managed aircraft systems, calculated performance data, conducted exterior preflight inspections in the snow, and brought the front-seaters their coffee. I didn't take to the job easily. Being used to flying alone, and in a military environment, fitting into the system required more than just learning the machine. The development of effective checklists for emergencies had been neglected by the company. The dreaded "two-engine-out landing" required the engineer to address each lost system in different sections of the manual. Later, a single checklist was developed for such emergencies. In an industry with such a long history, initiation rites existed to torment the new hire.

18. Airline New Hire

One such trick involved the replacement of a green light bulb with a red one. Just before takeoff, as power was applied, a light for one of the safety systems should illuminate green. When it illuminated red, the neophyte was mystified, resulting in a sort of paralysis.

727 Engineer's Panel

Check rides and examinations in the B-777 today emphasize knowledge and procedures on a need-to-know basis. That is, if you can't do anything about it in the air, you don't need to know how it works. Not so in 1977 in the B-727. More of an initiation that a learning experience, the oral exam and simulator check rides were brutal. Emerging from that ordeal with such in-depth knowledge of the systems certainly was not detrimental, and teaching it provided job security for a huge cadre of instructors.

The President of Delta at the time, Dave Garrett, insisted that each new engineer and pilot receive a flight in an aircraft before reporting to their assigned bases. That was in addition to the FAA requirements, funded entirely by Delta, and later discontinued as an economy move. Two of my classmates while on their trainer ride almost made it their last. They were busy learning about the engineer's panel while a new copilot received instruction in the front right seat. An important emergency procedure is the emergency descent. The instructor notified everyone that there was a simulated cabin depressurization and that an emergency descent should be initiated. The new copilot, fresh from the DC-8, where such things are part of their procedures, reached to the throttles and pulled all three engines into reverse thrust, which was prohibited in the 727. The reverser handles were immediately stowed, but the engines remained in reverse! Sinking like an anvil, they began to look for a field to land. I believe they shut down one engine and managed to get its reversers stowed, saving the day. No one ever mentioned the human factors involved in that incident. How could such a deeply ingrained habit from flying the DC-8 have gone unnoticed in that transition? As we shall see in later chapters about aircraft design and accident investigation, it was simply dismissed as pilot error.

After barely getting by ground school, oral exam, and simulator check came the initial operating experience (IOE). Engineers, the same as pilots today, receive an FAA airman rating after a successful simulator check with an FAA examiner or designee.

18. Airline New Hire

However, the rating is not valid until the newly rated pilot or engineer flies with a line check airman on a few flights. Therefore, unlike the rumor, it is not possible for a passenger to be on a flight with neither pilot having flown the actual aircraft. My IOE with Chris Walker was productive and laid back, a welcome relief from the schoolhouse.

Two-and-a-half months after beginning, I flew my first revenue trip as the only engineer on board. Imagine my surprise when, sitting in the engineer's chair, with happy anticipation of performing well, I was told by the captain, "At Houston, we don't use checklists. You can read it if you like, but don't bother us with it."

Well, OK, I can do that, I thought, recalling the notion among fighter pilots that few single-seat pilots use one. The joke is that when the standardization-evaluation examiner asks to look at one's checklist, it is completely unworn, having resided in the lower right pocket of the fight suit and never opened.

Coming from the strict atmosphere of the Delta training department, I was shocked at the casual approach demonstrated by the Houston pilots. Surely, they were competent. Many had ten thousand hours or more in the 727.

Becoming bored and stale at any job is predictable when promotions are slow or nonexistent. The entire airline industry had stagnated in the 1970s, leaving a cadre of pilots stuck in a job that had become too routine. Much of the mischief was harmless, such as playing pranks on the flight attendants, and making long and clever PA announcements. However, conducting an idle-power approach and landing from one hundred miles out, given the slow engine acceleration, bordered on the suicidal. Yes, they were cowboys, a less-than-endearing term for such non-standard behavior.

"You may think we are crazy, but we haven't had an accident, so we must be OK" was their refrain. I shall show how that attitude failed and became corrected.

Drinking on layovers was a cat-and-mouse game played by the senior pilots and the management "Gestapo." The FAA rules called for no drinking for eight hours before a flight. Delta, in their strait-laced wisdom, chose to extend that rule to twelve hours. The spy network from the company fought vigorously with the anti-spy network of bar owners at layover points. It was a game that the cowboys loved. A few years later, the company aligned their policy with the FAA at eight hours. Unlike the clever PA announcements heard on Southwest and other airlines, Delta insisted that their flight attendants read or memorize the required announcements verbatim. Management perceived the more formal approach as more elegant and classier. Little did they know the pilots were making crazy announcements.

On one sunny day (I was not on board), a Houston captain conducting a B-727 flight from Bangor, Maine, to Boston decided to make his route low altitude following the coast line. Although completely illegal, the passengers were ebullient with praise. He was quite proud of himself until one of the passengers wrote the company, thanking Capt. Schwinnaker for such a wonderful flight.

On a flight with that same captain, from New York to Houston, late at night, we pilots were in a deep discussion about something that seemed important at the time. The flight attendant call button flashed and I answered the call.

"Don, this is Jeanie. Could you make it a little bit warmer in the back?"

"Sure, I'll take care of it." I dialed the heat up a little in the aft section of the passenger cabin.

18. Airline New Hire

A few minutes passed and the call button flashed again.

"Don, (slightly exasperated) it's still cold back here."

"OK, sorry, I'll warm it up." I dialed the heat up a little more and went back to the badinage.

After a few minutes had passed: *Bang, Bang, Bang*, someone loudly knocked on the door.

I got up and looked through the peephole in the door, and saw that it was Jeanie. I opened the door and sat back down. Jeanie entered and pulled the door closed behind her.

"OK, just who do I have to f*** to get some cold air back here?"

Of course, it was just a figure of speech, and we all laughed. But considering the intense and litigious working environment of today, that seems like a different world.

As the junior-most engineer at the base, my flight schedule was sub-optimal. Someone in marketing had a brilliant idea for flying airplanes that were sitting idle in the middle of the night by offering low fares. Called "Owly Birds," the theory proved to be unprofitable and was soon abandoned. For the first few months, my only trip left Houston at 1:40 a.m., flew to Atlanta, and returned mid-morning. After a steady diet of those and the $800/month pay, I began to wonder if the airline life was for me. The pay got better after a year. During the first year, I was paid a flat salary. After one year, I was awarded increment pay. That meant that I would be paid on a flight hour basis. That raised my salary from $9600/year to $25,000/year. The catch, however, was that I had been paid in advance before, and on increment pay I was paid in arrears. I went almost three months without a paycheck!

The trips included Montreal in the winter. I had a lot to learn about cold weather operations, and flying in general. De-icing, very low ceiling/visibility approaches, thunderstorm avoidance, radar interpretation, and fuel management were areas of expertise absent from my repertoire. What better way to learn than from a seat behind two crazy ten-thousand-hour pilots?

First Delta Paycheck (don't spend it all at one bar)

During my first year with Delta, I remained a part-time guard pilot at Ellington. I managed to wrangle a cross-country training flight to Edwards AFB to see the first flight of the Space Shuttle as it separated from the B-747 carrier. It was successful and exciting.

That evening at the Officers Club bar, Joe Algranti, the chief of the NASA Astronaut Office, held court. Surrounded by dozens of fighter pilot/astronaut wannabes, he spouted grandiose plans for the shuttle program and its pilots. I couldn't even get close. Many members of the audience held better qualifications than me.

That evening, I decided that a promising career with Delta would be better than pursuing possible astronaut adventure and fame. After going on increment pay in 1978, I rethought priorities. I decided to give up either graduate school or the guard. Forty-plus

18. Airline New Hire

years later, I still don't know which choice would have been correct. Choosing to continue graduate school, two things happened that suggested I had made a good decision.

My languishing Master's Degree thesis received enough of my attention to see completion.

In October of 1980, an Ellington F-101 exploded on takeoff. The tail had separated from the rest of the aircraft, causing such a severe pitch down that neither crewmember survived. The investigation concluded that a void in the structure had slowly accumulated fuel and on that day had sufficient volume to ignite, causing the explosion.

Every squadron to which I had been assigned had lost an aircraft, a crewmember, or both. In all cases, the cause remained unknown to the aircrews when resuming flying.

The obvious question, "Am I next?" occurred to everyone. My solution was to convince myself that the victims lacked the skill that I possessed, and that it couldn't possibly happen to me. True or not, that enabled me reluctantly to climb back into the cockpit. If I could have flown as cautiously for the rest of my career as I did on those days, I would have been the safest, most conscientious pilot in history. The loss of two friends saddened me. However, I felt a secret relief for avoiding another "fly and hope I'm not next" day.

While anxiously waiting for promotion to copilot or "first officer," I joined the dual pool at Delta. That program allowed pilots to serve in two different capacities simultaneously. The logic of the program was that if aircrews for a particular position, e.g., B-727 first officer, became unavailable, then second officers who were qualified could step in. So, I became qualified as copilot and waited. One of the

727 Houston captains was dual qualified as a B-747 second officer! When the anxiously awaited day finally came, it was a terrible flight, late at night, poor weather, and a challenging airport. The captain, also a dual pool member, ordinarily flew first officer. The first officer (me) had not flown in that capacity for over a month, and the second officer was on his first trip. One wonders how we survived with such limited experience. I never heard of an incident involving a dual pool pilot, and it was later discontinued. The good news: we were paid for the upgraded position all month, regardless of the position flown in other flights for that month.

Promotion to first officer happened in November of 1980, after three and a half years on the engineer's panel. Looking back on the systems of the 727, a few major differences from modern designs emerge. Being mostly analog, every quantity, sensor, and setting involved a "plus or minus" tolerance. Fuel gauges wandered (sometimes to zero and back), radar returns depended on the "tune" of the set, and emergencies were triggered by leaky sensor lines. Inaccurate as it was, system information such as temperatures, pressures, and voltages were readily available. Modern transport design involves a constant battle between the engineers and pilots as to what information is to be revealed to the pilots. The B-767 design had been sharply criticized for denying pilots enough system information. The B-777 corrected that trend by integrating users into the design team. (They won the Bendix Trophy for that).

I loved the 727 best for its strength and reliability. I never worried when some of the Houston Cowboys flew through some very turbulent weather. Many landings severely tested the structure (it was a difficult aircraft to land, but more on that later). I never saw a popped rivet or skin wrinkle after a flight. Other than electronics, dispatch reliability was high. I wouldn't know whether to give credit for that to Delta's maintenance, or Boeing's design and construction.

18. Airline New Hire

After three and a half years as second officer, I was happy to escape the cold-weather exterior preflight inspections, takeoff performance computations, and blame for everything that broke on the airplane.

Delta Boeing 727-232

19. Early Retirement

No, I didn't really retire, but flying copilot was so easy that I felt like it. As a newly minted B-727 first officer, I was happy to be flying jets again. The pay improved, the captain had to make all the decisions, the engineer conducted all the exterior preflight inspections, and all I had to do was fly every other leg. It soon became obvious why so many pilots chose to remain first officers so long into their careers. The joke about the duties of the first officer was to learn to say: "Clear right, I'll eat the chicken, and I'll take the ugly one." It wasn't so funny when one of the cowboys decided to do something with the aircraft that exceeded one's safety envelope.

Before 1987 and Delta's "year of shame," the management frequently espoused the notion that we were a captain's airline. That generally was accepted to mean that anything the captain wanted to do should be accepted by the rest of the crew. Also implied in that philosophy was that company management would support any decision that one of their godlike captains made. The reality: The Flight Operations Procedures Manual lacked meaningful guidance for unusual situations, and the company was unwilling to devote the resources to create a good one. Later, as we shall see, that obsolete philosophy gave way to the modern Delta.

Sometimes, finesse and tact became the most important skills possessed by the first officer. Some three-day rotations left me

19. Early Retirement

wishing that I could have flown alone again. I can't remember a single exception to the notion that the unpleasant captains possessed lower than average flying skills.

Of course, there were the good ones. Kind mentoring and pleasant company frequently happen in multi-crew cockpits. In single-pilot aircraft, advanced learning happens mostly by trial and error. In the 727, I was privileged to observe masters at work and emulate them. Learning was not limited to flying techniques; developing a harmonious team with fellow pilots and flight attendants demands sophisticated skills also. As most first officers eventually become captains, that was the time to embrace some behaviors and discard others.

The 727 presented a completely different personality to me as a pilot than it did when I was a second officer. A fast airplane, the high-speed warning usually sounded about Mach .90 and maximum indicated airspeed, VMO, happened about 400 knots, depending on altitude and temperature. Normal cruise speed varied with the price of fuel, but Mach .84 was common. The large speed brakes functioned very well. Due to its T-tail configuration, the turbulence generated by the extension of the speed brake panels on the top of the wing did not cause unpleasant buffeting.

An apocryphal exchange between a 727 pilot and an air traffic controller:

"Delta descend to cross twenty miles north of Macy Intersection at one two thousand feet."

"Unable, we're too close to make that."

"Don't you guys have speed brakes? Why don't you use them?"

Aeromorphosis

"Yeah, we have 'em, but they are for my mistakes, not yours."

With speed brakes deployed and landing gear down, the 727 would descend 1000 ft. for every mile forward travel, a 1 to 1 descent.

Smooth landings eluded me and most new pilots. Looking at photos of it, one can see that the main landing gear is positioned unusually far back along the length of the airplane. I believe that this resulted in a strange airplane behavior near the ground. Just before touchdown, if the pilot sensed too great a sink rate, they would normally pull back slightly on the yoke to arrest that sink. However, as in all aircraft, anything behind the wing necessarily goes down before it goes up. With the main landing gear so far back, that small increase in yoke back pressure actually lowered the main landing gear, producing an unexpected early touchdown. The worst landings I have seen in any airplane took place on the 727. After a particularly poor one, yellow oxygen masks would be shaken from their compartments, creating an orange grove in the cabin. I had good luck with landings by trimming a little nose up and holding forward pressure on the yoke until near the ground, then releasing a little pressure to flare for the landing.

The dinosaurs (ancient creatures that perished due to an inability to adapt) encountered another artifact of remaining too long on the airplane: an increasing mistrust of the normal final approach speeds.

"Someday, this airplane will just fall out from under you for no good reason," they whined.

"That's why I always fly final at ten or twenty knots faster than book."

19. Early Retirement

It never did. In fact, flying book speeds resulted in a higher deck angle at touchdown, which terrified some of them. That certainly resulted in shorter roll-out distances.

"There are two kinds of airplanes, the 727 and all the others," they said.

I agree that it was unique.

Fighter aircraft and transport aircraft both have large, powerful rudders. Although the function of yawing the aircraft about the vertical axis is the same, their use varies considerably. In fighters, rolling the aircraft using rudder rather than ailerons is encouraged. When maneuvering with high-G loads, any aileron used induces yaw, which is likely to cause an out-of-control situation or a spin. In transport aircraft, pilots seldom use rudder except for crosswind landings. Use of the rudder at any other time results in uncomfortable sensations for the passengers. The overuse of rudder habit that I had brought from fighters was soon beaten out of me. Later, an accident was caused at American Airlines by just such a latent habit, emerging during an emergency.

Looking through my logbook, I see names of pilots of another generation. Besides the quality role model people, there are personality types and behaviors that are mercifully absent today.

During a descent to Seattle, with the captain flying the aircraft, the turbulence shook us violently. He continued at near maximum speed, which exacerbated the discomfort. The obvious move would have been to slow down to produce a more comfortable ride. He did not. After arriving at the layover hotel, he said, "Meet you at the bar, I'll buy you a drink."

After only a few minutes to change clothes, I entered the bar. There sat the captain with two empty martini glasses and a half-full third in front of him. He had hurried the arrival because he was thirsty!

The perpetrators of the following tale swore it was true. I wasn't there. Captain X made everyone in his crew miserable. His constant nitpicking and complaining wore very thin after a few days. That part I can vouch for, because I had a difficult time getting along with him also. During a night flight between New York and Miami, the routing called for a leg between Wilmington and Bimini over the Atlantic along Atlantic Route 7. Captain X dozed off during that leg. The calculating copilot changed the compasses from "slaved" to "direct gyro," enabling him to slew the compasses to indicate a heading of due east, while they were actually on course, heading south. Next, he instructed the engineer to push and hold the fuel gauge test button until the gauges read nearly zero. With that indication, he pulled the fuel gauge circuit breaker, rendering the fuel gauges stuck at a very low level. He then quietly called one of the flight attendants, requesting that she call the cockpit in a few minutes. Instructing the engineer to feign sleep, he also pretended to be asleep. When the call from the cabin arrived, it woke Captain X. Arousing, he found what he thought was two sleeping crewmen, an aircraft heading for Europe, and an aircraft with little to no fuel. Accounts of his reaction vary, but suffice it to say, he was extremely upset. The moral to this story: Be nice to your copilot.

Several of the married captains would frequently bring their girlfriends or wives on their trip. Getting their names correct and remembering the difference proved to be critical for first officer well-being. Charlie, one of our best, had he courtesy to choose a girlfriend with the same first name as his wife.

19. Early Retirement

Aside from the flying, I believe that being a member of an airline crew is unique among occupations for another reason. Where else does one get crammed into a small cockpit with strangers for twenty hours and observe their behavior for three or four days? All this while being subjected to stressful situations from weather, unruly passengers, and faulty equipment. It's true: put someone under pressure and you can see into their soul.

The same automation that so much changed the way pilots fly their aircraft pervaded all quarters of the industry. Crew scheduling became a huge beneficiary of the computer age. Atlanta headquarters published lines of time, which specified a series of trips for crewmembers for the upcoming month. Each line of time complied with the complicated contractual and regulatory restriction on maximum hours on duty and minimum rest time. A typical line of time might have a three-day trip followed by four days off, then repeated four times for the month. More likely, an extra short trip had to be included to make the hours add up to the most efficient numbers. These regular lines were followed by reserve lines, which specified only the days to be available to fly. In order of seniority, pilots chose which schedule they preferred.

At times, the casual conversations in the cockpit became contentious or uncomfortable. Late one night on a flight from New York, Captain Pete, a known Bible-thumper, and I became alone in the cockpit when the engineer temporarily left for coffee.

"Don, have you accepted Jesus Christ as your Lord and Savior?" asked Captain Pete.

Startled by this, I took a few moments before answering.

"No, Pete. I'm a Deist; I'm not superstitious at all," I answered.

"What? How can you deny the Bible as the holy word of God?"

"I don't believe that. The God that I know is kind and created all the beautiful things that I see in nature. How can such a God advocate in his Bible such things as homophobia, misogyny, slavery, and genocide?"

With that, the engineer returned. We never spoke about it again.

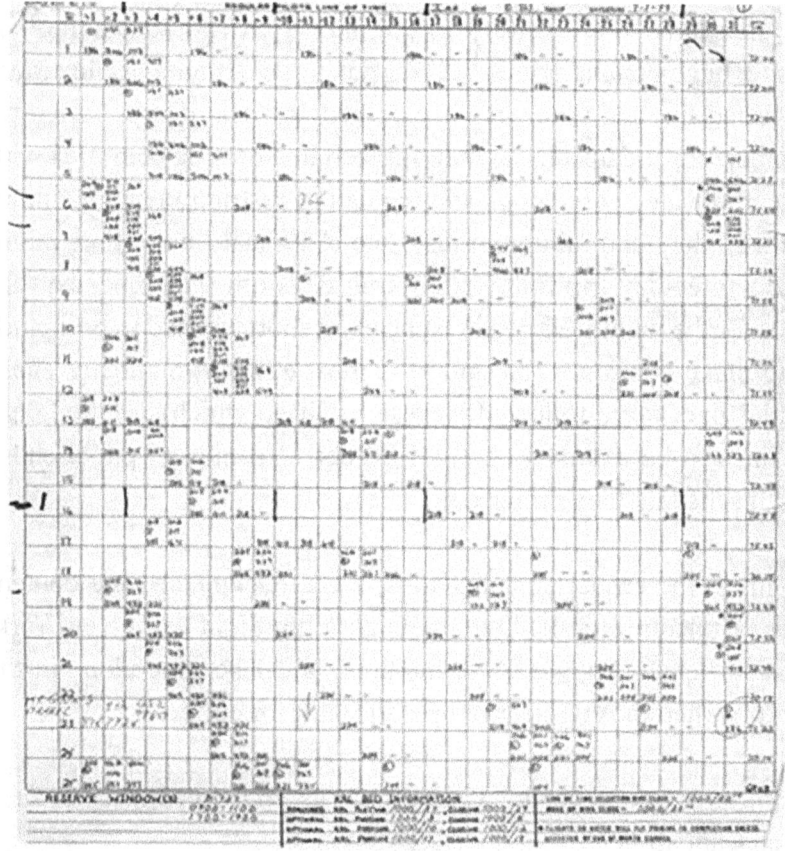

Lines of Time

19. Early Retirement

Houston trips

A senior pilot might choose to fly midday trips with San Francisco layovers, and weekends off. More junior reserve pilots might be able to choose weekends off. A certain contractually specified number of the pilots at a base remained on reserve. Vacations, illness, and other unexpected events necessitated the use of reserve pilots to complete a crew.

As with all the pilot bases, Houston possessed a group of crew schedulers who managed the reserves to ensure a smooth execution of the published lines of time. Since it was done completely manually, a master book containing the lines of time and who was to fly them figured prominently in our lives. A reserve pilot's obligation to be ready to fly was allocated to a few periods of long notice and a few of short notice. A long-call reserve pilot might be asked to report the next day for a flight normally flown by a pilot who had been awarded vacation time. A short-call pilot might get a call to report in an hour because someone had suddenly become ill.

Aeromorphosis

Where there are humans, there is corruption. One of the captains ran an auto dealership and flew on the side. Busy with that, and although very senior, he bid reserve and bribed the crew schedulers to skip his name on the duty list. What was ostensibly a rule-based system became perverted into an empire with crew schedulers doling favors for supplication.

"Hardy, I don't know what to do. I'm out of reserves. I have a trip to cover and you're the only one left. You are just gonna have to fly it or call in sick. If I call in a dual pooler or out-of-base pilot, Atlanta will be all over me. Yes, I know what you have done for me, but I'm in a tight place." I overheard that conversation in Houston operations.

One of the ostensible benefits of the "empire" was the availability of blue trips. An off-duty pilot might call his crew scheduler and declare that he would be on one for the next three days. The scheduler would dutifully place a "BT" on that pilot's schedule for those days. Anticipating a call from someone needing contact with that pilot, the scheduler was obligated to reply that he was on a certain trip and would be contacted to get in touch with the caller. This enabled a philandering pilot to get out of the house for indiscreet or blue activities. On one occasion, the wife of one of the pilots called crew scheduling, desperate to contact her husband.

The scheduler replied, "Ma'am, I don't know how to tell you this, but your husband retired two years ago."

The automation of pilot scheduling relegated this ugly chapter of the industry to the past. Additionally, cell phones, location tracking, GPS, and other modern innovations made this sort of subterfuge and philandering more difficult.

19. Early Retirement

When I decided to transfer to the Dallas/Ft. Worth Base, one of the schedulers warned me that I would be miserable at that base since they did everything by the book up there. Special favors would not be available. Once there, I discovered that I had given much more than I had received from Houston crew scheduling. By the book proved to be not only simpler, but much to my advantage.

20. ROTORHEAD

In 1982, with G.I. Bill money available and spare time on my hands, learning to fly helicopters seemed to be a good idea. I located a training center at Hobby Airport in Houston that specialized in subsidized training. Using an ancient Hiller UH-12C and a Bell 47C, they suggested that learning on older, less powerful aircraft produced strong pilots. This was mostly true, as their low power demanded coaxing into the air.

"My best students have been farm boys with lots of tractor time," my instructor confided.

Not having been on a tractor much, I did take to hovering quickly. I considered hovering to be much like flying formation in a fighter. After I made good progress, my instructor invited me to accompany him in a Bell 206L, Jet Ranger on his flights to an oil rig off the coast of Galveston. He allowed me to make my first pinnacle landing there. Graciously welcomed by the personnel on the rig, they were anxious to show us how well they ate. After consuming a gourmet meal, I was asked if we might take a mechanical part back to shore. Agreeing, I asked how large it was. With a tape measure, we calculated that it would just barely fit in the rear of the helicopter.

"By the way, how much does it weigh?" I asked.

"About six hundred pounds," he said.

20. Rotorhead

What a joke, I had forgotten to ask the basic question. That would have been much too heavy for us to lift.

On one flight returning to shore, two employees strapped into the rear seats. My instructor confided over the interphone that he would perform the takeoff and not to be surprised. Lifting off in ground effect, then slowly moving away from the platform produces a falling feeling with the loss of ground effect until it is counteracted with additional collective (lift from the rotor). As we dropped toward the water, the tough guys in the back actually screamed. A cruel sport.

My training progressed well until the day I flew alone and a chip light illuminated on the instrument panel. That indicated that metal had been detected in the engine oil and total failure might occur. I landed in a field and summoned my instructor. Belittling my caution, he flew it back to base. Soon afterward, while flying solo, a loud clanking sound prompted me to land in a field again. A cooling fan shroud had become displaced, allowing the fan to strike it. Discretion being the better part of valor, I decided to transfer to a different school at Hooks Airport, north of Houston.

For training, they provided a Hughes 300, a much newer and more powerful helicopter than I had previously flown. That machine has very sensitive flight controls and low rotor inertia. The small rotor makes autorotations happen quickly. After an engine failure, the pilot has only a few seconds before approaching the ground. My training went well, and on the day of my check ride, the instructor who had flown me to the oil rigs showed up six hours late as the sun began to set.

With the normal maneuvers demonstrated, he said, "You land and I'm going to get out and observe you perform a 180-degree autorotation from the ground."

He was afraid to ride through the maneuver. The tough guy from the oil rigs had reached his limit. The first time I had tried an autorotation at night ended up OK.

Sadly, with thousands of experienced Vietnam-era helicopter pilots seeking employment, working in that industry eluded me.

21. Fluff

The glacial change at Delta finally sped up in 1984; they acquired the Boeing 737. We called it the "Fluff," meaning funny little fat fellow. Equipped with second-generation automation, it offered a little newness to the boredom of seven years on the 727. Although a small pay cut, I opted to transfer to DFW to fly first officer on the 737.

Modest by modern standards, the automation offered a performance data computer and a mode control panel. Knowing what the other pilot was doing or intending became less obvious when he was communicating with the automation. This confusion proved to be a precursor to more serious problems with the pilot-computer interface in the third-generation 767.

The 737-200 was a pleasure to fly. Unlike the quirky 727, landings came easy, and the flight controls were light and harmonious. Ostensibly for ease of maintenance, and cargo and passenger loading, the shortened landing gear gave the aircraft its squatty stance. Even today, no 737 has inner landing gear doors, allowing the main wheels to be seen as one flies overhead. The wheel bogies have a swiveling mechanism that allows the wheels to track straight down the runway while the fuselage points slightly to the side. I call this "crosswind landing gear," although I have never seen it addressed in the manuals. That feature contributed to the easy landing nature of the aircraft by smoothing the jarring effects of landing in a crab. The short landing gear proved to be problematic when stretched versions of the 737 were developed. As larger engines became available, ground clearance suffered. The Dash 300 and subsequent models employed a unique configuration placing the engine in front of the wing with no pylon. However, the most serious drawback of the short landing gear proved to be the limiting of the fuselage length. As the newer models necessarily had stretched fuselages to permit greater capacity, the danger of dragging the tail during takeoff and landing increased. The landing gear could not be lengthened because that would not fit into the wheel wells. The solution: fly faster. At higher lift-off and landing speeds, less rotation about the lateral axis is required to achieve the necessary lift.

Years later, I became friends with the late Brien Wygle in my work with the Aviation Safety Reporting System (ASRS). A Boeing vice president, he captained the first flight of the 737. He knew the airplane perhaps better than anyone. Regrettably, I never discussed flying the 737 with him.

Southwest Airlines invested heavily in the 737. Except for a brief foray into the flying of a few 727s, it is the only aircraft type they have ever flown. During the 1990s, a series of 737 accidents was attributed to their hydraulic rudder pressure valve. United 585 and USAir 427 crashed under mysterious circumstances. Initially attributed to mountain wave turbulence or other causes, a rudder hard-over was deemed the culprit. In the ensuing months, 737 aircraft were given permission to continue to fly, although with higher minimum flap speeds. This was thought to be sufficient to allow aileron control to overcome the rudder malfunction. That was never tested, but during the period before the replacement of the valves, the 737 continued to fly and produce revenue. In light of the recent grounding of the 737 Max, due to far more clear and preventable causes, that continuance seems outrageous. I believe that in order to save Southwest Airlines and a few others, the pilots and traveling public were endangered. The aircraft should have been grounded, just like the Max.

21. Fluff

Because it was the slowest airliner in the airways, pilots of larger aircraft frequently complained about having to slow down following a 737. We joked that the biggest danger flying the 737 was the threat of being struck in the tail by an overtaking bird. As the smallest aircraft in the mainline Delta fleet, we served smaller cities. That translated into shorter runways, operations with nightly control tower closures, and (non-company) contract maintenance.

Some of the DFW schedules flew entirely in Texas. One particularly short leg flew from Lubbock to Amarillo, scheduled for eighteen minutes, gate to gate. Since it was new to the Delta fleet, the captains also lacked the vast experience on the aircraft that had been the hallmark of the Houston 727. Some achieved their first captaincy on the 737. Soon, I had as much experience on the 737 as most of the captains.

I looked forward to flying with Charlie Bratton. An easygoing, talented pilot, he made the trips pleasant. However, on one trip, the subject of his wife's ex-husband came up. Discovering that he had been a physician and had perished in an aircraft accident at Ellington piqued my interest. Yes, it was the same Lindell that had died the night I had been on alert at Ellington. Charlie told me that soon after his marriage to Judy, the doctor would frequently call him to ask favors regarding the community property. According to Charlie, the conversation would always end with the doctor saying, "Well, if you don't want to do that, I'll just kill myself. I've been thinking of doing that anyway."

Charlie was only vaguely aware of the circumstances of the Ellington crash, since the accident report had never yielded much information. We compared stories and decided that Lindell had definitely overcome Otis on the controls and deliberately crashed the T-33 that night.

Later in my work as an accident investigator, I would recall that the first two aircraft accidents that I had known, involved lying, murder, suicide, or failed investigations.

They say that a copilot should observe captain behaviors, reject some, and adopt some for their future *modus operandi*. A plethora of dramatically differing behaviors became available for me to evaluate (in silence, of course). I anticipated that the 737 might be the first aircraft for my future captaincy. I flew with the arrogant, the fearful, the lazy, the underqualified, the combative, the whining, the suspicious, and lots of good ones.

One memorable flight had us arriving at Amarillo in a windy rainstorm. The captain, a former KC-135 pilot, bore watching. The runway there is 300 ft. wide and 13,500 ft. long, a former strategic bomber base. Crabbing into the wind until just before touchdown, he applied rudder to align with the runway, but failed to add any aileron into the wind. After touching down, we began to drift to the downwind side of the runway. With thrust reversers deployed, the closer we got to the edge of the runway, the more reverse thrust he applied. He didn't realize that with the nose pointed upwind, the reverse thrust was actually aggravating the downwind trajectory. With the edge looming near, I seized the controls, applied full upwind aileron, pushed the throttles out of reverse, and the aircraft magically straightened up. Jim taxied off the runway, stopped, and set the brakes.

I thought, *Well, that's the end of a mediocre career. I'll be fired for doing that.*

He looked at me and said, "Thanks."

21. Fluff

On trips that took me to Miami in the summertime, their approach control would ask us to descend to low altitude far from our destination, ostensibly because of the complex airspace and traffic load. That not only wasted our fuel, but put us in the middle of numerous small aircraft flying visually and uncontrolled in the area. We called that going to Indian Country. Piper Aircraft named most of their airplanes for Native American Tribes: Cherokee, Pawnee, Seneca, Navaho, Seminole, and others. The manufacturing plant was in nearby Vero Beach, and the air was thick with them. Avoidance required extreme vigilance; a few close calls happened anyway. The advent of *traffic collision avoidance systems*, or TCAS, in 1982, and improved in 1986, eliminated much of the risk in such flights. Thus, in my lifetime I have seen one of the most serious threats to aviation safety, midair collision, mostly eliminated. More stories about TCAS saves later in my career will follow in later chapters.

On one rotation, I was flying with Gary Ritter, an inveterate Texan-hater. Why he chose to be based in DFW remains a mystery. After two days of suffering constant criticism, Gary flew us out of Salt Lake City.

"Delta, climb on three six zero heading until reaching 10,000 ft, then turn eastbound on course," said Departure Control, citing a reasonable clearance to miss the tall mountains.

"Don, tell them we will assume responsibility for visually clearing the mountings and turn now," Gary said.

I asked and received the clearance. Gary turned up the valley leading to Park City, hoping to give the passengers a good view of the ski slopes.

Wham, wham, went the turbulence. Everyone on board was extremely uncomfortable for a few minutes.

"What a great idea, showing the passengers the ski slopes," I mocked. I didn't hear anything about stupid Texans for the rest of the trip.

The late Dan Boyd was as easygoing as any pilot I flew with. I kept many of his techniques for my future command.

He said, "After you land the airplane, tell me when you want me to take over to taxi it."

Since the copilot had no steering tiller, the only way to guide the airplane was with the limited steering offered by the rudder pedals.

After clearing the runway on the high-speed taxiway, I said, "Do you want to take over now?"

He said, "Only if you want me to."

I thought, *I'll just try to get it to the gate.*

I didn't quite get it all the way there without help, but it made me feel good that he would have that amount of confidence in me.

On another occasion, flying with Dan, we were landing in an extreme crosswind. I was working very hard on cross-controlling the ailerons and rudder to keep the aircraft pointed straight down the runway.

Dan said, "Try pushing up the upwind throttle and pulling back the downwind throttle to get rid of some of that rudder pressure." It worked perfectly; I use that technique to this day, although I have never heard any discussion of it.

21. Fluff

I had finished a PhD degree in the spring of 1985 and had yet to put it to good use. On August 2, 1985, I was on a flight from Lubbock to DFW when I heard chatter on the radio about a Delta Tri-Star having crashed at DFW. It was true. I felt an overwhelming array of emotions: denial, shame, and helplessness. I decided to throw myself headlong into aviation safety, either with Delta or the Air Line Pilots Association.

22. SOARING

Most of my flying in sailplanes took place during the time that I spent as a first officer in the 737. As the years in that position began to drag on, I recalled the enjoyment that I had experienced in sailplanes while in college. In the 1960s, Clover Field in Pearland, Texas, hosted a flight training business called Greenfield Flyers. Ted Mendenhall and his girlfriend, Wendy, taught basic flying, instruments, and gliders.

Ted had just separated from the Navy; his flying skills were mostly wasted on us. He later had a successful career with Grumman Aircraft and NASA in the Shuttle Training Aircraft program. Several members of the flying club at A&M spent our weekends there earning an add-on glider rating. I took my check ride in a single-seat Schweizer 1-26 while the designated examiner, C. C. Holt, watched from the ground. All of those flights stayed close to home field, while cross-country and high-altitude flights remained a challenge for the future.

The following year, 1969, I managed a few flights back at Uvalde, which offered excellent thermal soaring conditions. A few years after that, Ron Tabery, a world-class soaring competitor, "discovered" Uvalde as a good place to soar.

That same year, I flew from Caddo Mills Airport as a respite for the rigorous F-102 training at nearby Perrin AFB, Texas. The late Dick Johnson, holder of numerous world records, flew from there.

22. Soaring

Once settled in at my first operational assignment in Newport News, Virginia, I joined the Tidewater Soaring Club. To the west, the Dismal Swamp barred all but the very adventurous from attempting cross-country soaring from there. However, the club conducted an annual wave camp near Lexington. The strong winter winds crossed the mountains there, producing a mountain wave in which sailplanes could achieve very high altitudes. We flew from a grass runway, owned by a retired Air Force C-130 pilot, Lynn Becktel. The weather necessitated heavy clothes, and the high altitudes required supplemental oxygen. None of us achieved the coveted altitude diamond, which is a badge for climbing five thousand meters above tow release altitude. The squadron information officer published an article in the local paper highlighting the irony of my going very fast at work and very slow for fun.

On one occasion, I flew a solo test flight in an F-106 in the area. Not one to miss a chance to demonstrate the airplane, I flew low over Lynn's runway, lit the afterburner, and climbed away. I wonder if he enjoyed it.

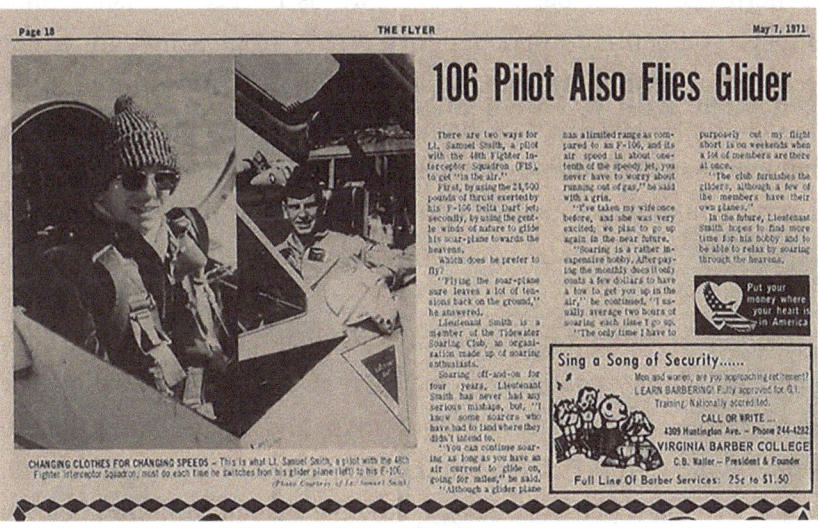

Mach 2 to Mach 0.2

After moving to Austin, Texas, I bought a half-interest in a Pik-20 sailplane in 1986. Made in Finland in 1976, the Pik, although of fiberglass construction and beautiful lines, was no longer considered high performance by then.

Yes, these crazy glider pilots have contests. Typically, they gather in the summertime and compete to see who can fly around a course the fastest. These people are *very* serious about their contests. On one occasion, I flew my sailplane among the contestants, flying along their routes, without being officially registered.

One of the contestants remarked to me, "Oh, you mean you're just here for fun."

I asked, "Aren't we all? There are no cash prizes here."

The Fédération Aéronautique Internationale (FAI) is the world governing body for air sports. With the Soaring Society of America (SSA) administering their soaring awards in America, a system of merit badges for beginners and awards for accomplished pilots attracts competitive-minded pilots. Aside from achieving a new record or an extremely long flight, the highest awards in soaring are the diamonds. The distance diamond is for a five-hundred-kilometer flight, the goal diamond is for a pre-declared triangle or out and return flight of three hundred kilometers, and the altitude diamond is for a 5,000-meter altitude gain above tow release altitude.

In the 1980s without any electronic navigation gear or glide computer, the flights challenged one in many ways. Navigation was accomplished using only a printed map, and occasionally the city name painted on water towers. Leaving from Uvalde and landing near Floydada (near Lubbock), I flew the distance diamond course in seven hours. With cell phones yet to be invented, I walked for an

22. Soaring

hour looking for a phone to use to call my crew to pick me up. The shorter goal diamond seemed easier after that.

The altitude diamond eluded me for many years. On one failed attempt near Texas City, Colorado, I launched without supplemental oxygen. Noticing that my fingernails had turned blue at 17,000 ft., I abandoned that attempt. Later at Minden, Nevada, the perfect winds and weather allowed me to climb to 27,500 ft. As an airline pilot, the lenticular clouds that evidence mountain wave create an apprehension of possible severe clear air turbulence. A forecast of "ACSL" or altocumulus standing lenticular, means rerouting for avoidance. However, in a sailplane, the air remains smooth due to the aircraft's slow speed. In fact, my position over the ground stayed stationary. As the wind speed increased with altitude, the performance of the sailplane limited the maximum altitude that could be achieved. At some point in the ascent, the aircraft could no longer climb at the higher speed required to remain stationary in the wave.

Even with spoilers deployed, thirty minutes passed for my descent. After cold-soaking at -30 degrees F, both myself and the windscreen had become less than optimum. The windscreen frosted over, and I shivered. I wonder why people do such things for fun.

FAI Diamond Soaring Badge

I finally graduated to flying contests, but never scored very well, a "bottom liner." Flying a contest at Littlefield, Texas, I came very close to my demise. Returning to the home field after successfully navigating the course, a thunderstorm began to form near the airport. A few miles out, I encountered extremely strong lift, probably associated with the cloud ahead. That should have been my clue to divert to Lubbock. Feeling very secure in my high altitude (and energy), I continued for home plate. I approached the runway 7,000 above the ground, planning to circle down. As I lined up for the approach, I entered what must have been a downburst, a sinking column of air. With little airspeed and sinking air hurling me at the ground, I retracted the landing gear and flaps and pointed the nose straight down in an attempt to recover enough airspeed to land. At first, I thought I might have enough energy to level out and land in the field between me and the runway. Soon I began to think I might have enough energy to pass under the power line and land on the airport, short of the runway. As I neared the ground, the downburst began to blow more horizontally. I lowered the landing gear and was able to land on the runway. Now the wind blew from my front and the rain pelted the windscreen. I locked the brake, kept the wings level, and attempted to keep from being blown backwards. The wind shifted to my left and the left wing began to uncontrollably rise. After I had resigned myself to being flipped on my back, the wing mysteriously began to lower to the ground. A young man had seen my plight, ran to my glider, and hoisted the wing back down. Completely stunned by the preceding events, I failed to properly thank him. Whoever you are, thank you.

22. Soaring

Pik-20 Over Southwest Texas

No, I did not quit after that. I joined the Fault Line Flyers in Georgetown, Texas. While there, I purchased a Bellanca Citabria to tow sailplanes aloft. Due to an unfortunate squabble, the city of Georgetown invited the club to leave its airport. Consequently, they purchased land nearby and began construction of their own airport. When it was partially complete, I decided to land my Citabria there, becoming the first to do so. It was a bad idea; that act spoiled their grand opening and incurred their wrath.

During my tenure with the Fault Line Flyers, I met the late Eddie Ross. At the time, he instructed and gave check rides in our gliders. Soloing in 1925, he had flown most of the aircraft of the "Golden Age" of aviation of the 1930s. Chief pilot for 25 years for Conoco Oil Company, he later became the personal pilot for Texas Governor Preston Smith. Notable personalities he knew: Wiley Post, Roscoe Turner, Jimmy Doolittle, and Walter Beech. My favorite story, however, involved Amelia Earhart. Eddie refueled her airplane in Oklahoma and performed a poor job of cleaning the windshield on her aircraft. Eddie recounted the blistering, expletive-filled dressing-down that he received as the most thorough that he ever received.

Aeromorphosis

I sold a half-interest in the Citabria to Kim Reniska, an accomplished sailplane aerobatics performer. For his airshow, he would be towed to 10,000 ft. (2,000 being the norm) and perform loops, rolls, and spins, surprising maneuvers for such a long-winged aircraft.

One cold day, Kim had difficulty starting the Citabria. He decided to pull the propeller through a few times to facilitate the start. Having erroneously left the magnetos on, the engine came to life and began to propel the aircraft toward a group of jets parked on an adjacent row. Sensing that the liability insurance would be inadequate, he ran alongside and grasped the strut. Pulling there turned the track 180 degrees, directing the aircraft back to the starting point. While trotting beside the cockpit vainly reaching for the throttle, the aircraft rapidly approached a hangar. Kim, visualizing a huge fireball when the collision happened, prudently released his grip and helplessly awaited the explosion. Unbeknownst to him, the targeted hangar was occupied by an aircraft homebuilder, working on the wing of his project. Fortunately standing on the side of the wing away from the door, the homebuilder witnessed a strange beast making circular incisions on his door, apparently attempting to eat its way through and gobble him up. Our insurance company paid for all the physical damages but got off easy, not having to compensate the hangar owner for mental anguish.

Most sailplanes can be disassembled for ease of movement. The Pik-20 came with a nice trailer and I kept it stored there, rather than paying for hangar space. In those days, Texas levied a tax on aircraft. When the Travis County Assessor sent me a bill, I responded with a letter claiming to base the airplane in Uvalde County at my farm. When Uvalde County sent me a bill, I claimed to base the aircraft in Austin. After three years, they finally conferred and demanded that I choose one or the other. That tax was later eliminated, eliminating the need for such subterfuge.

22. Soaring

The glider needed a wash and wax. I assembled it in my front yard in Austin. As I worked, a small crowd began to gather. The spokesman stepped forward, and loudly asked, "How did you land that here?" I think they were genuinely mystified about its arrival.

The Aircraft Owners and Pilots Association (AOPA) sent me a questionnaire. Among the questions asked: "Have you made an off-field landing." I responded that I had made twenty-two of them. I received a call from a curious statistician, wondering if I had the worst luck of any pilot he knew. I explained that such landouts are common within the glider community, and my luck was about average on that account.

I managed to beg a ride in a modern Pipistrel Taurus-M powered glider in 2019. It was difficult to taxi due to its wingspan, but easy to take off and climb with its strong engine. I noticed things had changed since I had last soared. With the engine secured, electronic displays revealed our position and locations of thermals, a far cry from the pilotage-only rules of my previous experience. The propeller cleverly disappeared in a retracting nose spinner, resulting in an extremely flat glide.

I recommend soaring for everyone. Regulations permit young people to solo at age fourteen, two years before legally soloing powered aircraft. On a day with strong lift, sailplane pilots enjoy a quiet environment, low pilot stress, and that "something for nothing" feeling. For the more competitive spirit, soaring offers a challenge for all levels of skill.

23. TriStar

Lockheed has a long history of producing fine aircraft. From the Vega in 1927 to the C-5 Galaxy, many of their products were named for heavenly bodies. Shooting Star, StarFighter, StarLifter, JetStar, and others became familiar names in the aviation world. Continuing today in that tradition after their merger with Martin-Marietta, they produce what is arguably the most advanced fighter in the world today, the F-35 Lightning II.

The first L-1011 TriStar was delivered to the launching customer, Eastern Airlines, in 1972. Delta received their first in 1973 and retired the last one in 2001, replaced by the Boeing 767-400ER. More expensive than the DC-10, it was certainly the queen of Delta's fleet. Delta began flying passengers on the Atlanta–London route in 1978, using the foreshortened -500 long-range model. Acquiring more North Atlantic routes necessitated the modification of its -1 models to the longer-range -250 model.

Delta had good success with the TriStar despite two occurrences. The first involved a jammed stabilizer which was miraculously landed safely by Jack McMahan, a veteran captain. The second, Flight 191, crashed at DFW on August 2, 1985 in microburst conditions. In spite of that, it was a favorite among the traveling public and highly praised among pilots.

Bored with the domestic copilot job, and with no upward movement in sight, I decided to try international flying. Unfortunately, the only

23. TriStar

seat available was flight engineer on the TriStar. Virtually unknown outside of America, this "downgrade" carried no stigma whatsoever. Because it was a complicated aircraft, ground school and simulators lasted six weeks. Soon enough I discovered the joys and miseries of international flying.

Like the Republic XR-12 Rainbow aircraft, the TriStar was the last of its generation. The XR-12 pushed the performance of reciprocating engine-powered aircraft to its limits. That aircraft traveled at over 400 miles per hour at 40,000 ft. with a range of four thousand miles. Even with every ounce of performance squeezed out of its Pratt and Whitney R-4360 Wasp Major engines, it was no match for the post WWII jet aircraft.

The TriStar was an incredibly complex, mostly analog aircraft. With its four hydraulic systems, all-flying tail, integrated drive generators, three-spool turbofan engines, direct lift control, and many other innovations, it was pleasant to fly or ride, but a heavy load on the engineer. It sported a galley below the passenger deck with a lift (the elevator was on the tail) providing passage between the two. On several occasions while flying near the middle of the North Atlantic, one of the fuel gauges would simply wind down to zero. To the uninitiated, that meant a fuel leak, dictating a diversion to Iceland. However, after a few minutes, the errant gauge would go back to its normal reading.

The TriStar was the first airliner certified in the US for Category IIIc, zero ceiling landings. On one such approach in Paris, all the computers, autothrottles, ground systems, radios, and autopilots were happily in agreement when the dreaded DANA Light illuminated. *Dual autoland not authorized* meant abandoning the approach and resetting most of the computers and autopilots and trying again, not knowing the cause of the problem. Always successful on the second try, it was just a quirk of the analog age.

Direct lift control (DLC) allowed the aircraft to maintain a constant deck angle on approach. That system allowed the spoilers to partially extend, and by modulating them, corrections to the glide path could be made without pitch changes. This concept was later embraced by the US Navy for their aircraft carrier operations.

Successfully entering the North Atlantic market, Delta decided that the -1 TriStars, with some modification, would be able to make a long trip. That didn't work very well. Marginal range and low fuel at the destination required close attention, lest diversion become necessary. The solution: the -250 model, with better engines and more fuel. The range problem faded. However, takeoff performance problems loomed.

Delta and most airlines compute takeoff performance on the "balanced field" theory. In that, the aircraft is loaded up to a weight that will permit it to accelerate to a point on the runway where an engine loss at the worst possible time will result in the ability to either stop on the remaining runway or successfully take off. In the B-777 when that speed is reached, "V1" is called by the pilot monitoring and the aircraft is flown from the runway with plenty of runway left for a possible aborted takeoff. In the TriStar, especially the -250, when "V1" was called, only a few short feet of runway remained. It would have been impossible to stop on the remaining runway. Rolling takeoffs were popular.

"Delta ten, taxi into position and hold," said the tower controller.

"We would like to remain in the number one position until cleared for takeoff," said the copilot.

Once cleared for takeoff, screeching around the turn onto the runway, a little extra speed could be gained for the dreaded long roll.

23. TriStar

I believe that an engine failure at or slightly below V1 would have been disastrous.

On a flight from Frankfurt to Atlanta, an emergency landing became necessary due to a woman going into labor. A physician aboard deemed it necessary to hospitalize her immediately. Nice weather greeted us at Goose Bay, Newfoundland and Labrador. After landing, the captain and first officer proceeded to base operations for flight planning and left me to supervise the refueling. Ed McHugh, the (very senior) captain, asked me what I needed from the company load planner. I told him that since the newly certified -250 TriStar did not carry the paperwork showing allowable takeoff weights for alternate airports, that I needed him to ask Atlanta. Soon they returned.

"What are the runway allowable and climb limit weights?" I asked.

"Oh s***, I forgot to ask. Do you think we can safely take off?

"Sure, with the cold air and long runway we can do that easily."

"OK, let's go."

Arriving in Atlanta, I had some apprehension about the semi-illegal takeoff. Before my flight home, I stopped into the load planner's office.

"Is there any way that I could have computed the takeoff numbers with what I had?" I asked.

"No, there is no way that you could have done that without Captain McHugh asking us."

"How about if I had come by your office last week and asked you what those numbers are?"

"Well, yeah, that would have worked, if you had known that you might need them."

"That's exactly what happened, don't you remember?"

"Well, OK, when were you here?"

"Just before we left on Wednesday."

I copied the correct numbers onto a takeoff data card and placed it into the pouch that we always turned in after a flight, asserting that I had known the correct numbers at the time.

Six weeks later, I was called into the chief pilot's office. Bill Rice said, "How did you know the correct numbers for that takeoff at Goose Bay? Captain McHugh said he didn't ask anyone."

I said, "Before the flight, I contacted the load planners and asked them what they were."

"You mean even though you didn't know you were going to divert, you got those numbers?"

"Yes, sir, that's my story and I'm sticking to it."

"Hmmm, (not convinced) OK, but I'm going to check your story out."

I never heard anything more about it, but I was stunned that he was so thorough that he caught it.

23. TriStar

In July 1981, a Presidential Task Force determined that a two-crew cockpit was safe for wide-body jets, which was a contentious issue. Unions and management fought vigorously about the crew complement. The unions, lobbying for as many members as possible, argued that three people were needed to effectively manage the workload of flying, systems management, and visually avoiding traffic. The managements contending that systems automation being sufficient to manage the workload, only two were required. The narrow-bodied jets such as the DC-9 had successfully operated since the 1960s with two-person crews. Thus, it was the alleged complexity of the wide-bodies jets at issue, rather than the risk to a greater number of passengers.

The subject of crew rest and tiredness became entangled in the arguments. Two-person crews operating such long hauls and managing more complex systems would experience greater stress, the union argued. Management prevailed. Delta's (two pilot) 767-200 arrived with a huge space in the cockpit where the engineer's panel originally stood in the early design. We called it the "dance floor." The -300 models, being conceived from their beginning as a two-person crew, eliminated that space.

In an enormous irony, my job got easier. While on the TriStar, Delta was legal to schedule a three-person crew for a continuous twelve hours. Many captains realized that a short nap by one of the crew members, although illegal, was a safer alternative to three sleepy-headed people conducting a low-weather approach.

I recall one trip which left Atlanta, made a stop in Paris, and continued to Stuttgart. The captain, the late Ralph Simmons, being a former chief pilot and stickler for the rules, did not allow any napping. After a long trip to Paris, and the inevitable delay there, we were three very tired zombie-like pilots landing in Stuttgart. Dangerous and very unpleasant, the company scheduled to the maximum permitted by the regulations.

Upon the advent of the two-pilot cockpit, the crew rest requirements changed to allow a relief pilot for all flights over *eight* hours. With the relief pilot on board, all pilots were able to take an hour-and-a-half nap on a typical Atlantic crossing, making the trip safer and much more pleasant. The union lost the battle, but the pilots won in a big way. I remember my experience later flying international routes on the 767, MD-11, and 777 as pleasant and quite safe.

I always wondered what would happen if one were to approach a stall in one of these behemoths. Coming from London with the copilot flying and the late George "Catfish" Flint in command, we were given a restriction to be level at a higher altitude at a certain point. Unable to satisfy that restriction, the copilot allowed our speed to diminish in a vain effort to make that restriction. The very heavy aircraft began buffeting, followed shortly by the flight attendant call light and chime.

"Are we OK, what is that buffet?" she asked.

I looked at George and he said, "I have the aircraft, tell control that we will not be able to make that restriction."

George began a descent, and it took one hundred miles to get the aircraft flying properly. The copilot, being a training department know-it-all, was properly humiliated.

The extravagance expended in hopes of accurate navigation is laughable by modern standards. A million dollars' worth of electronics on the TriStar could not pinpoint our location as well as my apple watch can today. Three inertial reference units (IRU) combined their inputs into two flight management systems (FMS) to provide a best-guess

23. TriStar

average of the current location. Coasting in just west of Ireland involved changing from Oceanic Control to radar approach control. Once close to land, the VOR navigation radio became very accurate. However, the approach control radar always had greater range than the VORs. When contacting approach control, we always hoped to be on course, because a navigation error of ten nautical miles or more is a "gross navigation error," and meant severe punishment for both the pilots and the airline. Most flights arrived less than three miles off course and received radar vectors to centerline.

While I flew engineer during the summer of 1987, a sensational incident occurred over the Atlantic when a Delta TriStar, through a gross navigation error, passed within 100 feet of a Continental Airlines aircraft. Just one of the five incidents of the "summer of shame" for Delta, this one struck home for me. The others, involving a wrong airport landing, a wrong runway landing, an inadvertent dual engine shutdown, and a blown-over baggage cart, also received national attention. These incidents, combined with the scrutiny that Delta received after the Flight 191 crash in Dallas, put Delta under the FAA's microscope. It appeared that the cowboy's chickens were coming home to roost.

The RB-211 engine moved a lot of air

24. Crash

Having just finished the drudgery of defending my PhD dissertation, I felt free to tackle new interests. I volunteered to work in the Air Line Pilots Association's (ALPA) safety division. I soon became an understudy of Dick Stone, a Delta Pilot, chairman of the ALPA Human Performance Committee. Part of that job entailed representing ALPA in the Human Performance Group of any accident investigation involving ALPA pilots. After the ALPA-Conducted accident investigators course, I became certified and a member of the International Society of Air Safety Investigators. My instructions: "If there is an accident, just go there. We will take care of your transportation and missed schedule." I was on ALPA's go team.

After an accident, the NTSB establishes working groups led by agency investigators in various technical areas such as operations, structures, powerplants, weather, air traffic control, human factors, and others as required. These working groups are made up of interested parties. The parties might be from the airline, the pilots' union, the airframe manufacturer, the engine manufacturer, airport management, and others with vested interest in the findings. The NTSB group leader must produce a factual report signed by all the parties in their group. I soon discovered that the group leader's desire to complete their factual report gave the parties some leverage in the interpretation of the investigation. Naturally, the ALPA party is focused on getting the pilots a clean break, without undue blame for something out of their control. My duties revolved chiefly around providing coffee for Captain Stone and the other investigators. This was my time to listen and learn.

24. Crash

The Delta Flight 191 findings of probable cause can be found in the NTSB final report, available on their website. My take on the accident: Lacking evidence to the contrary, the crew flew into a thunderstorm downburst which exceeded the performance of their aircraft. We all had flown into clouds that displayed the same image on the on-board radar, with impunity. However, the thunderstorm at Dallas that day contained deadly wind shears, unknowable from the cockpit or control tower. After such an accident, the NTSB conducts an extensive audit of the airline, especially the pilot training department and maintenance. Their finding of a few minor irregularities would figure prominently in another investigation three years later. Sadly, fatalities seem to be necessary for progress to happen. From that accident, the Terminal Doppler Weather Radar (TDWR) system received additional focus and became operational in 1994.

According to the FAA, "TDWR's primary purpose is to timely and accurately detect hazardous wind shear in and near terminal approach and departure corridors as well as to report this information to pilots and local air traffic controllers."

It works. Another one of the half-dozen or so things that can kill you in an airliner mostly disappeared.

In December of 1987, I upgraded to B-767 First Officer, then in July of 1988 I received the news that I had been awarded a captain's bid on the 737! Having completed training, I received my IOE on August 24, 1988. Before I could fly my first trip as a Delta captain, disaster struck. Delta 1141 crashed at Dallas/Ft. Worth Airport on takeoff on August 31 of that year. Reluctantly, I went there to represent ALPA in the Human Performance Group. I had been the apprentice on the 191 investigation, now my number had been called to lead.

Delta pilots loomed large in the ALPA safety structure. Had the accident involved United or Continental, the cast would have been the same: mostly Delta pilots. Reporting to the accident site, I was encouraged to see that the leading-edge devices in the front of the wing were partially deployed, indicating that the flaps were properly selected for takeoff. Later, I was disappointed to discover that they had been flung out by the impact; the internal mechanism indicated that the flaps were up for the takeoff. During the first meeting of the Human Performance Group, Jeff Gorney of the NTSB, the group leader, asked me to produce a duplicate copy of the printed takeoff data presented to the crew before every takeoff. That was stunning. After years of protecting those documents, I realized that it had not been necessary.

Paul McCarthy and Terry Mullane, both Delta pilots and attorneys, headed the ALPA delegation. The accident site investigation involved many disciplines and their associated groups. Paul was adamant about honesty. The admonition: just make sure that we discover any evidence favorable to the pilots. The first day of the investigation involved interviews with the crew by the NTSB. Chosen to attend the interview of Steven, the second officer, I was present much as an attorney to limit inappropriate questions. It proceeded like an interrogation, with the NTSB being harsh and aggressive, while Steven was obviously distraught. I intervened frequently, with the outcome establishing little about the flight, and mostly about his behavior leading up to it.

After the interview, Steven asked me to recover his suitcase from the evidence storage. I contacted the investigator in charge (IIC) and the request was approved. Retrieving the suitcase and his flight kit, I discovered that they were covered with mud. Sensing his sadness, I elected to retreat to a locker room to clean them. As I worked, the Delta chief pilot passed and asked about my actions.

24. Crash

He said, "Good for you, let me help."

As we stood there scrubbing mud from the luggage, I think we shared a poignant moment. Both of us felt the shame of the accident, the weight of the investigation, and the urge to improve in the future.

Finishing that, I loaded them into my car to present them to Steven at the nearby (secret location) Marriott. I visualized a sad young man moping in a lonely room with no one to bring him dinner. Arriving at his room and knocking, I could hear loud voices inside. Presently, a matronly woman answered the door.

"Yes, what do you want?" she asked in an aggressive tone.

Looking beyond her, I could see a dozen or more people laughing and talking in the room. Apparently, there was a party to cheer up the distraught second officer.

Taken aback, I said, "Steven asked me to bring his suitcase."

She turned around and spoke to Steven, who was seated nearby. "Steven, someone has brought your suitcase."

He looked at me, recognized me, and waved a chicken drumstick at me as a gesture of thanks. The woman took the bags and slammed the door.

Jerry Killian, the commander of the 111th F.I.S., once said to me, "When machines fail, it's always a surprise, but you can expect people to betray you." Exactly.

Steven, being a newly certified Delta second officer, emerged mostly unscathed from the investigation.

He said, "The way the media basically said: The crew did this. The crew said that. The crew joked about this; the crew forgot this. It hurt. When I felt all along that I had done my job." Perhaps, but as we shall see, in the reformed Delta, complicity became tantamount to the wrongdoing itself.

Delta fired all three members of the flight crew but rehired Steven. He flies as a Delta 777 captain, the pinnacle of airline prestige, today.

The focus of the investigation was the failure of the crew to extend the flaps for takeoff. Contributing to that, the captain and first officer carried on a continuous banter unrelated to the flight. In a long queue for takeoff, they were surprised to receive a shortcut and early takeoff clearance. Taxiing with an engine shut down for economy, the engine start and before-takeoff checklist became rushed, and they forgot the flaps.

All Boeing aircraft are equipped with a takeoff warning system. Functioning properly, an aural warning should have sounded as the throttles were advanced, indicating one of the conditions for a safe takeoff was not met. As proven by the cockpit voice recorder tape, it did not. I was present when power was applied to the takeoff warning computer; it made the appropriate sound. The airframe group determined that a faulty circuit outside of the box had caused the failure.

As Captain Larry pushed up the throttles, the autopack trip light (a safety system that reduces the electrical and bleed air loads on a failed engine) on the engineer panel should have illuminated green. Due to the retracted flaps, it did not. Judd said nothing. He later testified, "The autopack trip system is not a takeoff warning." Still, it should have been announced as something was amiss.

24. Crash

First Officer Wilson announced, "V one, V R," indicating they had attained sufficient speed to apply backpressure to the yoke to rotate the aircraft.

Captain Larry was known to aggressively pull back on the yoke for rotation. Most pilots (including myself) prefer a gentler interrogation of the aircraft. A sort of question of the aircraft, "Are you ready to fly?"

This one was not. Rotating the nose of the aircraft aggressively to a high pitch angle, well below the stall speed (with retracted flaps) resulted in a stall of the right wing, followed by a rapid roll to the right, dragging that wingtip. Captain Larry immediately countered the unexpected roll with full left aileron, which by design, enabled the spoilers to deploy to assist in roll. The turbulence generated by the upcoming spoilers of the wing propagated to the pod engine on the rear fuselage of the aircraft, causing it to surge, although the NTSB determined that it had continued to supply full power. Continuing to attempt to raise the nose, the high angle of attack stalled the aircraft; the flight was over. Runway 18L at DFW is 13,401 ft. long. Performance data proves that at their weight, flown gently, the aircraft could have easily flown from the runway without extended flaps.

ALPA, in the defense of the pilots, asserted that the flap handle had indeed been deployed, but due to a mechanical malfunction, the leading-edge lift devices did not extend. Delta wanted to test that theory by flying a 727 near stall speeds and observing the performance. I was asked to observe the flight and record data.

Upon arrival at the aircraft, I noticed that a few sandbags had been haphazardly thrown into the forward end of the forward baggage bin, to balance the empty aircraft. Having heard of the treacherous stall characteristics, I feared a pitch up, tail slide scenario. I imagined a high pitch angle with the sandbags sliding to the rear of the baggage bin, producing an unrecoverable situation. Insisting on securing the sandbags in place, I was humiliated by the loading personnel as being too cautious.

During the flight, the circuit breakers for the leading-edge devices were pulled out, simulating a configuration with trailing edge flaps deployed and leading-edge devices retracted. We recorded the test data and adjourned to Boeing Headquarters in Seattle to discuss the results. Although Boeing had never gathered data on such a configuration, the engineers did have data on the 757 in such a condition. They asserted that the results would be similar. Nothing much came of those discussions except what must have been an inadvertent revelation about 727 aerodynamics. The Boeing engineers passed around several charts showing the lift coefficient versus angle of attack for various flap configurations. Next came the drag curves. With everyone getting very bored at that point, they passed around the zero-flap pitching moment curve. Bill Melvin, affectionately known as the "Professor," and the resident expert on aerodynamics glanced at the chart and passed it to me. I was flabbergasted. It showed that in the clean configuration, once a stall had begun, the aircraft would continue to pitch nose up, a "pitch up."

I said, "Bill, look at this, it's the famous clean (landing gear and flaps retracted) stall chart."

He said, "Yeah, when I was testing the 727, the Boeing test pilot wouldn't let me get it slow when clean."

I said to the Boeing engineer, "May I have a copy of this?"

He snatched it out of my hand and said, "No, that's proprietary."

24. Crash

All that flap discussion was a weak defense, but it was the best we could do to defend the pilots.

Later at the public hearing, near DFW, we gathered for the bad news. The crew was criticized for conducting nonessential conversation, leading to the omission of items on the takeoff checklist. The failed takeoff warning horn was noted as contributing, and numerous deficiencies in the Delta training curricula were brought to light.

At one point in the hearing, Jeff Gorney, representing the NTSB, questioned Harry Alger, the then Vice President of Flight Operations.

Gorney accused Alger of stonewalling the recommendations from the Delta 191 accident.

"Captain Alger," Gorney shouted, "three years ago Delta lost a TriStar here at DFW. We audited your pilot training and noted many deficiencies. Training records were incomplete, we found too soft check rides, and you had no Crew Resource Management Program. After recently repeating that investigation, we find no progress has been made on our earlier findings."

Alger muttered something apologetic.

"Captain Alger, you can get serious about fixing your deficiencies, or we will shut your airline down."

That got everyone's attention. I believe that was the moment from which everything forward became the new Delta Air Lines.

In its final accident report, Jim Burnett, a member of the safety board, dissented from the probable cause statement. He added an additional probable cause, stating,

"Also causal to the accident was the failure of Delta Air Lines' management to provide leadership and guidance to its flight crews through its training and check airmen programs to promote and foster optimum cockpit management procedures, and the failure of the Federal Aviation Administration to correct known deficiencies in the training and check airmen programs of Delta Air Lines."

Delta decided that it was time for change. Training, check rides, and aircrew behavior were about to be dragged, under protest, into the eighties. A "Cockpit Resource Management Program," later renamed "Crew Resource Management," would be the star of the new Delta.

25. Holding Hands in a Hot Tub

"Don, this is Reuben Black, can you come by my office next week?"

Thus began a two-year-long project to transform Delta. After the humiliation of the summer of shame and two fatal accidents, Delta management finally decided that change was in order. Tapping the late Captain Reuben Black, former chief of training, to lead the effort, he began immediately—an onerous task for which I'm sure that Reuben negotiated strenuously before accepting. By the time that I became involved, it was a dream project—practically unlimited funds, guaranteed non-interference from above, and the challenge to produce the best Crew Resource Management (CRM) Program in the world.

Reuben's concept involved tapping a person from every quarter of the airline's activity. Having reached out to managers for nominations, we were called together to meet in his office that day. Present: a long-retired captain representing the old school; a flight attendant from in-flight service (whose husband was a psychologist); a very new pilot, representing first officers and flight engineers; a pilot/psychologist; a training department instructor; a line-check airman; a recently merged former Western Airlines captain; and me, representing ALPA.

All the factors miraculously aligned to enable us to build a program that, in retrospect, accomplished its goals well. Reuben was a master diplomat, who knew the organization like a thirty-year senator.

The team members were intelligent, highly motivated, and pleasant company. Highly anticipated by the rank-and-file members of the company, we were deluged with suggestions, many of them keepers.

Other airlines made similar moves in that period. Eastern Airlines pilots had crashed a TriStar into the Everglades when all three crew members became fixated on a minor problem and accidently disengaged the autopilot, flying into the swamp. United Airlines pilots ran a DC-8 out of fuel and crashed due to a squabble among them. Air Florida crashed into the Potomac River due to a deicing problem, and a disagreement between the pilots. United pioneered the new concept with their Command/Leadership/Resource Management (C/L/R) Program beginning in 1981.

Partially because of the desire to produce the best possible training, and partially because of the belief that CRM should be culture-centric, available off-the-shelf courses were rejected. However, considerable outside resources had become available, one of which was the workshop on the subject sponsored by the National Aeronautics and Space Administration (NASA) in 1979. The theme of that conference: "Human error contributes or causes the majority of air crashes due to failures of interpersonal communications, decision making, and leadership."

Delta had never hired an outside consultant. Promotions, even to senior management, had come from within the company. With the committee's blank check, we decided to break tradition and hire Richard Hackman, a distinguished professor of social psychology, at Harvard, and the late Robert Helmreich, principal investigator of the University of Texas Human Factors Research Project. With the team assembled, we proceeded to create what was to become a classroom course which changed the culture of the entire organization.

25. Holding Hands in a Hot Tub

With the benefit of the knowledge of the first generation of such courses, the anticipated resistance erupted from the senior pilots. The authoritative captains labeled the project "holding hands in a hot tub therapy" and "psychobabble in the classroom." The more junior pilots, whose only fault may have been lack of assertiveness, embraced the concepts. The new curricula emphasized team building, situational awareness, briefing strategies, error trapping, error mitigation, and decision-making. Concomitant with the revolutionary changes in aircraft hardware, CRM made the operations side of Delta of 1990 unrecognizable from that of the 1980s.

While CRM continues to evolve today, the shift from a "Captain's Airline" to a team-oriented one marked the welcome and necessary shift to an airline that the passengers had long expected and deserved. Much like racial bigots, some of the old-school members never embraced the concepts; they simply carried their obsolete habits into retirement.

Third- and fourth-generation CRM programs have been further integrated into training programs. A spin-off of CRM, the Advanced Qualification Program (AQP), allows airlines to develop training that fits the needs of the specific organization. Included in these custom training programs are line oriented flight training (LOFT), flight training with integral CRM, voluntary safety reporting systems, and flight data monitoring systems.

Validation of the effectiveness of CRM remains elusive. The accident rate for airlines is so low that its use in a statistical evaluation is impossible. However, in real-time mission simulations, using line oriented evaluation (LOE) techniques, the improved performances of flight crews handling simulated emergencies suggest that resources spent on CRM training are having the desired effect.

Declining an offer to teach CRM in the classroom, I returned to line flying, shortly thereafter to be upgraded to 737 captain.

26. In Command

No, I had no illusion about some newfound power; that was the name of the course given to all new captains. The photo below shows mostly forty-year-old white faces. Some of my original classmates were present. We were so happy to get the pay raise and left seat, we would have attended, no matter what the curricula had been. The older gentleman in the middle row is the late T. P. "Pre" Ball, the famously irascible former chief pilot and vice president for the airline. Long before my time there, but fresh in the memory of many senior captains, a reprimand from Captain Ball involved much shouting and derogatory language followed by, "Now get out there and don't do that again."

No secret handshake was revealed, but praise flowed freely, and we left feeling empowered. One of the speakers, Delta's chief attorney, spoke the words I most remember. He said that if we were to make an honest mistake, the considerable power of the company and its attorneys would protect us. However, if anyone were to be involved in an accident or incident in which we had done less than our best (meaning negligence or gross negligence), that not only would we be destroyed as individuals, but possibly the whole company could fail.

In Command Class

Having flown first officer from 1984 to 1986 on the 737, I enjoyed getting reacquainted with the airplane, especially remembering the tedium of the TriStar. Fred Goesphol, a Delta pilot and an FAA designated examiner, passed me on my final check ride. Fred was the antithesis of the gruff, demanding examiner. I asked him, "Why does such a nice guy like you want to do this job?"

He said, "I get extra pay, and I just like to have my name on your first airline transport pilot license (ATP) temporary certificate." I believe that the kind treatment that I received in that upgrade process exemplified a deliberate effort on Delta's part to make the process more pleasant, less an initiation.

My IOE followed with Bob Entrican, a senior captain and line check airman. We flew a three-day rotation with him in the copilot seat. On one of the legs, Bob flew, pretending to be an inept copilot.

My briefing: "When it's your leg, I will conduct the exterior preflight inspection. Pretend you are the captain, and I will do my best to support your flying. Make your own decisions—up, down, left, right, it's your choice. Manage the seat belt sign as you see fit.

26. In Command

If I see you doing something different than I would have done it, I won't interfere. If you do something that I really don't like, we will discuss it. If we can't agree, I will win."

Bob said, "Yeah, I've heard that from a lot of new captains. That will last about a month and you will get tired of it. It's much easier to just do everything the old way."

Bob, if you're reading this, it lasted eighteen years.

The other memorable thing that Bob told me, "Not all of the assholes in this airline sit in the left seat."

An FAA examiner rode on the jump seat on the last leg to finish the certification, only necessary because of my being a first-time captain.

Although I had flown the 737 for over a thousand hours as copilot, my first captain trip aroused strange feelings of anxiety. The old adage, "You haven't done it until you've done it," applied. Much like soloing an airplane for the first time, the authorities say you are ready, but self-doubt creeps into your mind. I have met many pilots who brag about flying a particular type of airplane. I always ask if they soloed it. Without having done that, they had an instructional flight; they might have been unable to solo.

Signing in for my first trip, I noticed that Bill Morgan was to be the first officer. Smelling a conspiracy, I asked the crew scheduler on duty if scheduling a new captain with the most senior first officer reflected some mistrust of me. He and Bill swore it was a coincidence. Bill was/is an excellent pilot, and the trip went fine.

It's no coincidence that airline pilots don't begin their careers on the biggest aircraft. The experiences on the 737 tested and educated me over the next six years. Of course, the senior pilots fly the international flights because the pay is better, but knowing your captain on that flight to Tokyo has *earned* the privilege should be comforting. Dealing with passengers, flight attendants, copilots, weather, maintenance, diversions, and the myriad of things that can go wrong is the education not available in the schoolhouse.

Flying the 777 was easy; flying the 737 was difficult. For example, the 737 flies into smaller cities where Delta chooses to hire contract maintenance, rather than station a company mechanic there. When a maintenance issue arises at such a place, a certified (non-Delta) mechanic is summoned to work the problem. In some cases, the airline's procedures and standards might differ from the Boeing/FAA rules that the mechanic observes. Decision-making on thorny mechanical issues frequently involves telephone conversations with company mechanics in Atlanta. However, the answer usually ends with, "It's your call, Captain." On the other hand, every place I landed the 777, a Delta 777 mechanic met me at the gate.

It's a different set of passengers too. On an early flight from Savannah to Atlanta, while preparing the cockpit, the head flight attendant entered the cockpit, "Captain, we have a problem." The Pensacola Penguins hockey team had lost a game the previous night, and most had chosen to stay up all night to drown their sorrows. The flight attendant informed me that a riot was happening in the cabin. Drunk and disorderly, most of the team members were harassing the flight attendants and other passengers, producing their own (illegal) liquor, and were acting loudly and boisterously. When I strolled to the rear of the cabin, everything became quiet. I noticed an elderly couple sitting in their midst, dressed in their Sunday best. Their eyes were wide as saucers; they looked terrified.

26. In Command

I said, "All the hockey team members raise your hands."

A dozen hands slowly arose.

"We can do this the easy way, or the hard way. Let me tell you about the hard way. If we do that, two or three dozen very large and mean-spirited police officers will come aboard in about ten minutes and drag every one of you off to jail. The easy way is for every one of you to sit down, be quiet, do not ring the flight attendant call button, do not touch the flight attendant, do not drink anything on the way to Atlanta, and most of all, continue to behave that way after I go back to the cockpit. Now, how many of you want to do it the easy way?"

The dozen hands again slowly arose.

"If the flight attendant tells me that you changed your mind during the flight, a different group of even meaner police officers will do the dragging and jailing when we get to Atlanta."

The flight attendant reported no problems on the flight.

The 737 arrived at Delta with the new digital radars. Appealing in their multicolored display, their low power rendered them poor in burning through any nearby rain. Thanks mainly to ALPA criticism, they were later upgraded to remedy that shortcoming. On a flight from Atlanta to Tallahassee late one night, we entered a rainy area. The rain slowly increased in intensity. Lulled into a false sense of security since no significant returns appeared on the scope, I was surprised when air traffic control asked," Would you like vectors around that cell ahead?"

Only then did I realize that we had become blinded by the heavy rain. I accepted their help, but even so, it was the roughest turbulence I ever encountered. After landing in Tallahassee, as is the Delta custom, I stood in the cockpit door to bid the passengers goodbye and accept any criticism. Expecting to be admonished for my stupidity, the opposite happened. Nearly everyone who deplaned thanked me for getting through such rough air!

An ice storm paralyzed the southern plains. With their considerable resources, DFW had been able to dig themselves out of it. Scheduled for a flight from DFW to Oklahoma City, I was happily anticipating getting paid for a canceled trip. Not so fast, they said, Oklahoma City will be open by the time you get there. If not, just come back to DFW as your alternate. Always wary of an airplane or automobile that "will be ready when you get here," I suspiciously launched toward Oklahoma. After a smooth flight, approach control cleared us to "hold at the outer marker." The outer marker beacon is about five miles from the runway threshold. Holding there at 1500 ft. above the ground is stressful because of the proximity to the ground and the short notice given to commence the approach.

"How is the runway clearing going?" I asked.

"Stand by, it's in progress," they said.

After twenty minutes of circling, ATC said, "We've got a little problem with the runway. The ice is so bad that the snowplow driver just called, in unable to get to the airport."

"OK, we have fuel to hold for another thirty minutes before going back to DFW. I'll see what the dispatcher says."

Dispatcher: "We have decided to send you to Tulsa, where the runway is clear. We will bus the passengers back to Oklahoma City."

26. In Command

With that, we turned and climbed toward Tulsa. Although the roads would probably be impassable, that wasn't my problem.

Tulsa tower declared, "Cleared for the approach, cleared to land. Runway is plowed fifty feet either side of centerline full length, braking action reported 'good' by truck."

Well, this is going to be easy, I thought. After an uneventful landing, I turned onto a taxiway which connected to a long taxiway parallel to the runway, leading to the terminal. It appeared shiny and, once on it, I discovered that it was glazed ice, with absolutely nil braking!

"Hey, tower, Delta is clear of the runway, but the taxiway is really slick."

"Yeah, none of the taxiways have been cleared. What are your intentions?"

"We'll call the company and get a tug to tow us in."

"Sorry, 1103, we don't have any chains for the tug. I guess you're stuck for a while," said operations.

Contemplating shutting down and caring for the passengers for what might be hours, I said to myself, "I can taxi this airplane in using reverse thrust."

Moving forward to the parallel taxiway very slowly, I was able to stop on it, facing perpendicular to it. Like a twin-engine boat, I applied reverse thrust to the left engine and a little forward thrust to the right engine. It pivoted in place nicely. I reversed that process to stop the turn. Luckily on flat terrain, idle thrust was sufficient, and we were on our way. Inching down the taxiway, we began to drift to the left a little. I pivoted a little nose left and applied reverse on both engines to stop on the centerline. Repositioning the nose back to the right with differential thrust, I headed down the taxiway again. It was slow. After what seemed like an eternity, we arrived at the huge parking apron.

I told the copilot, "OK, you try it. Don't hit anything. You will never get another chance to do this."

The gate crew had heard of our adventure and warmly greeted us. The trip was canceled and we got to the hotel much later. I never heard how the passengers fared on their bus trip to Oklahoma City.

All turbine-powered aircraft have a distinct advantage over reciprocating-engine-powered aircraft with respect to the threat of airborne icing. Part of the process of producing thrust from a jet engine involves compressing air before it enters the combustion chamber. Some of that hot, high-pressure air can be used to keep the engine inlets, wings, and control surfaces free of ice. Of course, using that bleed air incurs a performance penalty on the engines, but is gladly accepted for the capability that it enables. The bleed load to warm the engine cowls being modest, it is frequently used, normally when visible moisture is present and the outside air temperature is below 50 degrees Fahrenheit. A more powerful system warms the wings. Its use is prohibited on the ground to prevent overheating.

Late one night, after a deicing delay for a short flight from Cincinnati, Ohio (the airport is actually in Kentucky) to Lexington, Kentucky, we encountered heavy icing during the flight. With all of the anti-icing capability operating, we experienced an uneventful trip and landing. However, upon a post-flight inspection, I discovered that in the short period between lowering the landing gear and landing, the wheels, struts, and gear doors had accumulated so much ice that there appeared to be a large ice cube attached to the bottom of the wing with the bottom of the wheels protruding. Although much heavier for the ice, I did not notice any adverse flying qualities.

Early Air Mail history documents the uncomfortable and sometimes tragic flights in icing conditions. Since the 1950s, anti-icing (and deicing) technology has matured as well as our approach to its implementation. I remember holding high at the initial approach fix, low on fuel, at Keflavik, waiting for better weather. Once cleared for the approach, a descent through 20,000 feet of icy clouds loomed. Already tense about a low-fuel situation, I was always startled when the master caution light illuminated, advising me that the automatic engine anti-ice system had detected ice formation and had engaged.

Those early systems performed well. Although modern aircraft anti-ice systems remain similar in principle, they have evolved in effectiveness and efficiency. More importantly, pre-takeoff deicing procedures began to be codified and taken more seriously since the 1970s. In those days, the appraisal of airworthiness of an ice or snow-covered airplane used the TLAR (that looks about right) method. After a spate of accidents due to attempted takeoffs with freezing contamination, various governmental authorities and the airlines agreed on guidelines for such situations. Today, when precipitation continues to fall, the time allowed between deicing and takeoff (holdover time) is presented to pilots in a chart which considers the type of deicing fluid used, the outside air temperature, and the type of precipitation that is falling. In the absence of precipitation, extant frost is permitted to accrue up to 1/8" on the bottom of the wing (caused by cold-soaked fuel) and on the fuselage if the paint lines can be seen.

Since the implementation of these strict standards, I have complete confidence in flying (or riding in) an airliner that has been properly deiced before entering icing conditions aloft. A few general aviation aircraft have been certified for flight into known icing (FIKI). Since mine has not, my only tool to combat airborne icing is *avoidance*.

I never tired of hearing the stories my fellow crewmembers told about their flying. From Navy Top Gun Instructors to super-secret Area 51 test pilots, like Forrest Gump's box of chocolates, you never know what you were going to get. Pilots who had formerly flown the F-111, A-6, B-52, F-4, RF-4, C-130, F-16, F-14, A-7, F-15, P-3, KC-135, A-10, C-141 flew with me. A few had seen UFOs. Nearly all were highly motivated, and a few flew better than the others.

In 1991, the chief line check airman at DFW invited me to become one of them. I immediately accepted, knowing about the pay raise and prestige. Having received IOEs and line checks from check airmen, I vaguely knew what the job entailed. The school informed me about the pass/fail standards for line checks and how to conduct an IOE. Highly emphasized in the class was the notion that we represented the flight standards department in our everyday flying.

Conducting an IOE was rewarding. The candidate in all cases had received an upgrade from their former position. Since the 737 was among the most junior of aircraft, most of the captain IOEs involved first-time captains. Every one of the captain IOEs that I conducted was a joy. Like myself, they were very happy to become a captain, had plenty of experience, and knew the aircraft well. However, some of the first officer upgrades presented more of a challenge.

"Don, I've given Mike three IOEs and he's not getting it. You can try to get him through if you want, or I'll just send him back to the panel," said Les, the chief LCA.

26. In Command

"Sure, I'll give it a try," I said, knowing that Les conducted his IOEs more like check rides than learning experiences.

I said, "Mike, there's no way you can fail this. We'll just fly until you feel comfortable. I'll take the first leg and you just relax and talk on the radio, OK?"

There could hardly have been a worse rotation to do an IOE. The first leg flew DFW to Shreveport, a fairly short leg busy with traffic. The second leg only lasted twelve minutes between Shreveport and Monroe, followed by several other short legs.

I advised Mike to get his airport information (ATIS) and outbound IFR clearance while we taxied in, because of the short turnaround time. I volunteered to conduct the external inspection so he could prepare the cockpit for his leg. When I returned, he had done almost nothing. It was going to be a long day.

Sadly, he flew the airplane well, but had no plan or priorities for accomplishing the preparations. Les had failed to instruct him on the things that happened on the line that were different from the simulator. I instructed him in the three "Cs": hang up your Coat, get some Coffee, get the Clearance. Not exactly, but he did need a framework. My advice: (1) build your nest: adjust the seat, get your manuals out, check your oxygen mask, get pencils and paper out, find your rotation sheet so you will know when we are supposed to push back. (2) Gather your information: listen to the terminal information on the radio, get the flight plan and fuel information, call for the IFR clearance. (3) Load the information into the airplane: everything in the flight plan and clearance could be dialed into a setting on the airplane.

The problem with being too generous in passing an IOE candidate lay in the animus toward me from the captain who was given a weak copilot. However, Mike did just fine. In fact, after I retired, I passed Captain Mike in the Atlanta Airport. He didn't recognize me.

Besides giving IOEs, line check airmen give line checks. Receiving a twice-annually required line check has always been unpleasant. Becoming the dispenser of that proved to be just as unpleasant. At that point in Delta's transition, I believed that nearly all the pilots possessed the required skills and motivations. Thus, a line check, in my mind, consisted of a briefing on any recent changes and perhaps a suggestion on improving safety or efficiency. Not so in the minds of the pilots. I represented a threat to their job and livelihood. Perhaps I was a mean-spirited person looking for some minor discrepancy to embarrass or fire them. The response I always received was one of strained uneasiness.

I never failed anyone. The worst thing that happened to me occurred when observing a crew landing at Louisville. The captain, flying the approach, got a little low on short final. The Ground Proximity Warning System, sensing that, announced the aural warning, "too low, pull up." Everyone knows that necessitates a missed approach, although in visual conditions many of us make a correction and continue. It was a safe approach and landing, but violated procedure.

"You are getting a line check; don't you know that you should have conducted a missed approach?" I probably had an edge in my voice.

"Yeah. It looked safe, so I continued."

"Here are my choices. I can forget the whole thing, I can fly the airplane back to Atlanta and send you in for some training, or we can fly a few more legs and call it all good."

26. In Command

They, of course, opted for door number three. After three more flights with satisfactory performance, I legally approved the check. After that, I called Les and asked to do mostly IOEs.

I believe many pilots, myself included, have some small violation that we are willing to tolerate as a form of protest against apparently ridiculous rules. For some, it is the requirement to wear our shoulder harnesses for takeoff and landing. Another might be the requirement to have the airport diagram in front of us during taxi in or out even at the most familiar airports. The requirement for the wearing of the emergency oxygen mask when flying above 41,000 ft. might be forgotten. The problem with that behavior lies in having to remember the difference between one's normal routine, and the "road show" when getting checked. The simple solution is to fly by the book all the time. But that is easier said than done. I remember the first time I flew copilot for the infamous Don S.

He said, "I believe that it is easier on everyone to just fly by the book; that makes understanding each other very simple."

I agreed that was a reasonable approach and vowed to do my best to comply. Although not required, Don taxied the airplane *exactly* on the yellow line. To him, if anything was not expressly permitted, it was forbidden. On an approach to Kansas City in visual conditions, I advised him that I intended to fly one dot low on the glide slope to achieve an expeditious landing and turnoff. No, he would not permit that. From that point, the challenge for him was to fly perfectly, because I was determined to find a fault. No one can fly perfectly, and as we shall see, every flight consists of little mistakes that we notice and mitigate.

Some trips required us to fly seven legs in a day. I remember flying a three-day trip composed of twenty legs. Even though I was in my early thirties at the time, it took several days at home to recover from such a workout.

It was during that time that my marriage fell apart, mostly due to my failure to understand that being absent from family life in order to provide resources is a poor choice. After a few years of single life, I met the love of my life in New York. Martha Evitt, a flight attendant, was waiting for the flight we were to work to San Diego. It was love at first sight. She was tall, beautiful, and had a happy disposition. We were married in 2000.

It's no accident that pilots and flight attendants, like doctors and nurses, frequently find each other. Working in the same demanding environment creates an appreciation for each other that is impossible to convey through words alone.

It was a time for me to learn too. Perhaps the worst mistake I made in my airline career happened on a flight into Cleveland Hopkins Airport. The first officer, who had some experience on the airplane, flew the leg. On arrival, he misjudged the descent and had too much energy for the approach. He was "high and hot."

I said, "You're too fast."

"It will be fine," he said.

At that moment, I should have said, "I have control, extend the landing gear, please."

I did not say that, wanting to prove my correctness by allowing a bungled approach. And it was: too fast over the landing threshold; we barely stopped using the whole runway. I never allowed my ego or an arrogant copilot to put me in danger again.

26. In Command

After the merger with Western Airlines, things changed at Delta. As I was soon to discover, mixing crewmembers with diverse backgrounds demanded tact and patience. However, one pleasant aspect of that change required DFW 737 crews to fly more westerly routes. We had been flying mostly to sea level or flatland airports. Suddenly, Salt Lake City, Missoula, Jackson Hole, Helena, and other mountainous airports appeared in our rotations.

One night we were flying on a radar vector about halfway between Salt Lake City and Missoula when the air traffic controller said, "Delta, cleared to Missoula, cleared for the approach of your choice, tower is closed, good evening."

For a flatland pilot, the clearance demanded much. It necessitated capturing an airway, observing the minimum obstacle clearance altitudes (MOCA) during descent, selecting an approach appropriate for the existing wind, notifying local traffic of our presence, and most of all missing the mountains. We landed without incident, but that level of autonomy felt different.

Early on, the FAA had air carrier inspectors (ACI), pilots with ratings on the airplane in which they gave us check rides. Additionally, they had airworthiness inspectors, mechanics who specialized in the condition of the aircraft. Both were authorized to ride in the cockpit jump seat, checking our operation. In their questionable wisdom, the FAA combined the two groups into a single ACI designation. Arriving at the gate for an outbound flight from Miami, the Delta agent asked me to see what was holding up boarding. When I entered the airplane, I could see a man talking to the flight attendants, who were standing at attention holding their "red books" (their manual for operations, requiring frequent updates).

I said, "What's going on here?"

The man turned around and I noticed he was wearing a nametag that said only, "FAA."

He said, "I'm an air carrier inspector, and I'm here to give you a check ride."

"OK, fine, but we have a flight to conduct, so the flight attendants need to get back to their job."

We proceeded to the cockpit, where he proceeded to ask to see our licenses and physical examination certificates. Curious as to whether he was a pilot or mechanic, I asked, "Are you an airworthiness inspector?"

He answered, "I'm an air carrier inspector and I am giving you a check ride and that's all you need to know."

Not giving up, I asked, "Are you rated on this aircraft?"

"I'm rated on the King Air," he replied.

"OK, I think I get the picture."

"Captain, I don't like your attitude, I'm going to write you up no matter how the flight goes."

"Well, that makes us even. I'm writing you up for your attitude."

Ordinarily, a captain can refuse to allow a person to ride on the jump seat of his aircraft. Not so with the FAA. They have the influence to occupy the seat and give check rides no matter how badly they misbehave.

26. In Command

The gauntlet had been thrown down; he was determined to nail us for the slightest infraction. The flight was nearly perfect. I filed a complaint about his behavior, but never heard any more about it. Lesson learned: be nice even to mean-spirited people who can deal you misery. Yes, I remember his name.

I felt it my duty when conducting IOEs to expose the recipient to a wide spectrum of aircraft capabilities. The 737 is designed and built to fly slower than most airliners. The ones I flew seemed to be best suited to speeds about Mach .77. Flying faster produced a Mach buffet that felt much like light turbulence. The limiting Mach number, depending on altitude, displayed on the Mach/Airspeed indicator was about M .84. Most of the pilots with whom I flew became anxious at the onset of the light buffet. I liked to demonstrate that flight at M .84 was perfectly safe. The airplane would only achieve such numbers at medium altitudes such as 27,000 feet. Level at 27,000, at full power, the buffet increased but not extremely unpleasantly as we accelerated to M.84. Perfectly safe, the airplane had been flown in certification tests to much higher Mach numbers. Cruising at that speed would be a poor idea due to increased fuel consumption and the bumpy ride. However, if unusual circumstances prompted, flight at that higher speed is easily done.

Boeing aircraft have amazingly reliable cockpit windows. They are easily opened and closed on the ground, and yes, in the air too. They seal the pressurization well, and rarely require maintenance. An option for clearing smoke from the cockpit in an emergency is to open one of the windows. Desiring to demonstrate that, and to have a little fun, I liked to surprise the newbie by opening my window in flight.

"It's going to get a little noisy in here just before we land. Just ignore it and make your best landing," I said.

With that, I would turn off the pressurization and open my window on short final approach. The boundary layer of calm wind, being about four inches thick, allowed me to casually put my elbow out the window.

"See, nothing to it, just land the jet," I said.

27. A Book Review

Stranger to the Ground
By
Richard Bach

Part I

The date is September 1965. Dell has recently published a book entitled *Stranger to the Ground*. It is a paperback and contains 188 pages. The promising young author, Richard Bach, has autobiographically told a story about a single flight in an Air National Guard F-84G over Europe. The New York Times says, "The incredible story of one man alone in the sky facing awesome challenges of speed and space... penetrating... stands with the works of Saint-Exupery... Masterfully told." Your reviewer is almost nineteen years old. He is very focused on a career in aviation.

Richard Bach exudes everything a young fighter pilot should be. He has total familiarity with his aircraft. He has an unflinching devotion to duty. He has the courage to do, and courage to admit his fear. Most of all, he has an eloquence to describe his experience vividly. Lt. Bach is a New Jersey Air National Guard pilot assigned to fly a special cargo of top-secret documents from Weathersfield, England, to Chaumont, France. The mission is important and the weather is daunting.

Bach's narration of the flight includes a background into the details of his aircraft, his training, the Air Traffic Control Environment, and his philosophy. That, of course, is how he is able to expand a single flight into a book-length story. During the idle moments in the flight, Bach reminisces about exciting missions, inspiring people, and dead friends. An intensely proud person, he carefully develops his points, which come together in a compelling view of military aviation.

The flight is an exciting one. At one point he enters a thunderstorm, loses control on his aircraft, and barely recovers in time to save himself, his aircraft, and his precious cargo. He battles ice formation, radio failure, and a variety of unforeseen problems to accomplish his mission.

This book is a riveting story masterfully told. It offers an incisive view of the USAF, and the Air National Guard. Surely Bach is the epitome of what a pilot-patriot should be.

Part II

The date is September 1989. A dusty, almost forgotten book has been retrieved from long ago. Richard Bach, author of Jonathan Livingston Seagull and other successful books, wrote an autobiography of his aviation career in the mid 1960s. Stranger to the Ground describes him as a lieutenant in the New Jersey Air National Guard before his huge success as an author. Your reviewer is a former fighter pilot. Now a captain on the B-737 for a major airline, he describes his impressions of Lt. Bach's book in a different light than he was able to when the book was first published.

Lt. Bach was a fool, a very eloquent, highly trained, dedicated fool, but still a fool. This is the story of a young man who risks his life, his aircraft, and likely those of people on the ground to fly a bag of papers from England to France. This book describes a single flight of a young pilot who cannot know the importance of his mission. No

27. A Book Review

one will thank him or even remember its success or failure. Neither can he know that he will likely die if he flies it as assigned.

The effect of this is a huge irony. That is, how can such a proficient, highly trained young man come so close to destruction? It is a study in being confident and enthusiastic to a fault. I should know. I read this book twenty-four years ago and attempted to become a pilot exactly like that one in the book. While perhaps not as technically proficient as Bach describes himself, I shared his poor judgment.

In those days, I considered anyone over thirty to be better suited to a nursing home than a cockpit. Now at forty-three I can see a pattern. Some of us survive our inexperience and overconfidence to accrue some degree of wisdom. They say that there are no old, bold pilots. Maybe better said: "There are no old, still bold pilots."

28. World Record Flight

The National Aeronautic Association (NAA), calling itself "The Aero Club of America," is the only organization authorized by the Fédération Aéronautique Internationale (FAI) to certify distance, speed, and altitude records for powered aircraft in the United States.

Soon after becoming an airline captain, the urge to set a record became my raison d'être. Setting a speed record over a course where none exists is easy. Since the Los Angeles to New York records had been set by speedier aircraft than the humble 737, I chose Omaha to Atlanta. The requirements have been well documented in the NAA literature: Join the NAA, purchase a "sporting license," apply for a sanction, arrange for takeoff and landing times to be communicated to NAA, and fly route.

On the appointed day (my fragile schedule had not changed), I notified Omaha tower that the flight would be a record attempt and to expect a call from the NAA confirming my takeoff time. Once airborne, I flew the leg exactly as required by the flight plan. I anticipated the chief pilot, upon hearing of this, would be disappointed if I had flown faster than the most efficient speed. I notified Atlanta tower about the record attempt, and waited for contact with NAA and the chief pilot, hoping that forgiveness would be easier to obtain than permission. I never heard from the company. The NAA sent me a couple of nice plaques and invited me to receive the award at their annual meeting, which I declined.

28. World Record Flight

In 2000, I decided that an international record would be good to have. Having received the sanction for an Atlanta to Madrid attempt, Pedro Rivas, Bruce Doberstein, and I flew the very routine trip. However, the documentation proved much easier than before. NAA had approved the use of the on-board ACARS system for proving the details of the flight.

ACARS, Aircraft Communications Addressing and Reporting System, is a datalink system for communication between aircraft and ground stations. ACARS automatically reports the "out" time from the gate when the passenger doors are closed and the brakes released. "Off" and "on" times are reported automatically upon takeoff and landing. *In time* at the gate happens when a door, cargo or passenger, is opened. Short messaging enables critical communications between dispatchers and pilots. The system became much more sophisticated with the advent of CPDLC, or controller to pilot datalink communication systems.

"Captain, could you release the brakes? We just have a few more bags to load, and we sure would like to get an on-time departure logged today," said the driver of the tug waiting to push us back. When that request received compliance, the inefficiencies of baggage transfer and loading went unnoticed.

"No can do, Kemosabe. Did the machine that breaks the passengers' bags go down, or is it something else?" I replied.

In 2005, I applied to a sanction for a record flight from Tokyo to Atlanta on the 777. That went well, too, and as of 2021, the records remain. I attended the awards ceremony for that one, and met the keynote speaker, the late Scott Crossfield, the first person to exceed Mach 2. None of the three flights were especially fast, no high-power settings were used, and no huge tailwinds were encountered.

Until all the city pairs have established speed records, I expect that most future record-setters will, like me, choose a route with no established record.

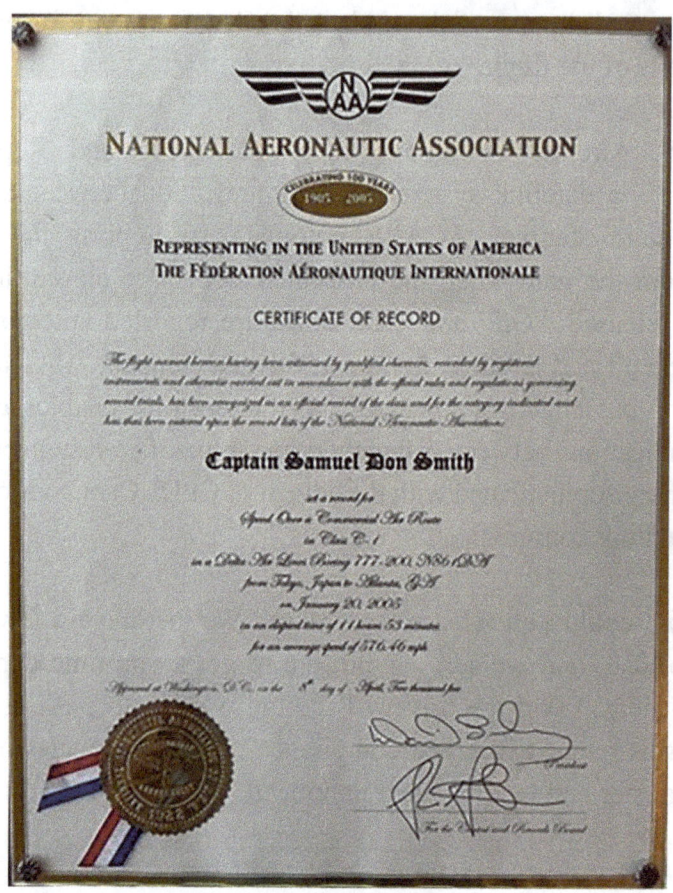

NAA Record Plaque

29. Get Out of Jail Free

The giant Boeing 747s engines wound up and it moved toward me. As I stood under the tail of the TriStar which I was soon to crew for a trip from Frankfurt to Atlanta, it approached, then turned sharply toward the runway. Seated high above me in the cockpit, I could see Jim McIntyre waving at me. Resplendent in shiny paint, the TWA 747 moved slowly by, a moment etched in my memory. TWA, Jim, and even the 747 would soon be but a memory.

Ironically, the captain of that giant aircraft stood only five foot six inches. We had met the year before at the annual ALPA Air Safety Forum in Washington, DC. The previous evening in Mainz, we had shared dinner, drinks, and stories. Highly energetic for an "old" guy, he chaired the NASA Advisory Committee for the Aviation Safety Reporting System. That position and his experience as an accident investigator placed him among the most dedicated to aviation safety.

The flash was so bright that I suspected an explosion had happened. I stood at the rear of the room housing the ALPA Air Safety Forum. At the dais sat Jim McIntyre holding a laser pointer and grinning from ear to ear. After his presentation, I sought him out.

"You jerk, you could have blinded me," I ranted.

"Really? This is the first time I have used one. Did it really hurt?" (Innocently)

"Damn right. Do it again and I will have to kill you."

"I just did it to get your attention. There's something I want to talk to you about. I'm retiring next year and I need someone to do the ASRS thing for me. Would you consider it?"

He said that it wouldn't take much of my time and that he had already gotten approval from the ALPA president. Accepting the honor would mean trips to NASA Ames at Mountain View, California and working with some very talented people. Attempting to conceal my delight, I was in.

From the ASRS web site:

"The ASRS is an important facet of the continuing effort by government, industry, and individuals to maintain and improve aviation safety. The ASRS collects voluntarily submitted aviation safety incident/situation reports from pilots, controllers, and others.

The ASRS acts on the information these reports contain. It identifies system deficiencies, and issues alerting messages to persons in a position to correct them. It educates through its newsletter "Callback", its journal "ASRS Directline" and through its research studies. Its database is a public repository which serves the needs of the FAA, NASA, and those of other organizations world-wide which are engaged in research and the promotion of safe flight. The ASRS collects, analyzes, and responds to voluntarily submitted aviation safety incident reports in order to lessen the likelihood of aviation accidents."

Foreseeing the unlikelihood of pilot and controllers submitting potentially incriminating information, the "waiver from enforcement action" emerged. The exact verbiage shown below became known

29. Get Out of Jail Free

as the "Get Out of Jail Free card." Initially refused by the FAA, the concept finally became regulatory after much arm-twisting.

As stated in Paragraph 9. c. FAA Advisory Circular No. 00-46E

"c. Enforcement Restrictions. The FAA considers the filing of a report with NASA concerning an incident or occurrence involving a violation of 49 U.S.C. subtitle VII or the 14 CFR to be indicative of a constructive attitude. Such an attitude will tend to prevent future violations. Accordingly, although a finding of violation may be made, neither a civil penalty nor certificate suspension will be imposed if:

1. The violation was inadvertent and not deliberate;

2. The violation did not involve a criminal offense, accident, or action under 49 U.S.C. § 44709, which discloses a lack of qualification or competency, which is wholly excluded from this policy;

3. The person has not been found in any prior FAA enforcement action to have committed a violation of 49 U.S.C. subtitle VII, or any regulation promulgated there for a period of 5 years prior to the date of occurrence; and

4. The person proves that, within 10 days after the violation, or date when the person became aware or should have been aware of the violation, he or she completed and delivered or mailed a written report of the incident or occurrence to NASA."

NASA, long considered an unbiased scientific agency, was selected to administer the program due to the general mistrust of the FAA by pilots. However, funding was channeled through the FAA coffers.

As the old saying goes, "There was a helluva lot they didn't tell me when I signed up for this job."

Traditionally, the ALPA representative became the chairman of the advisory committee.

There were fifteen other members, representing large aircraft manufacturers, general aviation manufacturers, general aviation pilots, aircraft maintenance, air traffic controllers, airlines, business aviation, flight attendants, and helicopters. Many organizations sent their top executives, such as the FAA administrator, Don Engen.

As chairman, I organized two meetings a year at the venue of my choice. That usually alternated between NASA Ames and Washington, DC. The likelihood of assembling fifteen such powerful people at one place at the same time proved to be impossible. After attempting to schedule around them, I finally just chose a date and sent an invitation.

The meeting agendas included discussions on budget, confidentiality breeches, staffing levels, computer resources, and much boring and mundane material. Two main issues had remained unresolved for years.

The make and model of the aircraft involved was absent or intentionally removed from the incoming reports and database entries. This emerged in the beginning as a precondition for the manufacturer's participation. The General Aviation Manufacturers Association (GAMA), the Aerospace Industries Association (Boeing and Lockheed), and the National Business Aircraft Association (NBAA) remained pleased that their aircraft names were never mentioned in any report. The rest of the aviation world desperately wanted to know which aircraft were experiencing

29. Get Out of Jail Free

problems. Every meeting dragged out the old "make/model" discussion to be stonewalled by the manufacturers. The implied threat was withdrawal of program support. Brien Wygle, then Vice President of Operations for Boeing, approached me at one meeting.

"Don, I think AIA can support make/model. We have a lot of confidence in our product and see only upside and improvement with more information," he said.

"Don't you think GAMA and NBAA will quit if we do that?" I asked.

"No. After I promote the upside, they will be shamed into submission."

Brien was head of his organization. The other two took their orders from above. After giving them plenty of time to discuss it with their superiors, the committee voted to include make/model, with two votes against. They both continued to come to the subsequent meetings.

The other thorny issue: public access to the database. Safety researchers were obligated to correspond with ASRS staff requesting data for their projects. Cumbersome for the researchers, expensive in resources for ASRS, and slow in the process, the carefully amassed information remained mostly hidden. The simple solution would be to put the entire database online and allow researchers to browse for their subject. Cyber security was in its infancy at the time. The thought of corruption of the database terrified NASA. Finally, a hotshot spook from Washington assured that with a shadow database he could guarantee the integrity of the system. With all the known safety features implemented in the public-access database, a new copy from the isolated primary database would be uploaded periodically. That was almost twenty years ago, and although I don't correspond with them, I haven't heard of any problems.

We discussed some of the most interesting reports. The ranged from the ridiculous to the sublime. Such discussions invariably prompted stories from our own members. Admiral Engen and Brien Wygle, being famous test pilots, often entertained us. During one such exciting story that waxed a little long, I said, "Admiral Engen, I hesitate to ask this, but can we postpone the rest of the story until we finish with the agenda?"

Of course, ever the gentleman, he apologized and bore no grudge.

The late Bill Reynard should be held up as the person who made the Aviation Safety Reporting System happen. He shepherded the Aviation Safety Reporting Program through its early years when the conflict with the FAA was highest. An attorney, his diplomacy, focus, and humor made the program what it is today.

Among the early heart transplant patients, he frequently opened his presentations with, "I want to thank you from the bottom of somebody else's heart."

Today, a pilot, controller, flight attendant, or mechanic can file a safety report online and receive a hard copy response, time stamped and identifiable only to NASA. If that report satisfies the above criteria, that slip of paper is good to avoid certificate action or penalties. Further, after thirty years of success, one may be sure that one's identity will never be revealed to anyone outside of NASA.

As I write this, I hold in my hand five NASA form receipts, representing my most serious errors in forty years of flying since ASRS became available. Three are for "Deviation from clearance," one is for "near midair collision," and one for "airspace violation."

29. Get Out of Jail Free

Looking back into my journal that I kept, I see the narrative of the flight that generated my first NASA report. During an IOE, Artie failed to turn at an intersection, and I missed it. He was waiting for the inbound radial to come alive but it never did because he didn't tune the proper frequency. I missed it too.

I wrote in my journal, "Artie is the most insidious threat in that he does some things extremely well, then loses focus."

Number two happened in 1997 in the 767. We were on downwind to runway 27L at Atlanta, being vectored at the very base of the Class B airspace. TCAS warned of traffic approaching, then turned into a resolution advisory, aurally announcing "Climb, climb." It was a Mooney single-engine aircraft flying under the Class B (at the very top of the uncontrolled airspace). I abruptly pulled up, jammed the throttles forward, and it passed *very* closely beneath. I returned to our assigned altitude as smoothly as I could manage, pulled the throttles back, and noticed that the engines did not accelerate at all, because it all happened so quickly. None of the passengers saw the Mooney, and apparently thought we had hit a bit of turbulence, since no one complained. I suggested to ATC that such vectoring at the base of the controlled airspace needed change. I don't know if they did anything about it, but forever after I became extremely focused when flying in or near uncontrolled airspace. A true TCAS save, in my mind, is marking the reduction of the threat of a midair collision to nearly zero.

Number three says "Deviation from Clearance." I don't remember that one.

Number four involved a runway change at Las Vegas. We had been cleared by the tower to perform an unusual maneuver after takeoff. For some reason we were asked to take off on a different runway and given clearance to taxi there. After takeoff, everyone got confused as to whether the earlier clearance remained valid. The lesson I learned there: never assume, always clarify at the risk of looking dumb. It's a sort of readback. Many times after that, I would say, "Just to make sure I understand, I intend to (e.g. perform a procedure turn when we arrive at the fix)."

Number five happened just last year (2019). I had recently installed ADS-B in my Bonanza and launched for a few practice instrument approaches. Climbing to the initial approach altitude, I crossed vertically into Class C airspace. Monitoring guard (the emergency frequency) on my second radio, I heard, "N…. you have entered the San Antonio Class C airspace, turn to three six zero heading to exit." More on ADS-B later, but suffice it to say that if you have it, everyone knows exactly who you are and what you are doing.

30. MOOSE

Jack Hofbauer, who passed away in 2017, started Jack's Air Service at Moosehead Lake, Maine. A fellow Delta pilot based in Boston, he offered us a "Delta Discount." That usually meant quadrupling the regular price then halving it for a deal. However, this offer was too good to pass up. For $400, one could obtain an add-on single-engine seaplane rating, including a hotel room.

In July of 1983, I signed up for the deal. After an hour-and-a-half drive from Bangor, I checked in to my room and met my instructor, Bob O'Brien. The perfect weather suggested a swim in the lake. Having endured some winter flying in Maine, I cautiously approached the water. To my surprise, the water near the surface warmed me like a bath. A few feet below, however, lay the Maine I remembered: very cold.

Seaplane flying merges the joys of sailing and flying. Like sailing, an acute awareness of the wind facilitates docking, taking off, and landing. Our airplane, a Cessna 172 on conventional floats, sported a high wing, enabling docking. Seaplanes with pontoons near the wingtip are difficult or impossible to dock. They are usually amphibious and simply lower their landing gear in the water and taxi up a ramp.

After a thorough briefing, Bob and I launched to try it. Moosehead Lake is twenty-six miles long. After dozens of takeoffs and landings, we reached the far end of the lake. At that point I had all the basics;

only finer points such as on-step turns and glassy water landings remained.

The next day, I rode on a powerline patrol. Jack had a contract to fly the electric power line right-of-way looking for potential problems. I accumulated some flying time, and Jack double-dipped with the power company. While cruising the power line, I spotted a moose family in a nearby bog. Receiving permission from Bob for a closer look, I flew over them as the cow and calf scampered into the woods. The bull remained in place. Recognizing the challenge, I circled around and descended to a few feet above the bog. Lining up with the moose, I was determined to frighten him into retreat. A movie director might have flashed back and forth from the view from the cockpit and the view from the moose. Closer and closer we came until…I pulled up and flew over it. As I turned to see, it was standing in the same spot, only with his head turned toward me. A bull moose is truly the king of the woods, afraid of nothing.

On the third day, we practiced step turns and other details. Bob asked me to dock near a house on the far end of the lake. He disappeared into the house and returned about forty-five minutes later.

"Do I want to know what happened in there?" I asked.

"Don't ask," he answered.

As we taxied away, I felt a bump as the water rudder hit a rock. Taxiing back, we got out and discovered one of the water rudders had a significant bend in it.

"Jack is going to be really mad about this. Let's fly over to my friend's house where he can fix it," he said.

30. Moose

And so we did. We removed the damaged part, pounded it straight, and replaced it. No one would know.

"Bob, I have a theory about soloing an airplane. I think that if you haven't soloed it, you haven't really been checked out. After all, you might just be humoring me," I said.

"No, our insurance doesn't cover your soloing it, we can't do that," he said.

"How about we alight near that island, you get out, I fly around a few minutes, pick you back up and no one will ever know about my soloing or your bent water rudder," I said.

"OK, I get it, blackmail. Well, OK, let's do it," he said.

That flight went fine, and I took my check ride the next day from a nice lady who had been an examiner for many years.

My research shows that airplane is still being used by Jack's Air, providing tours and charter flights from Moosehead Lake.

The Winner

31. The Mighty Dog

Delta had acquired the MD-88 in 1987. Affectionately known as the "Mad Dog," it proved to be less popular among the pilots than Boeing aircraft. Thus, when the company decided to become the first US carrier to buy the MD-11, several not-so-flattering names arose. Names such as "Mighty Dog," "Mega Dog," and "MD 911" (that was before 9/11/2001) stuck despite management protests.

Coming online in 1990, the process experienced serious problems. Being the first of the third generation of automated aircraft, traditional training in automation management proved inadequate. Just how deeply pilots needed to understand the behavior of the computer-controlled systems remained unknown as pilots rushed to certification. On a technical level, maintenance of the landing gear proved so complex that a misunderstanding rendered smooth landings impossible. Service of its triple hydraulic-pneumatic strut was conducted erroneously, causing it to be so stiff that no shock absorption was available. Flight attendants began to consider commonplace what were previously unacceptable landings. Its reputation for being difficult to fly persisted throughout its tenure at Delta.

Having missed the Vietnam War, I developed a curiosity about experiencing the Orient. Flying the MD-11, based in Los Angeles and the newly opened Portland, Oregon, base presented just the opportunity I wanted. First officer, that is. For about the same pay, I would be able to hold a very senior first officer schedule, see the Orient, and escape the rut I had created.

31. The Mighty Dog

First officers necessarily qualified with captains' credentials because of the swapping of seats for crew rest purposes. Becoming rated on the MD-11 required more of me than any other rating. As I previously noted, little consensus existed as to the required level of systems knowledge. The automation pervaded every system. Having eliminated the engineer from its predecessor, the DC-10, the "pilot monitoring" or "pilot not flying" became extremely busy in the event that one of the systems reverted to manual mode.

"When they invented the MD-11, they didn't eliminate the engineer, they eliminated the copilot," was the often-heard refrain.

Its fuel system typified the extreme complexity of the systems. In order to achieve greater economy, longitudinal stability was sacrificed with the help of automated flight controls. With fuel in its tail tank, proper pitch control required electronic augmentation. As a flight progressed, the fuel computer moved fuel among the tanks to achieve lateral and longitudinal balance. Sometimes the tail fuel would become unacceptably cold, requiring it to be circulated to a forward tank for warming, lest it freeze.

Frequently as the computer performed several functions simultaneously, the comment was made, "It wears out the fuel before it uses it up."

The electronically augmented flight controls mystified some of the dinosaurs. In normal mode, pitch control was achieved much like control wheel steering in other aircraft. That is, slight pressure on the yoke (less than ten pounds) produced a gentle climb or descent. Applying more pressure resulted in entering direct mode territory with much greater authority. To me, it was like flying a fighter or helicopter; only tiny corrections were required to precisely pitch the aircraft. However, a few of the more senior pilots never quite acclimated to the concept, resulting in a fore and aft thrash of the yoke, resulting in a very uncomfortable ride.

"This airplane was designed to be flown on autopilot, it's not possible to smoothly fly it manually," they whined.

Arriving at Taipei or Bangkok, we were often cleared high speed at low altitude. That meant, unlike America, flight at 365 knots indicated airspeed at 2,000 ft. was perfectly acceptable. My favorite trick to torment the dinosaurs was to disconnect the autopilot while at high speed and low altitude, and fly manually. That would produce a startled reflex and wide eyes from some of the guys who had declared such maneuvers impossible.

My favorite trip lasted twelve days and included stops at Taipei, Seoul, and Bangkok. It was as if we were based in Taipei, going back and forth to the other cities during the rotation. Bob McKinney, at the time the most senior pilot at the airline, and I flew together well. He was universally misunderstood among the copilots, but I enjoyed his dry sense of humor and excellent piloting ability. We had many memorable experiences, such as drinking snake blood in Taipei and touring Patpong in Bangkok.

Captain Larry from the Training Department arrived one day for the preflight briefing for a trip to Seoul. I asked if he had flown the trip very often, he replied that he had not done it previously. I advised him, as nicely as I knew how, that I was happy to help, as I had flown it many times. In no uncertain terms he let me know that he knew everything that he needed to know and that I was to keep my opinions to myself. Twelve hours later, we found ourselves coasting in to Vietnam at midnight. Since I was flying, Captain Larry managed the radios. After passing over most of the country, Danang Control, in perfect English, advised us to contact

31. The Mighty Dog

Vientiane Control. Knowing full well that Vientiane closed down at midnight, I said nothing.

"Vientiane Control, Vientiane Control, this is Delta one five over." No answer.

In a voice two octaves higher, "Vientiane Control, Vientiane Control, this is Delta one five over." No answer.

I imagined that since Larry had flown in the Air Force in Vietnam, that he considered Laos a dark and threatening place. I wondered if he feared being shot down. I said nothing.

"Hell, I'm going to try some other frequencies on the high-altitude chart." And he did, to no avail.

Failing that, he produced some high-frequency channels (a different radio) and tried calling on several of them. Sweat was streaming from his face.

I said, "Larry, we are over Thailand now, why don't you just call Bangkok Control?"

He did, they answered, and I never told him.

Flying into Nagoya, Japan, Catatonic Captain Ben slept a lot and talked even more. Being the lazy type, he expected the first officer to do everything, including loading the flight-management system for the arrival. Having done that, and approaching the top of descent, Captain Ben decided to brief his approach.

Delta loves acronyms, and the one to prepare for an approach is "NATS," meaning NOTAMS, Approach, Terrain, and Special Pages.

When he said "NATS," he suddenly realized that he had wasted hours of time at cruise without reviewing the Notices to Airmen. In a frantic effort to catch up, he produced the printed notices which ostensibly advise us of any irregularity with the airport or en-route facilities. Unfortunately, on international flights, the list of NOTAMS is extensive and printed on twenty feet or more of computer paper. Total chaos ensued, with Nagoya Approach Control placing us in a holding pattern until we were ready. As a copilot, one encounters a broad spectrum of behaviors; some of them are keepers, while some need rejection.

Those were the days of Seoul's Kimpo (Gimpo) Airport. Now Seoul passengers fly into the shiny new Inchon Airport and ride to Seoul in a taxi for two hours instead of one. Kimpo lay only a few miles south of the DMZ. With the runway oriented southeast-northwest, our flight path usually took us westbound, south of the airport with a right turn back to land. Flying on base leg, perpendicular to the final approach aroused anxiety among everyone. Going stupid and continuing northbound meant being shot down by the North Koreans. Adding to that anxiety, we entered heavy rain. Most of the runways in Asia are extremely slick when wet. That is because of the reverted rubber left by the tires of landing aircraft.

Captain Tom, sweating bullets, floated the landing. On and on we went down the runway, just barely above it, wasting precious braking opportunities. Finally touching down halfway down the almost 12,000 ft. runway, he slammed on the brakes and commanded full reverse thrust. Nothing happened. The airplane seemed to accelerate for lack of braking. When we stopped, the nose was hanging over the end of the concrete and the engines were still in full reverse (contrary to procedure). Something caught my attention on the right side of the aircraft. The powerful engine at full power was sucking in huge amounts of water and producing a swirling, not so small,

31. The Mighty Dog

tornado. Tom sat motionless as I pushed the throttles out of reverse. Little was said during the taxi in.

Departing Seoul, Delta had little priority with the Korean air traffic control. In their defense, coordinating an eastbound climb through the busy Japanese airspace and transitioning into the North Pacific Tracks involved many agencies. However, it seemed that "Queen Air," as the Koreans pronounced Korean Air, always received their requested clearance. Seoul to Portland, being a long trip, required the MD-11 to climb to high altitude for good fuel consumption. We were offered the leftover altitudes.

"Delta, the only altitudes available are 27,000 and 41,000."

Tough choice: fly for very long at 27,000 and land short of Portland for fuel; early in the flight the airplane is too heavy to climb to 41,000.

"OK, we'll take 41,000, with a slow climb."

An hour later finds us at 35,000 climbing at a very slow 200 feet per minute. The MD-11 primary flight display shows an electronic airspeed tape on its left side. At the stationary cursor, the existing calibrated airspeed is displayed. Above that, the Mach limit is shown as a red shaded area. Below that, the stall limit is shown as a red shaded area. As altitude increases, the two red areas converge. This is known as "coffin corner" or the "jaws of death." In smooth air, not much space is needed to safely fly. However, when the margin is narrow, and turbulence is encountered, bad things can happen. And then the turbulence begins. Should we admit our over-optimistic plan and ask for lower altitude and probably necessitate an Alaska refueling, or just hope it doesn't get any worse? A really unhappy Japanese controller usually gives us a lower altitude and vectors off the Oceanic Tracks until we can climb. Later, arriving on our track, the oceanic clearance must be renegotiated, but a Portland landing remains likely.

Captain Jerry had been the manager of the MD-11 program during its integration into Delta operations. Before the first purchase, he had steeped himself in the intricacies of the aircraft and had figured prominently in the options that Delta chose. Knowing his background, I looked forward to flying a trip to London with him. With his deep knowledge of the flight management system, he delighted in entering obscure commands into the FMS that would produce a surprise for the other pilot. Relying on the aircraft automation, he had received a violation from the British authorities previously when departing from Gatwick Airport. The setup happened when he departed eastbound with a strong southerly wind. The departure procedure called for a left turn after takeoff to enable passing about halfway between Gatwick and Heathrow. The strong wind had pushed him into Heathrow airspace.

"Don, let's hear your departure briefing," Jerry said.

It was the same setup that had gotten him violated. A strong southerly wind threatened to push us into Heathrow airspace.

"I'm going to leave the flaps at fifteen, keep the airspeed down to 220, and manually use thirty degrees of bank instead of the autopilot's twenty-five," I said.

"I think you should just clean it up, accelerate, and use the autopilot," he said.

I'm thinking, *Is he nuts, that's exactly how he got a violation.*

31. The Mighty Dog

I said, "OK, Jerry, you're the captain, we'll do as you like."

"But you can do it any way you like," he said.

Repeating, I said, "OK, then, I'm going to leave the flaps at fifteen, keep the airspeed down to 220, and manually use thirty degrees of bank."

"But I think you should just clean it up, accelerate, and use the autopilot," he said.

After a pregnant silence, nothing more was said. The departure went just fine.

Crew rest facilities in the 777 border on the luxurious. Not so much in the early MD-11. On flights exceeding twelve hours, airlines are obligated to provide "fully augmented crews," meaning four fully-qualified pilots for two-pilot aircraft. Additionally, regulations require adequate rest facilities. The definition of *adequate* proved to be elusive. Early MD-11s came equipped with the "coffin." A completely inadequate device that opened a plastic cylinder into the forward section of the passenger cabin, it offered a cramped, noisy, and cold environment in which off-duty pilots could toss and turn, attempting rest. After a spectacular diversion due to fatigued pilots, a room was grudgingly installed midway in the passenger cabin, eliminating several rows of revenue-producing seats. Later, a more seat-efficient hideaway emerged as the solution nearer the cockpit. The most senior captain could split the rest time in a way of his choosing, but most chose to divide the cruise time into four periods. All four pilots were required to be present in the cockpit for takeoff to top of climb, and top of descent to landing. On a long flight, two naps of two and a half hours or more made for good crew performance at the destination.

Aeromorphosis

"Dozing for dollars," lucrative as it may sound, required some management when arriving at a destination twelve time zones from home. Westbound afternoon takeoffs, flying great circle routes, meant staring into the bright sunlight for the entire flight. (I think that's why my face is so wrinkled.) Arriving about the same hour as takeoff on the following day made the body beg for sleep. If one succumbed to the urge, later you would awaken in the middle of the night, resulting in beginning the next flight exactly when the sleep urge hit again. Forcing oneself to stay awake for five or six hours did the trick, but it was difficult.

Eastbound from Asia challenged the senses also. An afternoon takeoff in the sunlight soon flew into darkness. After a short night, sunrise usually happened approaching the west coast of America, landing the same day as takeoff. The most confusing of all, crossing the date line at midnight.

Two hours after takeoff, and in total darkness, we encountered what must have been a city, with the lights of streets neatly laid out in a parallel fashion and cross-streets woven into them. The only sense I could make of it: we must have been flying in the wrong direction and now were positioned somewhere over China. No, the Japanese fishing fleet, in the middle of the Pacific, was hard at work.

I am a dedicated flightseer. By my calculations, I have spent more than two years of my life looking out the front window of an airplane. Some of my most memorable experiences happened while flying the MD-11 to and from Asia.

Late one night while crossing over Vietnam at high altitude, I warily watched an enthusiastic thunderstorm rising to our height and producing nearly constant lightning within. What I saw only lasted for a second, and luckily, I happened to be looking in the proper direction.

31. The Mighty Dog

Out of the cloud top, a cylinder of bright reddish light, a quarter of the diameter of the cloud, rose to perhaps ten times the height of the cloud and then spread out in all directions. I believe that I saw a Cloud-Ionosphere Discharge (CI). The National Academy of Science has an informative description of these on their web site. They are very rare and have been verified only in the last thirty years.

Cloud-Ionosphere Discharge

Returning to America from Asia usually involves passing near the Arctic Circle in the middle of the night. Aurora sightings are common. While enjoying an unusually spectacular aurora show, the sun began peeking over the horizon ahead. What had been aurora remained as the sunlight grew brighter, revealing multicolored wisps high above us. After further research, I concluded that they were polar stratospheric or nacreous clouds. Sometimes called mother of pearl clouds, they rank among the rarest of atmospheric phenomena, and despite their beauty, contribute to the breakdown of the ozone layer.

Aeromorphosis

Mother of Pearl Clouds

While on a domestic flight to the West Coast, the sun rose slowly behind us as we flew away from its chase. Flying along a path roughly along Interstate 10, hundreds of miles of road signs suddenly illuminated as the sun rose to the perfect angle to reflect back to the cockpit. Red "Do Not Enter" signs alternating with green information signs formed a perfect line of polka dots pointing the way to Los Angeles.

Occasionally, due to unusual winds, we flew deep into Russia after passing the arctic regions. Punctuated by smoldering volcanoes, ice, snow, and a few abandoned airstrips, there is little else to see. Void of any signs of life, hours would pass while talking to someone on the radio who sounded as if they were in a big tin can. Alternate airports? Yes, in case of a serious emergency, we could land at one of the abandoned airstrips. Help might be available in a few days. However, if we landed and ran out of fuel for an engine or APU, we would all surely freeze to death. What,

31. The Mighty Dog

I asked, is the difference between that and ditching in the ocean? "Name your poison" is the answer.

One morning I rose early in Nagoya, Japan. Wandering off the beaten path, I soon discovered that I was hopelessly lost, as the English signs existed only on the main streets. I stumbled into a gigantic fish market where fishermen had begun to unload their night's catch. In the middle of the covered area lay a stone block about fifteen feet in diameter. As I watched, a huge tuna was heaved upon it by several small men. Immediately, four Japanese men dressed only in loincloths and carrying sharp meat cleavers pounced on the carcass and began cutting steaks. In a matter of less than ten minutes the fish appeared to have been eaten by piranhas, leaving only a few bones. I understand that each of the hundreds of steaks cut there brought hundreds of dollars (or equivalent Yen) at the sushi market. To the side, an array of large barrels formed a twenty-by-twenty-foot matrix containing smaller catch. Despite the total language barrier, I was greeted by smiles and friendly-sounding words as I wandered the area. The barrels were arranged in one direction by type such as shrimp, octopus, or tiny fish of some kind. In the other direction the contents were arranged by size. Beginning on the octopus row, the first barrel contained tiny octopi, perhaps an inch long. Moving along, the barrels contained progressively larger creatures until arriving at the last, which contained sea monsters! Not really, but they were very large.

Still lost (pre-GPS), I wondered how to find the hotel. In a divine inspiration, I recalled the Japanese affection for McDonald's and the existence of one near my hotel. Asking a friendly-looking lady about "McDonald's."

She replied, "Ahhhh, McDonaldo." She pointed me in the proper direction, and I survived.

On another day in Japan, I was returning to the hotel when I encountered a mynah bird in a cage in front of a shop. Recalling an experience I had as a child, I remembered that some of them can talk.

I said, "Hello," in my best exaggerated bird voice.

To my great surprise, the bird said, "Konnichiwa."

I suddenly realized that I had always erroneously assumed that the bird from my childhood had understood the words it was saying, and that birds inherently spoke English! I burst into a hysterical fit of laughter, much to the wonderment of the shop owner.

Becoming a captain on the MD-11 seemed far out of reach. Little did I know that a strange turn of events would make that possible in a few short years.

32. Bottom of the Barrel

In early 1997, I was surprised to receive a domestic captain bid on the 757/767. Although pleased to get the promotion, I was relegated to very low seniority. The checkout went smoothly, as I had been an enthusiastic fan of the airplanes as a copilot. As a reserve pilot, I had periods in which I would be given a day's notice (long call) and periods that required me to report in two hours (short call). The schedule often assigned me a trip for the following day, absolving me from the dreaded short-call days.

"Don, we have a Lima trip for you tomorrow," advised the crew scheduler.

Great! Last month I was a copilot, now I am an international captain, I thought.

Little did I know it was the worst trip on the schedule. Although it crossed national borders, it was considered a domestic trip. Scheduled for seven hours and fifty-nine minutes, it did not qualify for the eight hours needed for a relief pilot. Flown with a long-range 757, it departed around midnight and flew through the night. Most people think of Machu Picchu and mountains associated with Peru. However, Lima lies on the coast, no mountain flying being required. Eight and a half hours later, two sleepy pilots landed in Lima. After several Lima trips, having not yet seen one shorter than eight hours, I questioned the chief pilot.

Aeromorphosis

"It's not possible to fly to Lima in eight hours. Surely your statistics show that the averages are longer. It's not fair to deny us a relief pilot just for the company's bottom line," I whined.

"Fly faster or change airplanes if you don't like it," he responded.

Fast-forward to my next Lima trip. We had just passed over Grand Cayman.

"First Officer, I am hereby advising you that I have become uncontrollably sleepy. You will be alert and fly the aircraft to overhead Panama, where I expect you to become uncontrollably sleepy," I stated.

And that became my *modus operandi*. Critics reading this story may condemn me, but I still believe my solution to be safer.

While in Lima, I received a frantic call from operations. Ecuador's Guagua Pichincha Volcano had erupted, spewing ash clouds along our proposed route home. We were to fly an extreme westerly deviation to avoid the ash. About halfway between the mainland and the Galapagos Islands, we entered some high clouds. Being near the Intertropical Convergence Zone (ITCZ), the clouds held considerable amounts of moisture. Large transport aircraft like the 757 have elaborate environmental control systems. After having been flown in dry conditions, contamination accrues in the ducts, much like lint. Upon entering the clouds, moisture is routed through the ducts, causing a musty odor.

"Oh, no, we have gotten into the ash cloud!" exclaimed the copilot.

"No, I think it's just moisture going through the packs," I said.

"We need to turn around right now."

32. Bottom of the Barrel

"If it were ash, it would smell a lot worse."

"I disagree," he said.

"Remember the briefing? We will discuss it, and if we can't agree, I'll win."

We continued and survived unscathed. However, that conversation typified many that I have had in the cockpit and, I believe, many others have had. On the one hand, lay the company priorities: safety, comfort, economy. On the other is the lack of common experience between the two debaters. Certainly, the company could not exist if safety or economy were ignored. If we were to agree on just what is safe and what is economical, then the subtlety of defining passenger comfort is the only issue. Supposing the question is whether or not to penetrate an area of weather illuminated by the aircraft's radar. If both pilots were able to perfectly interpret the information and the degree of turbulence was known, then the only issue would be the degree of discomfort to which to expose the passengers. Avoidance of that discomfort adds miles to the trip and subtracts dollars from the company's profits. Since interpretation of on-board radar is part art and part science, uncertainty becomes a factor. A captain with 20,000 hours in the cockpit likely has a better chance of predicting the outcome. Should a captain deviate around weather that he or she deems acceptable when the copilot does not? That partially depends on the experience of the copilot. Accepting good advice is a virtue, humoring an inexperienced or tentative copilot is not. Of course, the captain has the privilege of being the most cautious member of the crew if they so choose.

The heavier, more senior equipment offered dramatic contrast from the 737 in both aircraft and human-factors evolution. Modern flight management systems (FMS) found on all airliners today began on the 767. Originally conceived as a way to eliminate the engineer on earlier designs, it has evolved to pervade every aspect of a flight. An airline's dispatcher usually sends a flight plan to the plots, either electronically or printed. If printed, the route fixes must be manually typed into the FMS, exposing the process to potential errors.

In the late 1990s, Delta pilots manually typed the flight plans. An error of a single digit might create an error of thousands of miles. Usually, the *pilot flying* entered the flight plan and the *pilot not flying* (now called the pilot monitoring) checked the work. If the total miles on the fight plan did not agree with the total miles on the FMS, an error had been committed. If the route map followed a zigzag pattern, rather than a smooth line, an error had been committed. Once approved, the autopilot could be coupled to the FMS to dutifully follow the entered plan, correct or not.

More modern technology enabled the electronic upload of the fight plan, eliminating at least one source of navigation error. Part and parcel of FMS systems, vertical navigation systems (VNAV) optimize the aircraft's vertical path. Using aircraft performance, weight, lateral path, cruising altitudes, and other parameters, the VNAV computes and (if coupled to the autopilot) flies the most efficient vertical profile. VNAV saves airlines millions of dollars when properly used. However, human intervention is frequently required to overcome the inefficient and the impossible. For example, flying westbound into DFW with strong headwinds, the FMS computer plans a steep descent due to the wind. With a mandatory crossing altitude, that profile becomes impossible to achieve as the wind decreases with altitude. Ignoring that developing situation would find the pilots descending as fast as possible and still not being at the proper altitude. The remedy I used: lie to the FMS. I entered a 100-knot tailwind prediction for the lower altitudes, and the computed "top of descent" moved farther away from the assigned fix, leaving a more leisurely descent. More progressive airlines automatically upload the entire wind profile, negating the need for such tricks.

32. Bottom of the Barrel

I also encountered dinosaurs in the right seat. Relics from the pre-CRM days, many copilots chose to remain very senior and enjoy schedules that permitted other activities. Much like the captains I had encountered as a copilot myself, this group rejected most of the resource-management principles that Delta had embraced. On one such trip I was paired with an older pilot who had come to Delta from the Pan Am acquisition. Obviously angry at the hand he had been dealt, he intentionally violated nearly every procedure, demanding my intervention. He violently slapped the landing gear handle up after takeoff; he would not touch the yoke until V1, he would not hold the throttles; he tried to listen to music on the low-frequency radio. After setting the pressurization wrong, he lied and said he did it because he was used to flying from the old Atlanta terminal. (He had never flown from the old terminal.) He was to retire the following month; I did my best to fly safe and avoid a fight.

Mostly because of the great service our flight attendants provided, many passengers deplaned with gratitude for a pleasant flight. The illustration below is one of the perks that I valued highly.

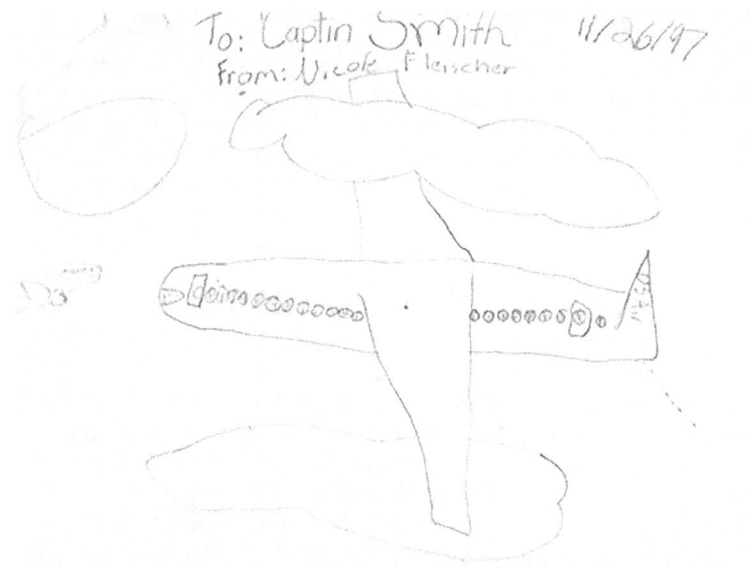

Nicole Fleischer Drawing

Occasionally, we junior pilots lucked into a trip flying the longer version of the 767, the dash 300. We gladly accepted the additional pay, although the larger one proved to be more challenging to fly into shorter runways. Late one night, landing at New York LaGuardia Airport, on runway 31, I experienced a terrifying illusion. Just before landing, at slower speeds, the aircraft is significantly pitched up, making the cockpit much higher than the landing gear. Even though the wheels were on the proper glide path, poised to touch down at the proper place on the runway, the cockpit trajectory appeared to be headed for the far end of the runway. The illusion being that I would touch down too far down the runway to be able to stop. Of course, the main wheels touched down on schedule, followed by a significant lowering of the nose, followed by an uneventful stop on the 7,000-foot-long runway.

A favorite clearance for a southeast landing at LaGuardia when approaching from the South, "Fly up the river and intercept the final approach to runway one three." A few inexperienced pilots chose the East River, rather than the Hudson. That made for a *very* tight turn onto the final approach. Transiting LaGuardia always seemed fraught with confusion. The good news: the ride into town was short.

The River Approach into Washington (now Reagan) National Airport in a 757 never ceased to thrill. The idea being to fly over the Potomac until very close to the airport and then make a sharp right turn to land. From the left seat, keeping the runway in sight was impossible. I always asked the copilot to make that approach, even though it was challenging. Most were pleased to be trusted and produced good results. The passengers never seemed to mind looking up at the USA Today Building as we passed nearby.

Even though Boeing achieved approval for a common type rating for the 757 and 767, the cockpits were a bit different. The 757, which

32. Bottom of the Barrel

stands very tall on its landing gear, would have presented a different landing picture to the pilots had it not been for the step down into the cockpit. Entrance into the 767 required a step up. The systems and flight-control characteristics achieved a remarkable similarity. However, the 757 possessed a nasty stiffness that produced a jerk on landing if the slightest crab remained at touchdown. One of the company's pilot-executives damaged one while landing in Miami. I believe it was an error on his part; the official story: landing gear malfunction.

True to my promise to Bob Entrican, I performed every other exterior preflight inspection, rain or shine. Traditionally, pilots took turns flying the airplane. Many captains would just rest easy with the upcoming first officer's leg, requiring them to perform the exterior preflight inspection and set up the cockpit. I think the copilots appreciated the efficiency of my method, especially when it was raining. Performing an exterior preflight inspection may seem incongruous on such a large, professionally maintained aircraft. Millions have been spent on maintenance not only for safety, but reliability. The extent and frequency of periodic maintenance on airline aircraft test the resources of even the best-funded airlines.

14 CFR § 91.3 - Responsibility and authority of the pilot ...

- (a) The pilot in command of an aircraft is directly responsible for, and is the final authority as to, the operation of that aircraft.
- (b) In an in-flight emergency requiring immediate action, the pilot in command may deviate from any rule of this part to the extent required to meet that emergency.

Once accepted, the aircraft becomes the pilot's responsibility. The inspection is part ritual, part practical. For the ritual, we are saying,

Aeromorphosis

"I have been given an airplane that has been deemed safe to fly. I will judge that and approve it."

Rarely did I find anything wrong with an aircraft. Our mechanics had a strong sense of pride in their work. The notion that a pilot, with their scant knowledge of the aircraft could possibly find an error, would be a huge humiliation. However, humans make errors. After reviewing the logbook and finding it approved by maintenance, I began my preflight inspection for a flight departing San Diego. I discovered part of an engine cowl hanging unlatched. Entering the maintenance control room, I encountered a very busy supervisor.

"I'll be with you in a minute, *Captain*," he said in a condescending voice.

"There's something you ought to see out here," I said.

"What is it? I'm busy," he said.

"Just come look at it."

Exasperated and slamming down the phone, he said, "Well, OK."

"Holy shit, I'm sorry," he said when I showed him.

Even though it is mostly a ritual, sometimes double-checking is a good idea.

Passengers watching a pilot inspect a B-777, shining a flashlight to the top of its 60-foot tail, might deem the process a waste of time. But perhaps a bit of ice or a bird strike could have gone undetected.

32. Bottom of the Barrel

I heard from a reliable source (the president of ALPA) that one airline whose demise was imminent began to reduce its maintenance to an unsafe level.

One captain who had refused to accept an aircraft for mechanical reasons was told, "Captain, you can take this airplane or we will find someone who will, and that won't go well for you."

A good rule for passengers might dictate: "Do not fly on an airline facing bankruptcy."

Although Delta did eventually file for bankruptcy, I was never questioned on my decision to require additional maintenance.

33. ICAO, IFALPA, AND HUPER

After the two accident investigations in the late 1980s, I began attending meetings of the US Airline Pilots Association Human Performance Committee. They were real snoozers. Dick Stone, who had recruited me, had retired, leaving the chairmanship to John. Mostly just waiting for another accident, we occasionally went to "show the flag," as John put it.

"Who wants to go to the Annual Manual?" he would ask. That meant attending the annual conference on manual control. No one wanted to go.

"Who wants to go to the G-10 Conference?" Everyone did. The Society of Automotive Engineers Aerospace Behavioral Engineering Technology Committee always met at Daytona Beach and offered good food and drinks, also the beach.

We attended such conferences ostensibly offering a user viewpoint, but were mostly ignored because of their intellectual nature. However, I did score a few points at a conference on workload management by bringing my PhD into play. Held in Seattle, the notion that cognitive workload could be measured physiologically, rather than by performance, was to be discussed. Tedious hours being spent on whether measuring eyeblinks or heartbeats is best, the academicians waxed eloquent.

When I was introduced (the only pilot in the room), one of the professors said, "ALPA, isn't that a dog food?"

33. ICAO, IFALPA, and HUPER

Incensed, I replied, "No that is an acronym for Airline Pilots Association, an organization of sixty thousand pilots that spends more than fifteen million dollars on research and aviation safety annually. And if you knew anything about nutrition, you would know that Alpo isn't much of a dog food, either."

The NTSB has been issuing recommendations on pilot fatigue since 1972, but it took until 2011 for the FAA to issue a final regulation on the subject. In the meantime, the FAA moderated the debate between the Air Transport Association (ATA) and the Airline Pilots Association (ALPA). The ATA argued that more rest for pilots would cost millions of dollars in crew expenses, and that the current regulations were perfectly adequate. ALPA maintained that individuals required different amounts of sleep, nighttime duty is more fatiguing, pilots should be given the opportunity for eight hours of uninterrupted sleep, and that current regulations had adverse effects on aviation safety. That controversy raged the entire time that I served in ALPA.

NASA has been conducting research on the subject for many years in their Fatigue Countermeasures Laboratory. I enrolled in their course to become an instructor in the subject, taught by Mark Rosekind, recently the administrator of the National Highway Transportation Safety Administration (NHTSA). I learned valuable lessons for my upcoming international flying. Conducted at NASA Ames Research Center (ARC), Mark kept us wide awake during the course, partially due to his professional-level magic tricks.

Being a newly graduated authority on the subject, Dave Haas, the ALPA Central Air Safety Chairman, asked me to represent the association at an FAA public hearing in Washington on airline crew rest regulations. Steeling myself for the onslaught by the

ATA hordes, I prepared carefully. Imagine my surprise when I realized that I was the only person in the room besides the FAA. After my presentation, he said, "Since everyone here is in favor of the proposed regulation, I will move it forward toward its publication." Sometimes you can score points just by showing up.

The Air Safety Forum, held in Washington, DC annually by ALPA has been very productive. Attendees from industry, government, and airlines meet and discuss changes that improve aviation safety. Speakers from the FAA, aircraft manufacturers, airline management, and others present updates on their activities and field some tough questions.

One such question came from the floor from Jerome "Jerry" Lederer. Jerry, being well into his nineties at the time, shuffled up to the microphone and asked when the low-power digital radars in new airliners were going to become as safe as the old ones.

Jerry commanded immense respect, being well known as the person responsible for introducing blinking anti-collision lights and flight data recorders to aircraft. He also was the leader in overhauling NASA safety after the Apollo 1 fire. He passed away at the age of 101, and his memory continues to inspire me and many others to remain productive in our senior years.

33. ICAO, IFALPA, and HUPER

Capt. Bill "the professor" Melvin, Don, Jerry Lederer

Don Bateman, inventor of GPWS; Carlos Arroyo; Don at a grueling technical meeting

In the ALPA Human Performance Committee, things remained stagnant. Approaching retirement, John had no intention of expanding our role. Since he was rarely available for leadership, most decisions fell to Patsy, his wife. One of our members, Robert Sumwalt, became particularly frustrated by the restrictive leadership. Robert, a pilot for US Airways, conducted courses which led to accident investigator certification. Lacking support from John, he resorted to alliances with the ALPA Accident Investigation Board (AIB).

Yes, that is the same Robert Sumwalt who recently retired as the Chairman of the National Transportation Safety Board (NTSB). Robert would usually correct anyone who mistakenly believed that he preferred to be called "Bob." That resulted in his becoming known as "Robert 'don't call me Bob' Sumwalt." We shortened that to "Bobbert."

Soon after I became chairman of that committee, funding for an expanded presence became available. The opportunity to send our representative to the Icarus Committee arose. A little-known, but highly respected think tank of aviation leaders, Icarus had honored us with an invitation. I asked Robert to represent us there. Their next meeting was to take place in Kuala Lampur, Malaysia. His naivete being almost humorous, he asked, "How do I get there, when should I leave, what should I take?"

I said, "Just go. Get a jump seat or buy a ticket. We will cover all your expenses."

He attended the meeting on time and unsurprisingly was embraced by the committee. Whether he gained insight or political clout there remains a mystery to me, but I believe that experience helped vault him to the lofty position achieved with the NTSB.

33. ICAO, IFALPA, and HUPER

Boeing, in its development of the 777, chose to include experts from all quarters of aviation on its team. The 777 remains a hugely successful airliner. Because of that success and the uniqueness of the approach, the project was awarded the prestigious Robert J. Collier Trophy in 1995. In the words of the National Aeronautic Association, "…trophy is presented to those who have made the greatest achievement in aeronautics or astronautics in America, with respect to improving the performance, efficiency, and safety of air or space vehicles." In a magnanimous gesture, Boeing shared the trophy with the organizations which had participated in the design and manufacture of the aircraft.

That recognition was especially sweet for the ALPA Human Performance Committee, as we had worked closely with Boeing's Dr. Curt Graeber on the aircraft's automation design. The role of the flight crew in automated aircraft, or as we liked to say, "the role of automation in crewed aircraft," had morphed considerably since the advent of second-generation aircraft such as the 767. At ALPA, grave concerns began to emerge about engineering out the pilot in future aircraft. Some called it job security, be we called it safety. In response, the Human Performance Committee produced a document called "Automated Cockpits & Pilot Expectations: A Guide for Manufacturers and Operators." Authored principally by Michael Hayes, who succeeded me as Chairman of the Human Performance Committee, it established the ALPA position on new automation and continues to guide new designs today. Although it elaborated on each principle, the main ideas appear below.

Automated Cockpits & Pilot Expectations: A Guide for Manufacturers and Operators

1. Automation should not be able to remove the pilots from command of their aircraft.
2. Automation should not remove the pilots from direct involvement in the operation. Reduction in workload by performing mundane tasks is appropriate use, but some pilot involvement should be required in most cases, even when automation can perform the entire task.
3. Automation must keep the pilots informed of its actions. Only critical aspects of flight should be enunciated or those that affect the next state of flight.
4. Automation failures or malfunctions must be clearly enunciated to the pilots.
5. The automation behavior must be predictable to the average, trained pilot under all circumstances.
6. Automation should monitor the actions of pilots and should provide them timely warning when their actions pose a potential threat to safe continuation of the flight.
7. Automation should inform pilots of its intentions and should request consent for actions that may critically affect the conduct of the flight.
8. Automation involving modes of control known to be potentially hazardous should contain safeguards to prevent its use under inappropriate conditions.
9. Automation design should permit its use at some lower level of authority if stability augmentation systems fail. Even in the event of extremely improbable failures (e.g., 10^{-9}), controllability is paramount.
10. Marginally stable aircraft must be controllable even in the least capable flight control reversion mode. This is

33. ICAO, IFALPA, and HUPER

controllability backup.

11. Primary flight displays have become extremely complex. Certification and industry pilots must decide upon the appropriate level of complexity.

12. Particularly salient and flight-phase-specific information must stand out in displays. Discrimination of displayed information can be enhanced through the use of color, font size, highlight capabilities, line thickness and open space. Aural annunciation coordination between displays must also be considered as an integral part of display design.

13. The status of flight-critical automation should be obvious at all times, not only when some element has failed.

14. Flight management systems and their associated control-display units should be intuitive and provide cues for programming, particularly for seldom performed functions.

15. Reprogramming tasks which must be performed at high workload phases of flight should be simplified to minimize head down time (especially during terminal environments).

16. Flight management systems should incorporate the maximum internal error-checking to improve the error resistance of the entire system.

17. Automation management should be standardized across fleets to the extent possible, to minimize transition errors of pilots from other aircraft.

ICAO, or the International Civil Aviation Organization, sets safety standards and regulations for the global air transportation system. With nearly 200 member nation-states, it issues standards and recommended practices for airlines, airports, and air traffic services worldwide. As a signatory nation, the United States complies with the standards issued by ICAO.

IFALPA, or the International Federation of Airline Pilots' Associations, now headquartered in Montreal, has permanent membership on many ICAO panels and task forces to provide pilot input into technical areas such as aircraft design, airports, accident investigation, and human performance.

The US Airline Pilots Association, being an important member of IFALPA, plays a major role in the technical committees. Thus, by maintaining a strong presence in IFALPA, US ALPA and its representatives serve to develop policies and positions that are adopted by ICAO.

As head of the US ALPA Human Performance Committee, I traveled to Chertsy, U.K., to represent ALPA in the IFALPA Human Performance Committee (HUPER). What I found there at my first meeting surprised me. In a dreary building far from London ran an organization reminiscent of a World War II intelligence community. Strangled by obsolete tradition and cumbersome procedures, progress proceeded at a glacial pace.

An embarrassment of riches, I attended meetings that accomplished little, but enjoyed lavish hospitality. In the early days, meetings rotated between Chertsy and one of the member states. Capetown, Geneva, Stavanger, Auckland, Tokyo, Dublin, Singapore, all vied to be known as the best venue. The HUPER Committee had been led by European representatives for many years. Because of that, the tone of the meetings mostly reflected European interests, such as pilot licensing standards, which remain entirely different from those of the US. Sensing the unfairness of the focus on European issues, and in light of ALPA's funding the majority of the IFALPA organization, I complained to the ALPA President, Duane Woerth.

33. ICAO, IFALPA, and HUPER

Duane said, "Don, just stand down for a while. We must humor the Europeans. When the time is right, I'll advocate for you to become chairman."

In the meantime, I attended meetings chaired by a Sabena 747 captain. Loving the formality and tradition of the meetings, he wore his crown a little too tight.

True to his word, Duane managed to get me elected to chair the committee.

HUPER recommends policy to ICAO in three different areas: aeromedical, training, and human factors/ergonomics. We usually met for three days with a day devoted to each subject. A typical day for aeromedical might involve discussion pursuant to a policy on protecting pilots from ionizing radiation.

Several members of the committee combined their airline pilot careers with that of being a physician. Knowing their loathing for the term "quack," I always began those meetings by loudly blowing on my duck call.

Part of the cause of the pace of policy-making lay in the complete absence of communication between meetings. Typically, a volunteer working on a project would gather data and interview experts, then present a draft proposal at the meeting. After negotiating with representatives from thirty countries, they would retire and revise the paper, which would be presented again six months later. I suggested that for each subject, a working group should be organized, composed of everyone who might be interested. Further, that working group would communicate via email to produce a mature paper at the next meeting. That increased the throughput dramatically.

During the discussions on licensing and training, the committee devoted much time to the "Harmonization" of the new European Union (EU) standards with the extant British standards. With the emergence of Brexit, most of that was rendered useless. I suggested a more global approach to the subject, rendering the England/EU harmonization question to a lower level of priority.

In the ergonomics and human factors studies, ICAO was anxious to standardize the new electronic displays, especially the colors. Some of our work became adopted as standard. Also in its infancy, standards for crew resource management training for airlines needed attention. Our proposals eventually become ICAO policy.

In addition to meeting twice each year at wonderful venues for the HUPER meeting, as chairman, I was obligated to present our work at the IFALPA conference. This conference was an even more embarrassingly opulent five-day meeting in which the elected leaders allegedly made high-level decisions.

While performing these duties, I witnessed fundamental changes in the way pilots fly their aircraft. It proved to be one of the most rewarding periods of my life. The food and accommodations weren't bad, either.

As a safety geek, I had to keep the politicians happy. Here I am on the picket line.

33. ICAO, IFALPA, and HUPER

Walking the picket line

34. Big Dog on the Big Dog

On August 15, 2000, Delta took delivery of their first Boeing 767-400. The 21-foot stretch of the 767-300 provided increased capacity, range, and efficiency. Although almost 180,000 pounds lighter than the MD-11, the pay scale agreed upon between ALPA and Delta management gave the pilots more to fly the -400. Previously, pay scales had nearly always been on a per-pound basis. The dinosaurs flocked to the -400 from the unpopular MD-11 like rats deserting a sinking ship. Seeing an opportunity to sneak into a junior slot on the MD-11, I applied for the long shot. I had developed an appreciation for the airplane as a copilot, and was very happy to be selected to fly it as captain in the summer of 2000 (with the lowest seniority).

Having been awarded a rating on the MD-11 as part of my copilot checkout, I only needed a refresher course to become current. I noticed that the course had vastly improved since I had endured the long course in 1994.

Once fully qualified, I soon learned which trips were frequently thrown to the reserves. Short domestic trips to New York and Orlando allowed me to maintain my skills and visit with FAA air carrier inspectors, who were seldom seen on international flights. The next worst trip was to São Paulo, Brazil. Having to cross the intertropical convergence zone (ITCZ) near the equator, combined with the questionable safety while on the layover, made for a stressful trip.

34. Big Dog on the Big Dog

The ITCZ results from the eastbound trade winds on the north side of the equator meeting the westbound trade winds on the south side. Tall thunderstorms present challenges to those of us trying to provide a smooth flight for the passengers. Crossing the area in darkness necessitated reliance on the aircraft radar for weather avoidance.

Passengers usually noticed our passing over Venezuela and the northern coast of South America. This caused many of them to become anxious about our early arrival into Brazil. Not so fast, relax; we still have eight hours to go. Brazil is very large. Flying over the Amazon Basin felt little different from oceanic flights. The few lights could have easily been misinterpreted as ships at sea.

On one of those São Paulo flights, I was assisted by Randy and Joe, both former US Naval aviators. Obviously delighted at the reunion, they happily discussed their experiences both in the Navy and at Delta. When I left the cockpit for my scheduled break about two hours before the top of descent into São Paulo, they were still chatting enthusiastically. Later, when I returned, the chatter continued. However, the radios were silent.

"How long since you talked to Brasilia?" I asked.

"Oh, not long," they said in unison.

"Let's get a radio check."

"Brasilia, Brasilia, this is Delta five nine, do you read?" No answer.

"Let's try São Paulo on a different frequency," I said.

(On tuning to the new frequency) "Delta five nine turn right to heading two seven zero, descend to six thousand, and let me know when you are ready for the approach." Oops.

The Brazilian air traffic controller would have been completely justified in reporting us, but he never did. Thank you. Weasel and Snork (or whatever their Navy callsigns were) bought me dinner and we forgot about the whole thing.

Some of the Brazil trips continued to Rio de Janeiro the next day. On my first try at that, the copilot had some good advice: "Get slowed and have some flaps out before you drop down into the valley, it's like a fighter penetration." I'm glad he told me that. The procedure starts at 12,000 ft., calls for a steep dive down a valley, and ends with a sharp turn to an instrument approach and landing at sea level. Be nice to your copilot.

By my third year on the MD, trips had begun to improve. No longer relegated to the unpopular São Paulo and Mumbai, India, trips, I began to successfully bid to fly to Europe and Asia. In those days before electronic flight bags (EFB), pilots were obligated to carry paper maps and approach plates (instrument approach maps) for every destination airport and many alternate airports. That meant updating large binders full of dozens of sheets for each airport. With hours of updating the charts facing me before departing, I cheated. Updating only the charts for the departure and arrival airports and a few alternates, I concealed the remainder of the sheets in my flight kit. During the hours of boredom between reporting points over the middle of the ocean, I finished the job. Such activities, being potentially distracting, were prohibited. In reality, that kept me more awake than the quiet focus on the instruments. Modern cockpits are equipped with laptop computers with maps and much more information ready for quick access.

34. Big Dog on the Big Dog

My favorites: the Shannon Ireland Airport manager always gave the captain a free bottle of booze; I could fly the Tokyo/Narita trip and accrue twenty-six hours of flying while being away from home only three days; touring Paris and London while receiving pay seemed like stealing.

Zurich is nice, but the weather there isn't for sissies. In my career, I made five Category III landings (very low ceilings and visibilities), three of which happened at Zurich. Lying in a valley, the fog, although thick, is usually shallow. Category III landings require elaborate equipment on the aircraft and on the ground. To qualify for such an approach, the airport must have carefully calibrated and recently checked navigation equipment, as well as surface guidance lights embedded in the runway and taxiways. The aircraft is required to have triply redundant electronics such as autopilots, computers, and radar altimeters. No minimum cloud ceiling required, zero is sufficient. Horizontal visibility minimal requirements usually specify 200 meters. Once configured, the aircraft lands itself, with the pilot's duty being the initiation of a missed approach if any of the proper mode changes fail to happen.

It's a thing of beauty: with my hand on the takeoff/go around button (TOGA), the copilot announcing mode changes (flare arm, flare capture, touchdown, rollout) and radar altitudes (fifty, forty, thirty, twenty, ten, touchdown), the main wheels smoothly touch down and with the nose still high in the air, I can see nothing. The autopilot de-rotates the nose, and as the nosewheel touches down, I begin to see the runway. Auto-spoilers deploy, autobrakes deploy, I must select reverse thrust manually. The aircraft steers itself precisely down the center of the runway, and I begin to see the green lights embedded in the runway, leading off to a taxiway. I push the autopilot disconnect button on my yoke and follow the green lights, steering with the tiller.

Category III landings are restricted to being conducted with very little crosswind. What little that is permitted must be compensated for by touching down with a bank towards the wind and opposite rudder to prevent turning. This forward slip is used both in visual and instrument landings to avoid landing in a crab and overstressing the landing gear. During an approach, the computers accomplish this while still in the clouds. Just prior to landing (at 200 feet above ground level), align mode is entered, sometimes causing a strange "sideways" sensation among the passengers.

In an attempt to duplicate this process manually, I set up an approach in the simulator with no visibility and a strong crosswind. Trying my best to remain on the localizer course and glide path while aligning with the runway proved to be beyond my capabilities. Perhaps Chuck Yeager could have done it, but not I.

Following a pleasant layover in Paris, we flew on to Mumbai, India. Skirting north of Iraq, our track went over Romania, the Black Sea, Turkey, and Iran. Most of the controllers greeted us with a friendly enthusiasm, except for Iran. The standard procedure for transiting from one flight information region (FIR) to another involved contacting the next controller on a second radio to receive permission to enter. Entering the Tehran FIR usually went smoothly; however, the clearance from the Tehran AAA site always created anxiety in the cockpit. AAA means Anti-Aircraft Artillery. Before passing within fifty miles of Tehran, we were obligated to contact their military defense personnel for additional permission. The exchange always caused near panic.

"Tehran AAA, Delta four nine at flight level three seven zero, squawking 4350." No answer.

(In a higher-pitched voice) "Tehran AAA, Delta four nine at flight level three seven zero, squawking 4350."

34. Big Dog on the Big Dog

No answer.

We all had visions of a ground-based missile locked onto us, ready to fire if we penetrated the perimeter without permission. As we approached the arc of death on the navigation display, I spun the heading select around for a 180-degree turn, while getting ready to change from track to heading navigation mode.

As I reached for the button to command the change, "OK Delta, cleared into the Tehran Zone."

They had been waiting until the last minute to clear us. Whew, they really got us on that one. We should have learned better, because they did it every time. We usually transited Iran in the dark. Only one time, after a takeoff delay, we passed over the country in the daylight. I could clearly see the Azadi Tower.

The runway and the terminal building at Mumbai lacked many of the niceties that we have come to expect in America and Europe. Surviving the slick runway and claustrophobic corridors of the terminal, we were loaded into a bus to take us to our layover. The flight attendants all lived in India. Delta had negotiated a separate agreement to hire Indian citizens for the job. All four pilots boarded a bus which very much resembled a school bus from my childhood. A chain-link fence separated us from the driver and the uniformed guard, who held a shotgun. As we proceeded toward the hotel, we passed through some very poor sections of town. Fires burned for warmth along the streets, and large cardboard boxes housed many of the citizens. The windows of the bus rattled in unison with the pothole bumps, and a strange neon religious light fixture shone on us from the cab. Surreal in that moment, we eventually arrived at the opulent Taj Mahal Palace Hotel, the same hotel that was attacked in November of 2008. It and its staff could not have been more welcoming.

Hungry at 4:30 a.m., we usually gathered at the café. That is 4:30 because India time is a half hour from the rest of the world. At that early time, the café would be completely full of well-dressed locals, smoking cigarettes held backward and wearing white shirts. A daylight walk to the nearby Oberoi Hotel or the waterfront accosted the senses with sights, sounds, and fragrances. It was safe enough to browse the streets alone, but the street urchins tormented foreigners mercilessly. Ducking into a shop and sneaking out the back door would do little to escape the experienced beggars.

Taj Mahal Palace and Waterfront, Mumbai

34. Big Dog on the Big Dog

Mumbai Waterfront from my window

The flight back to Paris usually tracked a more southerly route over Oman, UAE and Saudi Arabia.

CRAF

The Civil Reserve Air Fleet (CRAF) enhances American military mobility resources. Dating from World War II, civil air transport has been used in wartime and other crises to help meet military needs. Generously compensated for their commitment, airlines agree to provide some of their resources when called upon. During the build-up prior to the Iraq War, Delta resources were summoned by the Department of Defense. Appealing to the patriotism of its aircrew members, Delta recruited volunteers to fly the missions.

My first mission began at Biggs Army Airfield (Ft. Bliss), near El Paso. That airport has its main runway parallel to and nearby to El Paso International Airport. After many years of carefully selecting the proper runway, I felt very strange landing at the other one. We delivered several hundred fully armed troops to Aviano, Italy.

Another pickup started at Manhattan, Kansas, near Ft. Riley. After loading and startup, the tower advised us that the parallel taxiway had been closed. That necessitated a 180-degree turn at the end of the runway. Happily accepting the clearance, I envisioned a wide area in which to reverse course. Arriving at the end of the runway for the turnaround, I realized that there was no such help. Facing a shutdown and tow back to the chocks, we scoured the manual for the minimum turn radius of the MD-11. The answer: 145 ft. The runway: 150 ft. wide. That assumed that the outboard main gear tire was precisely on the edge of the runway, and that the nose gear would swing the 145 ft. arc. On the MD-11, the pilots sit fifteen feet forward of the nose gear. I positioned the left wheel very close to the edge, turned the nose steering fully to the stop, advanced the left engine, and began the turn. The right edge of the runway approached, then passed behind me; I was floating over the grass praying for the wheel far behind me to remain on the pavement. It was over in a moment, and I found myself with a pounding heart, much like previous experiences in which I was in real danger. *Next time*, I thought to myself, *I will get a person on the ground to marshal me through that*. That experience added credence to the adage: "A pilot would rather die than look bad."

Initially, the Italian government would not allow CRAF flights to originate from Rome. It did, however, allow departures from Aviano Air Base, in northern Italy. My first flight to Kuwait was the second Delta CRAF flight to arrive there. The operation began with a delayed inbound flight and deteriorated into total chaos.

34. Big Dog on the Big Dog

With a military call sign of Reach 830Y, the flight path took us over Cairo and down the middle of the Red Sea. That kept us far away from Iraq. I never knew whether that was just to avoid hostile action or to be secretive. At the south end of the Red Sea, we made a sharp left turn, continued for several hours eastbound over the wastelands of Saudi, and then turned north for Kuwait.

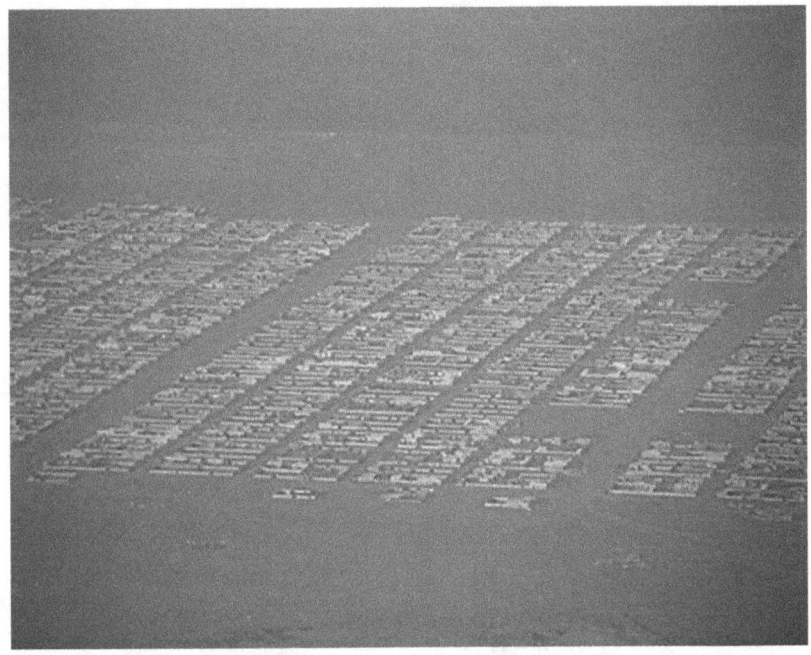

Troop Quarters near Kuwait City

Aeromorphosis

Kuwaiti Defenses

Landing Kuwait

34. Big Dog on the Big Dog

Lots of Cargo Arriving

Kuwait Nav Display

Aeromorphosis

"Reach" Flight Crew

Parked behind C-5, a shark look-alike.

34. Big Dog on the Big Dog

We were dispatched with two coordinators and a mechanic. The coordinators were nearly useless. They didn't have a cell phone that worked. Satcom was off and unavailable. I used my own cell phone to get some attention. We waited an hour for stairs to unload the troops. We waited two hours for fuel. We waited another two hours for a pushback. While waiting, we loaded the crew into a van and visited the nearby hotel. We bought sandwiches and T-shirts before leaving. Most disconcerting, a swarm of light utility vehicle (LUV) trucks mounted with 50-caliber machine guns manned by scruffy-looking teenagers paraded by us constantly. The most frustrating part was when the stairs were gone, no one would talk to us on the radio, and no tug appeared. We were trapped. Laying over there was a poor option.

Crew rest rules for commercial flying being not applicable, I began to plan a sleep schedule. Looking forward to a late-night approach into Aviano with poor weather, I needed someone to be wide awake. The excitement of preparing for departure from Kuwait City kept everyone wired. Halfway back, one of the copilots admitted to being a little sleepy.

"That's great, get some sleep and plan to fly the approach into Aviano," I said. Only then did I realize the value of having of a crewmember who is able to sleep amid the chaos.

This culminated in an approach to Aviano. We were fairly well rested considering the circumstances, because we had a very good sleep strategy. We were held high over Venice and told to contact Aviano Approach Control. At 10 miles from the airport, we were cleared for the non-directional beacon approach to runway zero five, a difficult and sometimes unreliable procedure. We had previously set up for the more accurate instrument landing system procedure, and no amount of begging would change the clearance. It is necessary to slightly overshoot the outbound leg due to the arrival geometry. There are 11,000-foot mountains on that side of the approach. Mercifully, we could see the terrain displayed on our navigation instruments. It was a challenging night, weather, non-precision approach, and First Officer Craig Stephens performed it flawlessly. We had been on duty for precisely 24 hours.

The CRAF duty got much better after that. The Italian government decided to allow us to base out of Rome, and the turnaround at Kuwait began to run smoothly. I volunteered to be temporarily based in Rome, exclusively flying the CRAF mission. Only after arriving there did I realize what I had gotten myself into. Most of the captains there were approaching retirement. Wanting to maximize their "final average earnings" for computation of retirement pay, they hogged all the flying. Nearly every day, I would drag myself into the scheduling office only to be told that there would be no flying for me that day. I would have to be content to spend another day touring Rome and the surrounding countryside. I flew a few more trips, once landing in a sandstorm. I'm still amazed that those engines can continue to function while ingesting that grit.

For the remainder of that year, I flew mostly Tokyo and Paris trips. On several trips, my wife accompanied me. Riding at reduced or free rates is an important benefit for airline employees. Utilizing available unoccupied seats, Delta has generously provided its employees with the ability to travel freely around the world, even though providing that privilege costs the airline due to extra weight, catering, and administration.

An apocryphal story that I love involved Tom Bebe, who retired as Delta CEO in 1980. In the early days, Delta executives always rode in the coach section. As the story goes, Mr. Bebe was seated in coach when the gate agent came aboard with an oversold problem.

34. Big Dog on the Big Dog

Not recognizing Mr. Bebe, and assuming him to be a freeloading "non-rev," the gate agent rudely commanded him to get his things and deplane. Bebe asked to speak to the gate agent in private.

"Just get your things and get off, like I told you," he said.

Bebe said, "Son, you no longer work for Delta Airlines. If we are going to offer this privilege to our employees, we are going to do it with dignity."

With that story in mind, the behavior of the personnel handling our gate in Paris had always irritated me. Their procedure involved seating the non-revenue passengers in a holding area far from the gate. Once the final count of passengers became known, the appropriate number of non-revs were dispatched to board. However, being far from the gate, they were told to run, lest they be left behind. On this particular trip, I instructed (or maybe suggested) to my wife that she should take her time getting to the gate, since I would not leave without her. Sure enough, it played out just as I had anticipated. As my wife slowly strolled to the gate, the agent attending the gate asked me if I would clear him to close the aircraft door.

"No, not until all the non-revs arrive," I said. He was beside himself for an on-time departure, but it was my call.

I don't know if I permanently affected their procedure, but it was certainly satisfying to dispense a little justice that day.

I bade farewell to the MD in January of 2004, finally accruing enough seniority to fly the 777. For all its quirks, I loved the MD-11. It had responsive flight controls, a comfortable cockpit, and, in the end, good reliability.

Aeromorphosis

Don in the MD-11

It was a big aircraft

35. T-Bird

"Don, do you want to buy half-interest in a T-33?"

"Yeah, Mark, that sounds interesting."

"Well, I did some work on a Cessna Citation for this guy in Brooksville, Florida, and he's out of cash and wants to give me the T-bird for the work."

"OK, let's go down there and look it over."

"No, you go look it over and either bail on the deal or bring it home. I'm too busy."

"OK, I'm on it."

Sandy Rosell was the FAA designated airman to grant pilots a letter of authorization (LOA) to fly the T-33. After looking over the airplane, I contacted him to fly the functional check flight (FCF) before accepting it.

The first flight was like the one at Holloman. Sandy was very reserved and a little grumpy, even though he was paid for the flight. After takeoff, there were several unacceptable squawks, including an inoperative pressurization system. Too heavy to land, he gave me the stick. I flew for a while and headed back to the field. As I rolled onto final (from the rear seat), I asked him to take over the landing.

He said, "Naw, you're looking good, just land it."

It was OK. I was confused about his behavior, though.

He explained: "The last dozen guys I have had in here were rich assholes who could not fly and demanded a thirty-minute LOA in an airplane that was going to kill them." We got along fine after that.

We flew two more FCFs before the seller reached his breaking point. Take it or leave it this time. The last one was my check ride. After a brief negotiation with the FAA, I was on my way to Texas with our new T-Bird.

It was a very special airplane. Rumor had it that the inventor of Nautilus Gym Equipment (a senior citizen) had bought a Canadian CT-133A Silver Star for his younger bride to fly. It was (and probably still is) the only T-Bird to sport an autopilot. Although it had been ten years since its rehabilitation, the black paint was shiny, and the avionics suite was modern. Being Canadian built, it had several features not found on the US version. The most obvious was the giant red light in the center of the instrument panel that illuminated for every takeoff. That was because the procedure was to select the emergency fuel control for takeoff, thus illuminating the light. I guess that was before human factors came up with the quiet, dark cockpit concept. The good part was the Nene-10 Rolls Royce engine, which had about 500 pounds more thrust than the J-33s found in the USAF T-33. The nose compartment had plenty of room for golf clubs due to the removal of the tube-driven avionics.

I managed to get it home to Uvalde that day, with only a few minor glitches. The first occurred at FL310 in the weather when the transponder failed. The controller graciously allowed me to continue in Class A airspace to Lafayette, LA. I managed to cock the nosewheel

35. T-Bird

there and get it uncocked (thanks, George). Arriving back home with too much fuel to land, I terrorized the tourists in the hills near the little town of Concan. Before I arrived, Mark (my partner and airport manager) had received several calls concerning a black jet flying low over the hills and maybe crashing.

There wasn't much left to do on the airplane. Its systems are simple and reliable. The engine was good for another 1000 hours. Maintenance was conducted according to its own FAA-approved plan, exempting it from the periodic inspections required by ordinary aircraft. I was obligated to get Mark up to speed for his LOA check ride. He had thousands of hours of citation time and was a world-class sailplane pilot.

After the ground school, we went flying. I gave him an excruciating lecture on the conduct of the SFO (simulated flameout) landing. He nailed the first one. I had forgotten about his sailplane experience.

N133AT

The T-bird was my ticket into the rich and famous club. I was invited to participate in the Rod Lewis T-28 formation clinic. In the beginning, T-28, T-6, and L-39 owners converged on the oil billionaire's South Texas ranch airport for formation flying training, whiskey drinking (only in the evening) and lying. The chief instructor was none other than the grand old man of aviation, Neil Anderson. I was his assistant. Neil has since passed, but in those days, it was fun to be around him. He, of course, was the guy who bellied in the #2 F-16 and walked away. Although famous for such a feat, he confided in me that it never flew again. Demonstrating the F-16 at the Paris Airshow brought him additional acclaim. Accompanying the entourage of diplomats and sales geeks, he helped consummate the sale of F-16s to Egypt. He told me a great story about flying the MiG-21 there. I have included that story in the blog found at www.aeromorphosis.com. His pilot license read like no other. It said this guy can fly anything he wants. He checked me out for my low-level airshow license.

Laredo Airshow Flyby

35. T-Bird

The whole entourage of about thirty airplanes would join up and fly to Laredo for their annual airshow. I led with Niel in the rear seat. I was to fly at 140 knots, which I did with some flaps extended so as to allow the T-6s to keep up. The conversation went so:

Neal: "Don, you are doing a great job."

OK, I thought, *what am I doing wrong now?*

Neal: "I see you are up to one hundred forty-two knots, watch that."

He always led with a compliment. After getting the gaggle to the airport and making a few passes, we split up, with the prop guys landing and Neal and I doing the airshow. It was mild by professional standards: Cuban eight, loop, barrel roll, four-point roll, tuck under pitch out. Even so, the crowd seemed to like it. We returned single plane. Arriving at the ranch, Neal asked what I planned to do. I responded with my plan for a mini-airshow. He agreed. As we got closer, the minimum fuel light illuminated, meaning 80 gallons left in the feed tank. I was already gang loaded, meaning every boost pump was on.

I said, "Let me rephrase that, I plan to do a straight-in, full-stop landing." It turned out that the main wing boost-pump circuit breaker had popped, but I couldn't figure it out in time.

Rod usually sent a jet to California to pick up Chuck Yeager. Chuck loved to shoot hogs while hanging out of Rod's helicopter on straps. Chuck has certainly been no stranger to controversy. In those days both he and his wife, Vicky, could not have been nicer. They both visited, laughed, and drank with the rest of us. He even acted interested in our amateur pilot stories. The opportunity to meet some of America's greatest heroes was certainly worth the price of admission.

Triple Ace "Bud" Anderson, Don, Flying Tiger "Tex" Hill

One morning, the T-28 pilots briefed their training flight and vanished, leaving only myself and the L-39 owner in the cabin. The previous night, he had regaled us with the prowess of the mighty L-39.

"It was perfect; it can go fast; it can go slow; it is so maneuverable, it can fly up its own asshole. It is the warbird to have," he boasted.

"Should we go fly?" I asked.

"Let's do it," he said.

I was to lead off. Once joined up, he was gyrating wildly, trying to fly fingertip formation. I suggested he go to trail formation. Once he called in position, I started a gentle barrel roll. He called out of formation. We tried it again with the same results. When I gave him the lead, I could stay with him through all his maneuvers. That night, I didn't miss the opportunity to remind him of what he had claimed

35. T-Bird

the night before and suggested he explain how an old T-Bird could do everything better that his L-39.

Someone said that 90 percent of T-Bird crashes happened because of fuel mismanagement. It was at once complicated and brilliantly designed. Without doing a complete ground school, a brief explanation follows: The two tip tanks held a total of 460 gallons. The two main wing tanks held a total of 154 gallons, the two leading-edge tanks held a total of 104 gallons, and the fuselage (feed) tank held 95 gallons. The only gauge was for the fuselage tank. Although it held 95 gallons, it could only read as high as 85 gallons, and when the dreaded low-fuel light came on, you had 80 gallons to figure out why it was getting low. The tips fed from pneumatic pressure from the engine and would feed before any of the other tanks. The remaining tanks had circuit breaker-protected fuel pumps.

Before takeoff, the fuel counter was set to 813 gallons. The system was gang loaded for takeoff, meaning everything on. After takeoff, the main wing and leading-edge boost pumps were turned off. The tips light was expected to illuminate at 350 gallons remaining. If not, the difference was trapped, unusable fuel. Usually, I forgot to watch for 350 on the counter and the low-fuel light would remind me to turn on the main wing boost pumps. After a few seconds, the light would go out and I would wait for 200 gallons, signaling they, too, were empty, and time to turn on the leading-edge boost pumps. That was a good time to think about landing, because the 95 gallons in the fuselage tank didn't buy you much time.

The feed tank principle allowed all the tanks to be completely used. It was a brilliantly designed system, but unforgiving for the careless. On local flights, I frequently removed the tip tanks. The airplane was 3,000 pounds lighter and had only 350 gallons for the flight. It was much nimbler in that configuration.

Aeromorphosis

In the book, *P-80/F-80 Shooting Star* by David R. McLaren, many photos of the F-80 appear in such a configuration. I highly recommend that book for a detailed history of that seminal jet. In that book, McLaren reveals the disposition of the first T-33. It is at the Lackland AFB museum in San Antonio. That is not a T-33, it's an F-94. Right, it's both. An F-80 was stretched to become the first TF-80/T-33. Later, that same airframe was converted to the first F-94. You can win a bet at the bar with that one.

The T-bird was a gas guzzler. A very accurate guess at fuel flow was simply to look at the airspeed indicator. Knots equals gallons per hour. Yes, whizzing along at 350 knots at 100 feet, you were burning 350 gallons per hour. Expensive? As the old adage goes, "When I signed on to this outfit, there were a hell of a lot of things they didn't tell me." Early on, fuel was 65 cents per gallon. Four hundred gallons cost $260—yes, it was worth it. I sold out of the deal at $2.00 per gallon. It eventually peaked above $5.00.

Air Force jets of the T-Bird vintage burned JP-4 fuel. Most civilian airports offer Jet A for business jets. Burning Jet A in the T-Bird resulted in "cokeing" or carbon buildups in the engine because of the lower flame temperature. The solution: fill the tanks with 2/3 Jet A and 1/3 Avgas (aviation gasoline) and you get "simulated" JP-4 or "homebrew." That procedure produced great results in the engine, but made for interesting conversations with the refuelers.

"I want you to put one hundred fifty gallons in the left tip tank, then put one hundred fifty gallons in the right tip tank (so it doesn't tip over). After that, top them off with Avgas," I usually said.

The response: "You're joking, right? You can't mix fuels; that will destroy your engine."

35. T-Bird

I don't know of any other airplane using such a procedure.

Shortly after one of the required inspections, Mark and I loaded up in the T-Bird to look at a citation that he was buying in north Texas. After takeoff, the hydraulic system failed. Aborting the flight, I turned back to home base. The emergency landing lowering procedure called for turning a valve to allow the emergency pump to pressurize the landing gear system. Having done that, I turned on the switch for the electric backup pump. In the three minutes that it took for the tiny pump to extend the landing gear, I suffered a thousand deaths thinking about the gear up landing in the offing. Once extended, I felt better, but the failed hydraulic aileron boost made the stick very heavy in roll. The winds were light, and we landed safely. I wouldn't want to try that in a strong crosswind, though. We rolled the airplane into the hangar, accusing the maintenance crew of forgetting to tighten something. The next day, we were told that they refilled the reservoir, went over the system, and could find nothing wrong! It performed perfectly fine after that. Raise your hand if you believe that!

The best part of owning such an airplane was giving rides. Going fast down low is one of the privileges of being a fighter pilot. My general aviation friends had no way to experience that rush until I showed up. My flight profile was preceded by a twenty-minute briefing on ejection seats and parachutes, which took 4 weeks in the Air Force.

"Just leave the seat pin in" was my advice. "If we need to eject, I'll send you out. If you think I am dead and you can't land the airplane, pull the pin and eject."

Dad and Daughter Lauren fly the T-Bird

After takeoff, we would climb up a bit and I would demonstrate some mild aerobatics and then give the passenger the stick. Most wouldn't pull enough G to make it work. Then we would get low and zigzag among the hills at high speed. I had a friend who owned a 25,000-acre ranch who agreed to let me fly low and fast over his place. I never had to explain my actions to the FAA. Among my passengers were my wife, my daughter, a retired admiral, my neighbor who built an experimental airplane, a future fighter pilot, a newspaper reporter, and a future crop duster. A few of them (including pilots) suffered mild airsickness. My advice: eat bananas before the flight. That won't keep you from becoming airsick, but they taste the same coming up as they do going down. One day I decided to fly without asking anyone or telling anyone. I pulled the T-Bird out of the hangar, fired it up, turned the radio off, and flew for an hour. Only in America.

36. 777

Anticipating the possibility of reaching the pinnacle of Delta's flying positions, I asked one of our 777 pilots, "Surely it can't be perfect. It must have a flaw."

"We don't have enough of them," he answered.

After spending some time flying them, I agree. All my complaints from previous transport aircraft had been recognized and resolved.

Its predecessors had an Inadequate Auxiliary Power Unit (APU): 777 APU can enable the air conditioners to cool a 130-degree cabin on the ground to 70 degrees in a few minutes. It can start both engines at the same time.

Accurate takeoff data: At 648,000 pounds, a V1 cut left plenty of runway to stop.

No surprising flight control gains: Landing in a 30-knot crosswind is much like landing a Cessna.

Others had inadequate crew rest facilities: The 777 "Condo" had bunks and first-class seats, good environmental control (quiet and cool), and a bathroom.

System reliability: All digital, most systems had on-board backups that could be switched easily.

Practically unlimited range: With capacity for up to 300,000 pounds, most of my trips loaded less than 225,000.

Rolls-Royce Trent engine with 90,000 pounds of thrust

Having participated in Boeing's *Working Together* group, I enthusiastically commend them for being good listeners. I remember discussing the cockpit design with Curt Graeber, chief of Boeing Human Factors. One item that I suggested failed to make the design. I favored the MD-11-style green light on the instrument panel which advised pilots that the aircraft had been properly configured for takeoff. Curt advised me that was incompatible with the quiet, dark cockpit, meaning that the absence of aural warning or lights meant "go." We also discussed the fly-by-wire reversion modes. I was concerned that the Airbus Aircraft do not allow pilots to easily select less automated modes of flight control. To his credit, the 777 has a prominent guarded red switch on the overhead panel that does just that. In the simulator, I selected the downgraded mode, and surprisingly, could perceive little difference in the flight controls.

36. 777

Few are even slightly concerned about boarding a twin-engine airliner for a transoceanic flight today. Such flights have proven to be very safe. Achieving this has been a long, cautious process call ETOPS, Extended range Twin engine Operations Performance Standards. In an abundance of caution, long overwater flights for twin-engine aircraft had been restricted to routes from which a diversion due to an engine failure could be accomplished in 60 minutes or less. As jet engines became more reliable, permission for routes farther from diversion alternates was granted. Airlines, seeking the efficiencies of twin-engine aircraft, and more direct routes worked tirelessly to prove the reliability of their aircraft and engines. Based on the IFSR, or in-flight shutdown rate ETOPS 120 (2 hours), 180 (3 hours), and eventually 370 were granted. Among the requirements for achieving ETOPS 180 or greater is an IFSR of less than 1 per 100,000 hours.

With a typical 777 engine costing about $24 million, airline managements are understandably conflicted when creating procedures for engine shutdown. On the one hand, the early detection and shutdown of a failing engine might result in the saving of millions of dollars. On the other hand, a reported engine shutdown might relegate the airline back to ETOPS 180, or less, extending the route length. Thus, an earlier procedure calling for an engine shutdown morphed into one calling for leaving a sick engine on a 777 at idle power. This kept the diminished engine available for any other emergency while avoiding an IFSR penalty. In my overwater operations, I never experienced any engine malfunctions at all.

By 2004, bankruptcy loomed on Delta's horizon. Many senior pilots, fearing the loss of their retirement, left early. I eventually retired just days before the official bankruptcy, but those early retirements opened the door for my promotion.

By a fluke of the promotion and training system, being between assignments, I was granted most of January off. Although anxious to begin training on the 777, avoiding January weather in the northern hemisphere is no small gift. I attended ground school and flight training in the simulator for most of February and began earning my pay in March.

Tom Richards gave me my transoceanic operating experience (TOE). A great instructor, his favorite expression: "I haven't ever crashed an airplane when I was wearing my lucky hat." I was afraid to ask him to try a landing without it.

Most of the Asia trips required a fully augmented crew, or four pilots, because the flight time was over twelve hours. Each crew consisted of two captains and two first officers, all rated in the aircraft. For the first time in my airline career I flew with my contemporaries as fellow captains: Gary Winsett, Jack Crofton, and others. I also encountered some old memes and a few new ones. One that I had not seen before was the weather expert. Rick, a part-time meteorologist, used his great knowledge of the weather to control the cockpit. Asserting that his data was superior to that provided to us by the company, he wanted to dictate speeds, altitudes, and courses. I prefer more reliable sources.

I flew mostly Atlanta to Tokyo-Narita trips. However, all of the 777 destinations offered pleasant layovers, such as Milan, London, and Paris and Frankfurt.

36. 777

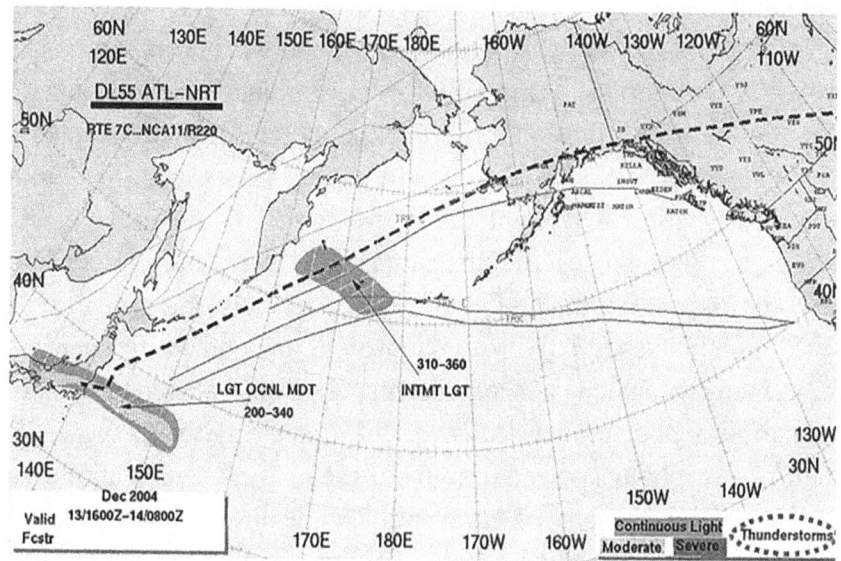

Follow the Dotted Line to Tokyo

The map above shows a typical track for the ATL-NRT route. Notice the "INTMT LGT" near the center. That shows that we were to expect intermittent light turbulence. On many trips, that area contained the dreaded MDT-SEVERE forecast. Although we diligently prepared for the worst turbulence, I never saw it. I think the weather forecasters placed those warnings there just to be super-cautious and for their job security. We frequently flew a more northerly route to take advantage of favorable winds. That took us deep over Siberia and over the Russian Sakhalin and Petropavlovsk Bases, a feat that had earned Korean Airlines Flight 007 a shoot-down in 1983. They had been deserted by the time we flew those tracks.

By the time I flew it, the 777 avionics had become very sophisticated. Satellite communications, both voice and data, enhanced the operation. As late as the 1990s, HF, or high-frequency radio communications, remained the norm for oceanic communications. Such communications, although sometimes able to span thousands of miles, have always been frustratingly unreliable. HF can travel via ground wave, in which line-of-sight between two stations is required. Sometimes, a ground wave curves under the ionosphere, and sometimes becomes a sky wave, bouncing off the ionosphere. Since the reflective portion of the ionosphere varies in altitude with sunspot activity and daylight, the sky wave may or may not connect two parties flying a specific distance apart. The resulting procedure calls for calculating the height of the ionosphere using time of day, season, and sunspot activity to choose one of a dozen frequencies for the attempt. Once chosen, a dead silence might be encountered, indicating a poor choice. Most of the time, a garbled, crowded, staticky cacophony spewed from the speaker. If communication was deemed possible, many others would also be attempting to provide their (mandatory) position reports. Told to stand by, we would wait until control called for our report. Amid the static, several repeats always became necessary. At that point we frequently had already arrived at our next reporting point, and just gave them two reports. We joked that even though we were flying the latest, greatest hardware, communication remained exactly as in the 1930s.

Many forms of information flowed via satellite. Intermittently, a chirp could be heard in the cockpit, indicating that a maintenance report had been transmitted to Atlanta, containing engine performance, flight conditions, and systems status.

"Are you as worried about that right engine oil pressure? It looks a little high to me," read the message from flight control. We hadn't noticed.

"No, we think it's nothing to worry about," we replied.

Controller to Pilot Data Link Communication (CPDLC) had only just begun. A typical interaction might start with a request by the pilots. Typing the request to the controlling agency (mostly Tokyo in the

Pacific), might ask for a higher cruising altitude due to turbulence. If approved, the return message would authorize the climb, and opened boxes, if selected, confirmed acceptance of the clearance, and automatically loaded it into the flight-management system. Once executed in the FMS and allowing the climb by changing the altitude in the mode control panel, the throttles advanced and the aircraft would begin its climb. Such clearances were made possible by the controlling agency exactly knowing our position in relation to nearby traffic. Automatic Dependent Surveillance – Broadcast (ADS-B) enabled that. Every few seconds, our aircraft would send its GPS position via datalink to the controllers, resulting in a very accurate display of the far distant aircraft on the tracks.

Today, ADS-B is required for all aircraft transiting large airports in America. However, the domestic system uses line-of-sight radio communication rather than satellite, resulting in a minimum useable altitude of a few thousand feet. CPDLC is required for oceanic operations as well. Aircraft lacking that capability must contend with less than optimal altitudes and routes.

Flying the North Pacific Tracks

Having fought the "Condo" battle with the company, ALPA prevailed in the configuration of the arriving 777 aircraft. Complete with a bathroom, two bunks, and two first-class seats, the forward rest facility was positioned above the forward part of the passenger cabin. Made possible because of the purely circular shape of the fuselage, the headroom measured almost six feet. Access was obtained via a door near the left forward entrance passenger door and a stairway. The rear rest facility for the flight attendants contained several bunks and no chairs.

Rest Break in the 777 (Dozing for Dollars)

36. 777

My favorite stop in Narita was the Jet Lag Club, owned and operated by Vincent Zimmerman, a former Sabena flight attendant, and his wife Sayaka. Newly opened when I first began flying the route, Vincent solicited our advice for making his club more welcoming. I suggested that he should offer popcorn as a snack to accompany beverages. Vincent complained that with Japanese tax, such a luxury would cost thousands of dollars. After some research, I discovered that I could purchase such a machine for a few hundred dollars, and that it would fit nicely in the forward coat closet of the 777. With his approval, I purchased it and brought it to work.

During the preflight briefing with the flight attendants, I asked the on board leader of the flight attendants (OBL, the chief flight attendant) if I might place a large package in her forward coat closet, requiring her to make a few changes. With her approval, I loaded it and launched for Tokyo. Arriving in Japan, and after all the passengers had deplaned, I announced to the station manager, Craig, that I had fulfilled my part of the bargain. His part would be to move it into town. I don't want to know how he did it, but he and the machine arrived at the club a few hours later. I became modestly famous for bringing the "Don Smith Memorial Popcorn Machine," and never was asked to pay for another meal or drink again.

Vincent Zimmerman at the Jet Lag Club

Aeromorphosis

The Illegal Popcorn Machine

Having requested early retirement and being granted such, I flew what I thought was my last flight on August 23, 2005. Deciding to cut and run with my 50 percent lump sum retirement pay and with little prospect of receiving the other half after bankruptcy, I made a difficult choice. A Narita trip, the experience went very smoothly, but it was bittersweet. The flight attendants announced to the passengers that I was retiring and most offered their congratulations. We had a small party at the Jet Lag Club, and awoke the next day for the return home. After we pushed back from the gate, all the Delta Narita ground crew

36. 777

lined up on the ramp, and as I pushed up the throttles to pull away, they all bowed deeply. An emotional moment, I will never forget that.

Leaving NRT

Back in Atlanta, I received the traditional water spray from the fire department and plaque from the chief pilot.

Hosed by the fire department. I thank them for being there all those years.

Aeromorphosis

Last Wave from the Cockpit

Don't let the gate bang you in the butt on the way out

But wait, it's not over yet. Delta, having had most of their 777 captains retiring, experienced a sudden inability to crew its largest aircraft. In a happy agreement with ALPA, Delta hired us back as

36. 777

contract pilots for a few months as they trained our replacements. We were to receive the same pay, but be on reserve. Being accepted into that program, I flew my last trip as a contract pilot on Dec. 21, 2005. During that period of reserve, I agreed to long-call duty, and a two-hour short call.

My relatives owned a beautiful cabin near Blairsville, Georgia, a 2 ½-hour drive to the airport. At first, when the short call window opened, I dutifully drove closer to the airport for the duty period. One day, while waiting for a call to report from the closer location, I had an epiphany. The odds of being asked to show up in two hours were practically nil. If that actually happened and I failed to report, what would they do? Fire me? I spent the rest of short call in the mountains. They never called.

My last, last trip flew to Narita. It began as a very routine trip until the landing weather uplinked. The winds had become strong and were gusting to 45 knots of crosswind. Since Narita has two runways, both running in the same direction, a diversion to Nagoya or Haneda loomed. How much crosswind can a 777 handle? The manual defines demonstrated crosswind as 38 knots. The exact definition of demonstrated crosswind is clear: test pilots successfully landed the airplane in that condition. To the pilots, the meaning of that is not clear. My interpretation: if you want to try to land in more that the demonstrated number, it is legal, but if it doesn't go well, it's on you. However, if it doesn't go well at less than the demonstrated, it's still on you.

I was reminded of the line in the Clint Eastwood movie, *Dirty Harry*, "Do you feel lucky, punk?"

A Nagoya diversion, although an approved airport, would leave the passengers at a place they didn't want to be. A Haneda diversion (the Tokyo domestic airport) would mean customs and immigration backlash.

Tough call: I decided to land at Narita. On final approach about 2 miles out, still in a crab, the nose pointed more than 30 degrees right. At a mile out, I banked into the wind and applied left rudder. Bless Boeing, the powerful flight controls easily performed the maneuver without coming close to reaching the stops. To lighten the rudder pressure, I added power to the right engine while reducing that of the left engine. Much like landing a Cessna in a 20-knot crosswind, the upwind main gear touched down first, and as the aircraft slowed, the left main landed. It was easy. Even if my superiors disagreed with my decision, that was my last trip in the 777; I never heard any criticism.

I felt good about my exit from the company. After 29 years, and 20,000 hours of flying, I had bent no metal, passed all my check rides, made good money, answered a half-dozen bad letters (balanced by about the same number of good letters), and enjoyed it tremendously. It was a good gig.

37. Fido

"Delta one two, cross thirty miles north of Atlanta at ten thousand, two hundred fifty knots," says the air traffic controller. Our aircraft is a Boeing 777, which weighs 500,000 pounds and is cruising at 82 percent of the speed of sound with a 120-knot tailwind. I type the crossing restriction into the flight-management-system computer. The top-of-descent marker appears slightly ahead on the navigation display. As we begin our descent, I am very aware of the tremendous amount of energy that the aircraft carries: by my calculations, the equivalent of about thirty tons of TNT.

Before September 11, 2001, the thought would not have occurred to me. Until then, the airlines' security training consisted mostly of preemptory procedures, avoiding gunplay, and politely accommodating a hijacker's demands. After 911, everything changed. Now we flew a potential weapon with the power of a small nuclear device. The cockpit had become a fortress which could not be breached under *any* circumstances. Additionally, pilots were authorized to carry weapons, after proper training and certification.

Called the Federal Flight Deck Officer (FFDO) Program, the nickname "Fido" quickly emerged. The program, authorized in 2003, was slow to mature. I volunteered soon after the program's authorization, but waited until 2004 for an invitation.

"The TSA collects information in order to evaluate an applicant's cognitive, psychological, medical, and physical skills before an applicant may enroll in training," says their impact assessment. In a paper shuffle reminiscent of my nuclear weapons clearance, my past received microscopic scrutiny. Surmounting that, I received a two-hour grilling by a professional psychologist in Atlanta. After that, I received an invitation to attend training at the Federal Law Enforcement Training Center (FLETC) at Artesia, New Mexico.

Arranging time off from my flying duties, I set out for the desert. Delta management, being reluctant to accommodate the program, had no choice but to allow it to proceed on its property, due to the strict wording of the Arming Pilots Against Terrorism Act. Strictly voluntary, none of us were compensated by our airline or anyone else for the training. In fact, we were required to pay for our accommodations and meals at Artesia. The room and meals satisfied our basic needs. The price was very low, $30/day, probably subsidized somehow.

Most days began with a few hours of classroom lectures, followed by shooting at the range in the afternoon. Nearly all of us brought a familiarity with firearms. Border Patrol veterans taught us at the range. Every one of them had been in a gunfight.

The sky marshal program proceeded alongside ours. However, our jurisdiction, being only the cockpit, only called for fast draw and rapid fire at close range. The sky marshal program demanded Olympic-level marksmanship from them. I believe we shot several thousand rounds during the week I was there. The evaluation of physical skills proved to be very modest. No strenuous hikes, or sweaty exhaustion sessions being required. We received some instruction in hand-to-hand combat, but as a twenty-five-year student of martial arts, I enjoyed it.

37. Fido

Considerable resources had been expended to make the cockpit training very realistic. A real Boeing 727 provided us with such an environment. As a left-handed captain, I had an advantage in the training scenarios in that the simulated intruder entered the cockpit from my right side. I was easily able to draw with my left hand and point the weapon across my right side. Left-handed copilots (sitting in the right seat), and right-handed captains enjoyed no such advantage. The two-second cockpit breach, even though simulated, managed to get the adrenaline flowing. We drew and fired wax bullets at an intruder wearing protective gear.

On one occasion, as a test for the copilot, the cockpit breach happened. He properly drew and fired. The simulated hijacker fell to the floor, whereupon my copilot proceeded to empty the remainder of his bullets into the attacker's crotch.

"Wow, that was really something, why did you do that?" I asked.

"I don't know, I guess I was just excited. It seemed like a good idea at the time," he replied.

At the end of the week, a graduation ceremony was held in which we received our credentials and a new Heckler and Koch (H&K) .40-caliber semiautomatic pistol. We had been promoted to Deputy Federal Marshals.

FFDO Class June 2004

Most law enforcement officers (LEOs) carry their weapons with them on airline flights. The gate agent for departing flights was required to attach a form to the usual paperwork if a person with a gun would be riding in the passenger cabin. Bypassing normal security, they entered the secure area of an airport via a special lane in which credentials were verified.

Every time I approached the official guarding that lane, a very bored-looking officer would say, "Captain, you're in the wrong lane. You should go through security over there."

I would show my credentials and pass. They never got used to seeing a pilot passing through the LEO lane.

Bypassing security was a sweet revenge for the harassment that I had received from the TSA previously. In those days, the pilot/TSA relationship was acrimonious at best. Federal regulations required

37. Fido

pilots to carry a flashlight, which the TSA considers a weapon. Wings and nametags frequently tripped metal detectors, requiring partial disrobing for access.

Returning from Paris into Cincinnati (as a flight crew member), their local protocol required me to pass through security. Non-standard as that was, their ancient metal detectors fired at the slightest provocation. After firing the lights on the metal detector several times, there I was with my shoes, belt, wings, hat, nametag, and epaulettes off, standing on one foot with my arms outstretched, while TSA checked the bottom of my feet. The awaiting passengers were amused.

The FFDO program encountered much opposition early on. The criticism arose from airline management and professional law enforcement. The objections from law enforcement agencies has mostly subsided, owing to the near-perfect statistics achieved by the FFSOs. No other agency can boast of only one accidental discharge in their history. While serious, that single incident occurred in 2008 aboard an USAir flight with no injuries.

Law enforcement officers with the largest egos and smallest jurisdictions

38. MRO

After retirement from Delta, I enjoyed flying my MX-7 Maule from the grass runway on my farm for a while. Growing restless, I applied for a job at a nearby maintenance, repair, and overhaul (MRO) facility. My friend, Jay Finney, a retired two-star admiral, had previously worked there and advised me to stay away. Disregarding his good advice, I signed up to be their director of sales and test pilot.

The testing mostly involved certification of avionics for Reduced Vertical Separation Minima (RVSM) and new engines on the Cessna Citation series. RVSM allowed aircraft flying above 28,000 ft. to be separated by only 1,000 ft. instead of the previous 2,000-foot minimum. This doubled the amount of aircraft able to fly that airspace. However, rigorous testing was required in order to receive clearance to fly there.

The test flights became routine, but sometimes almost comical. The typical test flight to certify an aircraft to climb into RVSM airspace often encountered a lack of understanding from air traffic control.

"November one two three four requests flight level four one zero for RVSM certification," I said,

"November one two three four are you RVSM certified?" ATC says.

"Negative, this flight is a RVSM certification flight, we don't have it yet."

38. MRO

"Unable to clear you above flight level two eight zero without RVSM certification"

Tedious at best, we eventually fulfilled the mission.

One of the modifications that the company installed was a short takeoff and landing (STOL) kit that enabled the Cessna 210 and 206 series to fly very slowly and improve takeoff and landing performance. Test-flying a Turbo 206 that had recently been modified, I was obligated to conduct stalls and slow flight to confirm the enhanced performance. One of the salesmen in the office, a flight instructor, accompanied me on the flight. The modification of this particular aircraft had been supervised by a relative newcomer to the process. Slowing to a speed that a docile, straight-ahead stall would be expected, the aircraft snapped into an inverted attitude. Although easy to recover, it certainly got my attention. The cause: the new mechanic had installed the cuff of the right wing a few millimeters too far back, creating a situation whereby one wing stalled before the other.

I said, "Ron, the bad news is that we are going to do that again with the flaps down."

Under extreme protest, he remained in the aircraft during the second maneuver.

As sales director, I received an initiation in an industry fraught with complexity. One of the aircraft that we had modified had been repossessed by a bank and remained in default for payments to us. I contacted the (lady) banker in charge of the matter and inquired about their selling it and paying us. I advised her on a fair price. After a long delay, we received payment. She had sold it to her boyfriend for half price.

After a year of that, the test flights became scarce, and the subterfuge of aircraft sales weighed heavily. I decided to move on.

39. JET SET

Curious about corporate aviation and business jet operations, I applied for a job with a San Antonio management group that flew a Socata TBM-750 and two North American Sabre 65s. A precursor to today's TBM-900, the TBM-750 offered good comfort for six people and a 230-knot cruise. I only flew it on a few trips, but one maneuver in the checkout remains vivid in my memory. Similar to many powerful propeller-driven aircraft, the throttle demanded a smooth hand. Advanced too rapidly, the engine would induce a torque roll that overpowered the flight controls. On a missed approach (go around), the procedure called for advancing the throttle to 80 percent torque and then waiting for the power to stabilize before further advancing the throttle to full power. To dramatize the necessity, the incorrect procedure was demonstrated. With the landing gear and flaps extended, I pushed the throttle to the stop. Anxiously awaiting the result, I prepared to apply full aileron and rudder when the roll to the left began. In a heartbeat, we rolled inverted against my application of full opposite controls, and I was really ready. No further urging was required for me to be gentle on the throttle.

I flew the North American Sabre 65 for three years. A refinement of the early Sabreliner 40, it was based on the USAF T-39 VIP transport. Being derived from the F-86, it is the only business jet certified for aerobatics. The 65 model that I flew came equipped with a supercritical wing and larger engines (Garret TFE-731), enabling higher cruising speeds. Plagued from its inception with poor steering and brakes, many of the T-39s were lost due to ground accidents. Even in the upgraded models, pilots were prohibited from the use of nosewheel steering on takeoff above a few knots for fear of a steering hard over. In a strong crosswind, the rudder being insufficient at low speeds, violations of the rule became necessary.

With seating for seven passengers, and a 440-knot cruise, the airplane performed well. My old friend, Dean Howard, and I alternated pilot/co-pilot duties. Frequent destinations included the New York area, Aspen, Cabo San Lucas, Florida, Bahamas, Toluca, Kalispell, and St. Maarten.

Preparing for a trip to Montana, the owners drove up to the aircraft in a large truck filled with hunting gear.

"Load 'em up, boys," they said.

What? I'm a 777 captain, you can't talk to me like that, I thought.

I thought wrong. We schlepped their baggage, tied it down, and flew the trip. I discovered corporate flying to be dramatically different from the airline life I had left.

On a flight departing Toluca, near Mexico City, with the owner sitting in the jump seat, Dean planned to fly through a rain shower.

"Don't fly through that rain, I just had this airplane painted, and I don't want it damaged," he said.

Such was the captain's authority. Humiliating as that was, the layovers were luxurious. Rather than incurring the expense of flying the aircraft back to home base, the owners often would invite us to stay at their destination without flight pay, but with generous accommodations. We logged several all-expenses-paid vacations at Aspen, Cabo, and St. Maarten.

39. Jet Set

Dean Howard in Sabre 65, photo by author

Preparing for a flight from Laredo to Houston, I noticed that one of the passengers spoke no English. Later, I discovered that she had been hired as a nanny, but lacked immigration credentials. Circumventing the border patrol highway checks for such illegals in a multimillion-dollar jet seemed to be "pound foolish."

Great range and plenty of power made it a pleasant aircraft to fly. Nonstop from Houston to St. Maarten was the longest flight in my log. Landing at Princess Juliana Airport at St. Maarten requires one to pass low over the beach when landing to the west. With a 7,600-foot runway, no necessity existed for us to land on the first few feet of the runway. However, larger aircraft needed all of it.

Air France Airbus 340 lands at St. Maarten

The Toluca, near Mexico City, at 8,400 ft. elevation, challenged the takeoff performance of many aircraft. The Garrett engines met that challenge easily.

Being an exceptionally clean aircraft, descent into Aspen became problematic. Even with all drag extended, the required descent was too steep, requiring some low-altitude maneuvering to land.

Insurance required annual recurrent training. We accomplished that at Flight Safety in St. Louis. The owners paid the $10,000+ training bill, but justifiably demanded that the pilots earn their keep by flying many hours. Lesson learned: if you are rated in a business jet and have not had recurrent training in the last year, you are not marketable.

Berkshire Hathaway acquired Flight Safety International in 1996. They also insured the Sabre. I suppose that it is fair for the company that insures your jet to demand that your pilots receive recurrent training at the place of their choice, even if they own that too.

39. Jet Set

If I were a young person considering a career in corporate aviation, I would, of course, first examine the pay and benefits. Perhaps more importantly, the way flights are scheduled can make one's life pleasant or miserable. Large flight departments and considerate private owners publish a *flight schedule* months in advance and stick to it.

"Don, can you get to Laredo in two hours for a trip to New York?"

"Since I can fly down there in my Maule, I think I can make that."

Such scrambles are best left to Air Force fighters on alert. Dean moved on to manage and fliy a PC-12 for a very considerate owner who published the flight schedule far in advance.

The job provided me with a window into the lives of the rich and famous. For about $1,000,000 per year, the owners were able to travel with the greatest of ease. A typical launch from New York found a stretch limo pulling up to the jet, which we had prepped for hours. As Dean closed the door, I engaged the engine starter switch, and soon were rolling. Not cheap, but very, very convenient.

With frequent late-night arrivals at Laredo, I headed for home in Uvalde in darkness. Buzzing the house signaled my wife to drive the runway, frightening the deer away. Accomplishing that, she would position her vehicle's headlights so as to illuminate the first part of the runway. Lacking runway lights proved to be unimportant because I could easily see the white caliche runway with the landing lights on the airplane.

40. Flunt

Retiring to the farm in Uvalde, I decided to build my own airport. The property is about a mile long and a half mile wide. A seasonal river lies at one end, and a highway at the other. It is roughly shaped like the state of Indiana. I decided to construct my runway along the side that looked like the west side of Indiana. However, a stream bisected the planned runway, and a power line passed over it, near the center. With a 32-inch culvert and yards and yards of fill, I conquered the stream. The local electric co-op offered to bury the wire for $20,000. I declined, planning to take off and land underneath it. After much earth moving, grass planting, and rock picking, I had a 5,200-foot-long by 150-foot-wide grass runway.

Early on, my friend from Delta, Paul Natho, landed his Cessna 180 there, becoming my first guest. Over the subsequent years I flew a Cessna 120, Maule MX-7, RV-6, BE-58 Baron, and V-35B Bonanza from there.

Surprisingly, the wire over the middle of the runway never impacted traffic. Departing, as one gathered speed, the wire passed overhead just before flying speed was attained. On landing, touching down in the first 2,500 feet was easily done, followed by rolling out beneath the wire. Many a fixed landing gear pilot flew down the runway and beneath the wire, but no one ever performed that trick with the landing gear retracted. No one ever damaged an airplane there, either.

40. Flunt

An avid bird hunter, I had hosted an opening-day dove hunt since the 1960s. Once the runway became complete, it only made sense to invite my friends to fly in for the annual hunt. Thus, the fly in and hunt was born, the "Flunt." Although never approved for airshows, the setting was sufficiently remote that the aircraft "demonstrations" never caught the attention of the authorities. Some of the more spectacular shows featured aircraft such as the T-28, T-38, F-16, P-51, T-33, UH-1, and Pitts S-2. Other demonstrations included formation flybys, toilet paper cutting, and flower sack bombing.

In the early days we drove the 70 miles to Mexico, and enjoyed dinner and drinks there. By the late "oughts" (2008), the cartel spoiled that. Bar-B-Que and a featured speaker highlighted the weekend. Neil Anderson of General Dynamics test pilot fame; Alan Price, Delta Chief Pilot; Marion Griffith, Braniff Concorde pilot; Lt. Gen. Steve Polk and others enlightened us about their unique aviation experiences.

Flunt Group

T-28 with Smoke

Ray Stallings and his CJ-6

40. Flunt

Conrad Huffstuttler in Waco

Pat Wilson and Waco courtesy of Larry Pullen

Aeromorphosis

Siai Marchetti on takeoff

P-51 Low Pass

40. Flunt

Mark Huffstuttler attempting to cheat during the flower sack bombing contest

Alan Bloxsom and his UH-1 Huey

Aeromorphosis

I wanna do that someday

The hangar; the Baron fit in it with 3-inch wingtip clearance.

40. Flunt

Don's Baron photo by Larry Pullen

1969 Hunt with Air Force Pilot Training Classmates Lafon, Webb, Schornstheimer, Huusom

Aeromorphosis

Early group 2004

Hangar 2002; Pullen photo

40. Flunt

Don in Waco by Pullen

T-28 climbing; Pullen photo

Retirement party 2005

Over the years that we gathered at the Flunt, little changed. Although the airplanes got faster and more expensive as we prospered, camaraderie and story-telling remained staples.

As a teenager, and a Boy Scout, I had immersed myself in aviation to the point that I looked forward to earning their Aviation Merit Badge. I bought the pamphlet and accomplished all the requirements on my own. I then contacted Art Chaney, a local insurance agent who had previously served as a DC-6 flight engineer. He was not aware that he had been "volunteered" to become a merit badge counsellor.

"I didn't know I was supposed to do that, but c'mon over and we'll work it out," he said.

We had a great time talking about airplanes, and he approved my work.

During the period of the Flunts, Jim Maixner approached me to become a counselor for the Boy Scouts of America and their aviation merit badge. Recalling my experience many years before, I agreed.

40. Flunt

After a very tedious application process, I was approved. On the appointed day, he brought ten of his scouts for their experience. Expecting them to show me their work, my concept proved to be severely outdated. They expected me to put on a show for them and then sign their applications. We meticulously satisfied all the requirements and I gave them a ride in the Bonanza. I think many of them were a little bored with my discussions. That is a change worth noting.

In 2011, I hosted the "First Annual Last Flunt." As the regulars and myself had grown long in tooth, the title proved to be prophetic. After more than 40 years of camaraderie, flying, hunting, storytelling, and partying, the time had come to pull the plug.

As President Lincoln said, "The world will little note nor long remember what we say here, but can never forget what they did here." While the Flunt was never intended to memorialize the brave pilots who gave their all for their country, it did honor those present who came sufficiently close.

41. ERISA

Since I was due to retire at age 60 on Sept. 17, 2006, the looming Delta bankruptcy did not seem to be too important. After all, the Employee Retirement Income Security Act (ERISA) of 1974 protected my pension.

According to the Department of Labor:

"The Employee Retirement Income Security Act of 1974 (ERISA) is a federal law that sets minimum standards for most voluntarily established retirement and health plans in private industry to provide protection for individuals in these plans. ERISA requires plans to provide participants with plan information including important information about plan features and funding; sets minimum standards for participation, vesting, benefit accrual and funding; provides fiduciary responsibilities for those who manage and control plan assets; requires plans to establish a grievance and appeals process for participants to get benefits from their plans; gives participants the right to sue for benefits and breaches of fiduciary duty; and, if a defined benefit plan is terminated, guarantees payment of certain benefits through a federally chartered corporation, known as the Pension Benefit Guaranty Corporation (PBGC)."

Properly vested and entitled to withdraw half of my retirement as a lump sum, I saw no need to doubt that my retirement would be safe. As the bankruptcy approached, the doubters began to retire as early as five years, fearing loss of their 50 percent lump sum.

41. ERISA

The doubters ranged from the most senior far down to the barely vested. The good news for me was that many senior pilots took early retirement, advancing my own seniority. (I retired as number four on the system seniority list.)

Delta's problem, like that of General Motors and other large corporations, was funding the defined benefit (DB) plan. Requiring billions of dollars to fully fund the promised retirements, the funds had become woefully inadequate. Unlike defined contribution plans (DC), in which the retirement funds are kept in the retiree's name, these corporations owned the accounts and became the "fox guarding the henhouse."

How were these corporations allowed to raid the pension funds when ERISA specified that they should fully fund vested benefits? In Delta's case, it happened in smoky backrooms filled with negotiators with questionable motives.

As the bankruptcy loomed, management began reaching out to the employees for concessions. Cash, of course, became a hot commodity. Where better to obtain huge sums than from reduced contributions to the retirement fund. I have never been privy to the details of the negotiations, but among the surviving ALPA members who were involved, I have gathered some rumors.

In exchange for underfunding the retirement fund, ALPA pilots received various compensatory concessions such as non-furlough and stable salaries. Explicitly stated in the agreement: in the event of bankruptcy, the beneficiaries of the underfunded DB plans would be "made whole."

We bought that story, but the bankruptcy judge did not. As debtors in a bankruptcy case, we pilots just had to get in line with the rest of the debtors. That promise made, even if in good faith, was technically illegal. The Pension Benefit Guaranty Corporation (PBGC), whose duty is to compensate employees for lost pensions, never planned to pay us the whole retirement. One of my friends who retired early had his monthly retirement check cut by a third. The second half of my retirement vaporized.

The result of that flurry of bankruptcies was the general abandonment of defined benefit plans in favor of defined contribution plans. For a young person just beginning their career, their company's offer of matching up to 6 percent of their salary offers a stable retirement, with all funds owned by the employee. However, the employee's participation is optional, possibly encouraging an extravagant lifestyle at the expense of retirement funds.

The possible words on my tombstone: "He took the hit so that DC plans might prosper."

42. AirVenture

Observing the Concorde land on an 8,000-foot runway initiated me to the thrills of the Experimental Aircraft Association's "AirVenture" at Whitman Regional Airport in Oshkosh, Wisconsin.

That happened in 1985, and I have had many happy returns.

According to the EAA: "Action, education, innovation, and everything in between makes EAA AirVenture Oshkosh your perfect, affordable, family-friendly destination!

"For seven days from sunrise to well past sunset, your days at Oshkosh are filled with dazzling displays of world-class aerobatics, forums and hands-on workshops, diverse aircraft spanning all eras of flight, historic evening programs, two-night air shows, and much, much more. Only in Oshkosh can you experience all of these activities in one week."

From my experience, all that is true. It's so big and elaborate, it defies description. With an attendance of 600,000+ people, 10,000 aircraft, 1,000 forums/workshops, and 1,000 vendors, one must see it to believe it. Originally conceived as an annual convention for homebuilt aircraft enthusiasts, it has grown to embrace every aspect of recreational, commercial, military, and astronautic aviation. It is an almost 70-year-old institution. My attendance began at its halfway point. Of course, it has grown, and that growth has necessitated procedural changes. For a week in July, Oshkosh is the busiest airport in the world. To accommodate 10,000 aircraft transiting the airport, the published procedures (NOTAM) are more than 30 pages long.

Daily airshows are scheduled Monday–Saturday from 2:30 until 6:00 p.m. For those of us flying 1,000 miles, arriving before the beginning of the airshow is problematic. Sometimes the airshows extend until later. Rather than flying the holding pattern waiting for the conclusion of the daily airshow, I prefer to land at a small nearby airport, refuel, and fly the short trip to Oshkosh when notified of clearance. Many others do too. Like a swarm of insects circling a nearby lake, we wait for a space between aircraft heading toward the airport and line up. Two approaches are usually active, one for the low and slow, and another for faster aircraft.

"Follow the railroad tracks and listen for someone to tell you to waggle your wings."

What railroad tracks? All I can see is a line of trees. That's it.

"V-tail Bonanza, rock your wings. (pause) Good wing rock, you follow the Baron for runway two seven, change to tower frequency."

The ground track is easy to follow. Once on downwind leg, tower tells me, "V-tail make close in base leg, land on the orange dot. Baron ahead landing on the green dot."

As many as three aircraft may be landing at the same time, on the same runway, at different points on it. A good trick, normally illegal, it seems to work there.

In years past, I was instructed to clear the runway by turning onto the grass as soon as speed permits. Recently I have been allowed

42. AirVenture

to roll out to a paved taxiway. I suspect that the spate of collapsed nose landing gear accidents happened partially as a result of pilots' premature turn onto the grass. Directed by some of the 5,000 volunteers, taxi and parking is tightly controlled.

Days are filled with airshows of aircraft doing seemingly impossible maneuvers, walking among the parked aircraft, and vendors selling everything even remotely related to aviation. Most civilian aircraft that have ever been built are represented. Rare indeed is the missing model.

It is impossible to adequately describe. I recommend the event to everyone. Inspirational to the young, nostalgic to the "mature," and informative to the curious, it has something for everyone. Few venues offer such an incisive view of the year-to-year changes in aviation. Not only can one experience the innovations since last year, but encounter examples of change spanning the entire life of American aviation.

Don and Doolittle Raider, Dick Cole at his book signing

43. Go Late, Leave Early

Early on, that was my mantra for dealing with simulators. I hated them. They rarely flew remotely like the aircraft, and frequently failed to function at all. Most of all, a simulator flight meant being tested. A typical flight meant dealing with simulated engine fires, engine failures on takeoff, system failures, dangerous weather, and other stressful situations. No one would volunteer for such punishment.

However, the effectiveness of simulators in aviation training has been proven since Orville and Wilbur's time. Not only do they allow practicing dangerous emergencies safely, but their operating cost is much lower than training in aircraft.

Even in the primitive simulators of the 1960s and 1970s, the ability to freeze and discuss and back up and repeat offered learning opportunities unavailable in the aircraft. Realistic training in the aircraft conflicted with safety concerns. Air Force and airline training accidents far outnumbered operational mishaps during that period. Simulated flameout approaches in fighters and engine failures on takeoffs in airliners raise questions as to the amount of acceptable risk in realistic training.

A Boeing 777 costs about $10,000 per flight hour. A Boeing 777 simulator costs about a tenth of that. A tour of any major airline's simulator facility makes one wonder how that could be so cheap. Modern full-motion, Level D simulators require mountains of com-

43. Go Late, Leave Early

puters, dozens of technicians, and simulator cabs on hydraulic jacks swaying with their victims inside.

From flight training devices (FTDs) to Level D simulators, their complexity and sophistication determine the privileges that may be granted from training and testing in each type.

FTDs greatly enhance the learning experience with respect to systems knowledge. The marginal cost for one to sit (sometimes alone) and learn where the switches are located and what lights are associated with them is practically zero.

As described in Chapter 26, I received my airline transport pilot license for the 737 without ever having been tested in the aircraft. After flying about 25 hours with a line check airman (on revenue flights), I was granted full privileges.

Advances in simulator technology represent huge financial savings for all operators of sophisticated aircraft. Have you seen any two-seat F-35s? There aren't any. How could the Air Force allow a pilot who has never flown one climb into an $89-million aircraft and fly alone? That is because that pilot is already experienced in similar aircraft, and especially because the simulators are so very sophisticated. The visual representations of flight are of such high fidelity that physiological measurements of the pilots reflect the stress of actual combat. Except for the vertical G-loads, the experience is remarkably realistic. The transverse acceleration one feels when power is applied is felt in the simulator by the pilot because the entire cab is tilted up. The high vertical G loads of combat be can simulated only in centrifuges.

In a recent briefing, I was shown how the future USAF trainer, the T-7 Redhawk, can be configured with software to imitate the flying characteristics of many different fighter aircraft. This training evolution further suggests that when that pilot climbs into our (the taxpayers') F-35 for the first time, she will be ready.

Since we don't pull many Gs in airliners, the Level D 777 simulator is nearly perfectly realistic. Pushback, engine start, taxi, takeoff, and landing are indistinguishable from reality. Line-oriented flight training (LOFT) began in the 1990s as a real-time training tool for aircrews. During a LOFT flight, realistic abnormal situations are presented to the crews and processed in real time. This is in sharp contrast to earlier techniques which called for multiple simultaneous emergencies designed to determine just how much load the pilots could handle. Crew procedures, system knowledge, and decision making are discussed at the end of the simulated flight. Measurements of the effectiveness and efficiency of LOFT training have shown favorable results.

At the end of my last simulator flight in the 777, my instructor congratulated me on the end of my career, and asked if I wanted to have a little fun with the simulator.

"Would you like to land on an aircraft carrier or fly under a bridge?" he asked.

"No thanks, this thing is so real that it would just give me nightmares," I said.

44. Childhood's End

I remember talking to air traffic control (ATC) controllers back when I was a student pilot. I landed from my first solo flight into a big city airport at San Antonio International Airport when I was 16. After landing, I turned off the runway in the wrong direction. After a few more turns, I was taxi-lost, on the wrong frequency, and worried. The calm voice on the radio advised me that everything was going to be okay.

I completely trusted ATC in those days, and for good reason. I was only a student and they were fully certified controllers who talked to those Godlike, superhuman airline pilots. They skillfully managed to shuffle my slow-flying puddle-jumper in with the jets. Their communications were flawless. They were wise, understanding, cool, firm, and trustworthy; a father image.

As my flying skills matured, my relationship with ATC changed. I became a system user, rather than the trainee.

ATC changed too. During the PATCO strike of 1981, when air traffic controllers went on strike, safety became diminished. I remember flying soon after the strike. ATC made lots of mistakes. I remember conversations like this:

"Uh, Approach…we usually are cleared to four thousand here. Do you really want us to go down to three?"

"Oops, descend to four thousand."

Today, we typically fly sophisticated aircraft into large, well-equipped airports using autopilots, and are told exactly what to do by ATC. After all, in this high-volume air traffic environment, there just is not enough time available on the frequencies to question a controller.

This is unacceptable; we must discard the notion from our aviation childhood that controllers are to be obeyed at any cost. Today, controller errors are so rare that we rarely question a clearance. However, our having eyes on the environment contributes an insight sometimes unavailable to the controller. A common understanding of weather, potential runway incursions, aircraft emergencies, and garbled clearances must be shared. The busy controller rattling nonstop clearances on a crowded frequency leaves little chance for questioning a clearance.

Controller to Pilot Data Link Communication (CPDLC) has vastly improved communications and safety. Although not fully implemented for domestic operations, every small step is a blessing.

The downside will be the loss of the party line, the eavesdropping of the communications between other aircraft and ATC. I believe that the improved precision in communication is worth that loss. After all, we still have voice communication available for verification or questions.

If we have any doubts as to the meaning of any communication with ATC, we are obligated to take the time to make it crystal clear. What is your image of a controller? If you see an infallible person there, then your situational awareness may be inadequate. They are human, and a little more so than they used to be.

44. Childhood's End

Our childhood is over in this respect. When we were student pilots, the airline pilots were old and always sounded so bored on the radio. Now they are young and enthusiastic like us.

45. THE YEAR 2053

The sesquicentennial of American powered flight may pass unnoticed. Perhaps, like nomads, we will have consumed the planet's local resources and moved on. More optimistically, we could be in the next golden age of aviation. Looking forward to the end of the third semicentennial of American aviation, what can we expect?

Safety

Airline fatal accidents have steadily decreased in the second fifty years of American aviation. According to the Bureau of Transportation Statistics, the airline fatal accident rate in 1960 registered 44.159 per 100,000 flight hours. By 2019, that had steadily decreased to 0.044, with the sharpest decrease happening in the late 1980s. Most of the things that can kill us have been corrected; controlled flight into terrain (CFIT), midair collisions, gross navigation errors, structural failures, and engine failures have become so rare that an occurrence becomes headline news.

Will the year 2053 enjoy even better safety? More traffic means more total risk. However, the accident rate stands to benefit from improved jet engine reliability. Of the few accidents and incidents in the last few years, structural engine failure has been at the top of the list. Improving the performance of high-temperature metal alloys will reduce the spate of compressor blade and turbine blade failures.

45. The Year 2053

General aviation has made significant strides in improving safety. Not the least of the innovations has been the Ballistic Recovery System™ (BRS), or Whole Aircraft Recovery Parachute System which enables a stricken aircraft to deploy and descend under a large parachute. Over 30,000 aircraft have received this system; manufacturers claim that over 440 lives have been saved. What may become a threat to pilot job security is a recent development by Garmin called the HomeSafe™ Autoland System. Once activated, it can land the aircraft completely autonomously. Designed for aircraft with sophisticated autopilots, its primary market will be operators of turbine-powered aircraft.

I believe that the remarkable reduction in accident rates since 1990 is mostly due to the human factors' effort to reduce pilot error. The harmonious interaction between humans and their automation will follow the favorable trajectory of today. For example, predicting turbulence from the airborne radar remains somewhat of a mystical art today. In the future, more accurate turbulence prediction by electronic means will surely enhance safety and comfort.

Comfort

Lie-flat seats now available on long flights enable well-rested arrivals. Many of us have squirmed in a coach seat on a long flight, wishing for a bed and rest. By 2053, the traveling public will demand such comforts. As engines become more efficient, breathing air recirculation ratios will be lower, cabin altitudes will be lower, and noise may be insignificant.

Propulsion

Electric jets: unlikely. Energy density, or the amount of energy for a given weight, prohibits battery-powered long-range aircraft. Unlike autos, aircraft must be light to perform. A 4,600-pound Tesla with a 400-mile range might be a little sluggish, but an equivalent battery-powered aircraft will not fly. Also weighing in is the fuel burn factor. In the latter part of a long flight, a 777 is 100,000 pounds lighter than when it took off. The lighter aircraft can fly much more efficiently. We will not be throwing spent batteries overboard. Barring a nuclear breakthrough, synthetic kerosene, or some other new high-energy-density source, we will remain stuck with noisy, polluting jet engines for a while.

Aircraft

Do not hold your breath for a $100 ticket on a supersonic jet. Although a few supersonic aircraft are being proposed, few will overcome the economic barriers. The Concorde proved that one must be in a helluva hurry to pay the price of dragging a Mach 2 shock wave across the ocean. Perhaps as electric cars proliferate, a lesser demand for fossil fuels will enable aircraft to burn less expensive fuel. If the price of jet fuel ever decreases to 65 cents a gallon again, I recommend buying a T-33 or maybe a T-38 for the adventurous traveler.

Epilogue

The first fifty years of American aviation brought change at a rate unprecedented in the history of mankind. From the Wright Brothers Flyer to the supersonic fighters of the 1950s, advances in structures, propulsion, and aerodynamics took "giant leaps for mankind."

The second fifty years, while dramatic in space explorations, might be considered more of a refinement process in aviation. Modern jet engines have become lighter, quieter, and more powerful than could have been anticipated long ago. Aircraft structures, using computer-aided design techniques, new metal alloys, and resin-filament materials have made aircraft lighter and thus more efficient. Due to advances in aerodynamics, modern fighters and transport aircraft are able to fly fast and land slowly.

The Global Positioning System, reliable digital avionics, and satellite communication, although technical innovations, have ushered in a profound change in the way humans fly their aircraft. GPS has reduced the pilot workload by orders of magnitude. Even the smallest aircraft of today likely carry a portable GPS device enabling the pilot to achieve situational awareness at a high level. Orientation using water tower fly-bys, eastward-facing tombstones, and celestial star-shots have vanished into the past. Reliable digital avionics have reduced spatial disorientation accidents with attitude heading reference systems (AHRS) with near-zero failure rates. The "It's only a bad gauge, we don't really have a problem," solution has disappeared. If the caution and warning system announces a problem, its validity is reliable.

Human factors in aviation has evolved apace with technical innovation. The age of "iron men flying iron airplanes" has passed. No longer the courageous, godlike men able to perform impossible maneuvers, modern men and women pilots are considered skillful and dedicated, but capable of human error. The disciplines of error trapping and error mitigation acknowledge human fallibility.

Automation in the cockpit has enhanced safety. From the mistrust and disuse of the 1950s to its reliable assistance today, pilots continue to debate the proper level of automation. Can a pilot become complacent or rusty from the overuse of automation? Do efficiencies demand the use of the automation constantly? The July 2013 crash of Asiana Airlines at San Francisco suggests that pilots must practice manual flying skills. Contributing to the debate is the near-perfect safety record of fully automated landings.

James Reason pioneered the "swiss cheese model," an illustrative representation of a much more complex process. In his model, all components of a safe flight such as design, manufacture, operations, and pilots have the opportunity to prevent an accident, each layer being able to prevent an accident unless the threat passes through a hole. Only when all of the holes line up, symbolizing a failure of all these components, does an accident happen.

As late as the 1960s, pilots, being the last possible ones to prevent an accident, frequently bore responsibility for accidents more likely caused by manufacture, design, or maintenance. Much like blaming the police for society's systemic failures, scapegoating the pilots after an accident was the cheapest solution to manufacturer or airline errors. This practice has become a thing of the past, thanks to an enlightened NTSB. The "Miracle on the Hudson" accident investigation and public hearing dramatized the human ability to properly analyze a complex situation. A true human save.

Most of the threats of the 1950s have been reduced or eliminated. Traffic collision avoidance systems (TCAS) virtually eliminated midair collisions. Landing accidents have become statistically insignificant thanks to Ground Proximity Warning Systems (GPWS). Combatting Controlled Flight Into Terrain (CFIT), Terrain Awareness Warning Systems (TAWS) have emerged. GPS and satellite data have rendered gross navigation errors to the past. Mature design and manufacturing techniques have (with proper maintenance) almost eliminated catastrophic structural and system failures.

Perhaps humans remain the most serious threat to aviation safety. However, the synergy created by the proper assignment of the roles of humans in concert with automation promises to further reduce risk.

"Before-takeoff check, please," I say.

The first officer reads the challenge and response to most of the items. I respond only to the flaps and window challenge.

"Delta five five, you are cleared for takeoff," says Atlanta tower.

As I push the throttles up, I can hear the engines, 50 feet behind me, make their characteristic whine and a few whooshes as the pneumatic valves modulate.

Lining up on the runway centerline, I ask, "Is everybody ready?" They are.

As I stand the throttles up to allow the engines to stabilize before applying takeoff power, I am mindful of the effort that has brought us to this moment. Not only does 100-plus years of progress and sacrifice pave our way, but recently, the rigorous training of four pilots in the cockpit. Equally important are 14 highly trained flight attendants in the cabin, intense maintenance procedures, reservation agents, baggage handlers, and gate agents. There are many more, but it's time to fly.

This flight to Tokyo Narita weighs 636,000 pounds. The runway allowable weight limit is 653,000 pounds—lots of slack. I press the TO/GA (takeoff/go around) button on the front side of the left throttle. The throttles automatically advance to takeoff power; the engine pressure ratio gauge needles slip perfectly into their target bugs; the engine noise increases slightly in pitch and volume. At 50 knots, I have an effective rudder.

At 80 knots, the first officer says, "Eighty knots, engine instruments checked." Any minor system warnings will now be inhibited by the Engine Indication and Crew Alerting System (EICAS). The engines began to growl, rather than whine as the fans reach speed. We now have 180,000 pounds of thrust pushing us into the sky. In the next 20 seconds I earn my pay. Between 80 knots and takeoff decision speed (V1) minus 6 knots, I must decide whether or not to abort the takeoff.

It's much like approaching a green light at speed in your car. Looking for the light to change to yellow, as you approach the point beyond which you cannot stop, the decision becomes more difficult.

"V1, VR," says the first officer. Whew.

With a little back pressure, the nose lifts off, soon followed by the mains.

Epilogue

"Positive rate," says the first officer.

"Gear up, please, heading select," I say. Flying at takeoff safety speed (V2), I wait for 1,000 feet above the ground.

At 1,000 feet, I say, "Flaps up, V-nav," and the throttles reduce to climb power. The engines lower their pitch and loudness, as if to relax a little after a strenuous takeoff. The weather is good, the airplane is performing well, I feel great. We are taking almost 300 happy people to a place that they want to be. What could be better than that?

INDEX

48th Fighter Interceptor Squadron 61, 73
48th FIS 63, 73, 79
57th Fighter Interceptor Squadron 84
111 Fighter Interceptor Squadron 197
111 FIS 83

A

AAA 338
ACARS 287
ACI 279
ACSL 239
ACT 27, 74
ADC 45, 73, 74, 77, 192
ADIZ 92, 109, 201
Adolla 112, 113, 114, 149
ADS-B 296, 367
ADTAC 45
ADWC 55
Aerospace Defense Command 45, 73
AFIT 195
AFRTS 92, 162
Agrarian Land Reform 23
AIM 58, 62, 136, 139
AIM-4 58, 62
Air Combat Tactics 27
Air Traffic Control 20, 283, 305, 380, 409
AirVenture 403
Akureyri 107
Alger
  Harry 259
Algranti
  Joe 212

INDEX

ALPA 252, 253, 254, 257, 261, 269, 289, 290, 292, 321, 322, 323, 324, 326, 327, 330, 334, 368, 372, 401
AMARG 71
Anderson
  Niel 354, 389
Apache 150 25
APU 310, 361
AQP 263
ARC 131, 323
Arroyo
  Carlos 325
Artesia 376
Asiana 35, 416
ASRS 230, 290, 293, 294
ATA 323, 324
ATP 266
aurora 96, 97, 100, 151, 309
Aurora 309
Aviano 342, 347

B

B-47 13
B-52 75, 79, 92, 103, 274
B-58 52
B-77 26
B-727 208, 210, 216
B-777 26, 35, 207, 214, 246, 320
Bach
  Richard 283, 284, 285
Ball
  Pre 265
Ballistic Recovery System 413

Bangkok 302, 303
Bateman
  Don 325
Bear 92, 99, 106, 107, 120
Bebe
  Tom 348, 349
Bell 47C 226
Bell 206L 226
Body haul 17
Boeing 737 229
Bonanza 16, 296, 388, 399, 404
boom log 41
Boyd
  Dan 234
Bratton
  Charlie 231
BRS 413
Burnett
  Jim 259
Bush
  George 82
Butcher
  Budd 102, 103, 106, 107

C

CAP 65
Caulkins
  George 91
CBPO 86
CCTS 55, 197
Cerisano
  Vinny 203

INDEX

Cessna 172 18, 31, 297
CFIT 412, 417
Chaney
  Art 398
Chauret
  Colin J. N. 43
Chertsy
  U.K. 330
Citabria 241, 242
Cloudcroft 28
Cloud-Ionosphere Discharge 309, 432
Clover Field 236
cloverleaf 42
Cobra 44
Cochran 27, 28
Cole
  Dick 405
Collier Trophy 327
Collins
  Howard 21
Combat pike 151
combat trim 160
Convair 55, 82
CPDLC 287, 366, 367, 410
CRAF 341, 342, 348
Crew Resource Management 259, 260, 261
CRM 261, 262, 263, 264, 317
Crofton
  Jack 364
Cronin
  John 84, 88, 158, 176

D

DANA 245
Dart 185, 186
Dayan
  Moshe 56
Delmar targets 154
demonstrated crosswind 373
DeStaffany
  Nelson 154
DLC 246
Doberstein
  Bruce 287
Dozing for dollars 308
Drainage Control 94, 96
Dual Pool 213
Duckbutt 142, 144

E

EAA 403
Eagle Scout 46
EC-121 112, 148, 149
ECCM 170
Echelon formation 157
ECM 48, 170
Edwards AFB 212
E&E 46
EICAS 418
ELINT 92
Ellington 82, 195, 197, 212, 213, 231
Emerson
  Malcolm 53, 55, 61, 72, 73

INDEX

Engen
  Don 292, 294
Entrican
  Bob 266, 319
EPR 95, 132
Ercoupe 24
ERISA 400, 401
ETOPS 363
ETP 143, 144
Evitt
  Martha 278
EWO 105, 170
Experimental Test Pilot School 181

F

F-15 Eagle 58
F-101 136, 181, 183, 184, 185, 186, 187, 189, 190, 191, 195, 197, 198, 199, 200, 201, 213
F-102 48, 51, 82, 97, 102, 104, 117, 130, 136, 139, 144, 153, 154, 155, 162, 192, 197, 198, 236
F-106 16, 28, 45, 48, 54, 55, 56, 57, 58, 60, 61, 62, 63, 67, 71, 72, 76, 79, 82, 88, 91, 127, 167, 183, 185, 190, 237
FAC 45
FAI 238, 239, 286
FAIP 45
Fairchild AFB 46
FCF 351
FFAR 51, 59
FFDO 375, 378, 379
FIGAT 183, 184
FIR 338
Firebee 172, 184, 185, 192

Flunt 388, 389, 398, 399, 432
Flying Kadets 20
Ford
  Mike 46
FTD 407
Fullerton
  Dan 84, 88, 89, 162

G

G-10 322
GAMA 292, 293
Garrett
  Dave 208
Garrison
  Vermont 48
Gatwick 306
GCA 69, 101, 183
GCI 13, 52, 57, 72, 76, 103, 111, 136, 140, 152, 160, 167, 177, 201
General Dynamics 55, 82, 389
Genie 58, 62, 187
Goesphol
  Fred 266
Goose Bay
  Labrador 130, 142, 165, 247, 248
Gorney
  Jeff 254, 259
GPS 31, 192, 224, 311, 367, 415, 417
Graeber
  Dr. Curtis 327, 362
Griffiss AFB 130
Griffith
  Marion 389

INDEX

Ground Observer Corps 13
Guss
  George 181

H

Haas
  Dave 323
Hackman
  Richard 262
Hallmark Aviation 31
Heathrow 306
Heimay 103, 174
Helmreich
  Robert 262
Hervatine
  Bob 85, 155
HF 365
Hill
  Tex 356
Hofbauer
  Jack 297
Hofn 152
Hofnafoðer 103
Holloman 27, 192, 195, 351
Holloman AFB 27, 192
Holmgreen
  Wrather 23
Holt
  C.C. 236
Homestead 56, 61, 63, 66, 67, 70, 73, 74, 75
Howard
  Dean 21, 22, 23, 84, 384, 385

Hudson
  Billy 58, 76
Huffstuttler 391, 393
Human Performance Committee 252, 322, 326, 327, 330
Hume
  John 202
HUPER 322, 330, 331, 332
Huusom
  Michael 395

I

ICAO 322, 329, 330, 331, 332
IFALPA 322, 330, 332
IIC 254
Inchon 304
Inuit 145, 146
IOE 208, 253, 266, 274, 275, 295
ITCZ 314, 334, 335
IWS 89, 171

J

J-4 18, 19
J-75 58
Jayhawk 39
Jet Lag Club 369, 370
Jones
  Bill 63, 67

INDEX

K

KC-97 13
Keflavik 82, 84, 109, 151, 162, 180, 273
Killian
  Jerry 82, 196, 255
Kimpo 304
King 280
  E. W. 25
Kinloss 121
Knowles
  Pete 16
Kuala Lampur 326
Kuwait City 343, 347

L

L-1011 244
LaGuardia 318
Langford
  Clancy 202
Langley 56, 60, 61, 63, 66, 73, 119, 131
Lanning
  Mike 119
Lederer
  Jerry 324, 325
LEO 378
Leuchars 118, 119, 123, 125
Lima 313, 314
Line Check Airman 209, 266, 407
Littlefield 240
LOE 263
LOFT 263, 408

LofthleÐir Air Line 118
Lossiemouth 90
Lynn
  Bart 86, 109

M

MA-1A radar system 57
Mace 139, 140, 141, 184
Mach 2 55, 59, 60, 237, 287, 414
Maier
  John 55, 127, 130
Maixner
  Jim 398
MARSA 94
MCC 57
McCarthy
  Paul 254
McChord
  Richard 41
McCormick
  Mac 193
McIntyre
  Jim 289
McKinley
  Art 25
McKinney
  Bob 302
McLaren
  David 358
MD-11 250, 300, 301, 305, 306, 307, 308, 312, 334, 342, 349, 350
Melvin
  Bill 258, 325

INDEX

Mendenhall
  Ted 236
Mercury Astronauts 80, 81
Mexico 21, 22, 23, 73, 75, 376, 384, 386, 389
MiG 62, 63, 72, 74, 354
Minden 239
Minor
  Bill, \ 46
Momeyer
  William 61
Monte 22
Mooney 21, 22, 295
Moosehead Lake 297, 299
mother of pearl clouds 309
MRO 380
Mumbai 336, 338, 339, 340, 341
Murmansk 92, 93, 109

N

NAA 286, 287, 288
Nagoya 303, 311, 373
NASA 212, 236, 262, 289, 290, 291, 292, 293, 294, 295, 323, 324
Natho
  Paul 388
NATO 92
NBAA 292, 293
Neely 36
Nelson
  Pinky 26
NESA 87
New Tigers 31
NHTSA 323

Nielsen
  Chester 18
Nixon
  Richard 63, 64
Njardvik 84
NOTAMS 303
NTSB 252, 253, 254, 257, 259, 323, 326, 417

O

O'Brien
  Bob 297
Owly Birds 211

P

P-51 43, 389, 392
Palace Chase 196
Panama 55, 58, 136, 314
Panama City 55, 58, 136
Parris
  Daniel 74
PATCO 409
PBGC 400, 402
PBI 200
Pensacola Penguins 268
Perrin 47, 52, 55, 181, 236
Perrin AFB 47, 236
Peru 313
Ph.D. 235, 252, 322
Phillips 31
Pik-20 238, 241
pilot-induced-oscillations 39

PIO 39
Piper 13, 17, 18, 25, 72, 233
Pipistrel 243
Polestar 96, 97, 112
Polk
  Steve 389
Portland 46, 300, 305, 306
Potomac 262, 318
Pottsboro 51
Price
  Alan 55, 165, 389
Pullen 391, 395, 396, 397, 432

R

Ramlo
  Orvin 195
Randolph 31, 43, 61
Randolph AFB 31
RAT 71, 144
RATO 139, 140, 184
Reagan 318
Reforma 23
Reynard
  Bill 294
Reynolds Number 191
Ritter
  Gary 233
Rivas
  Pedro 287
rocket beam 51, 59
ROE 52
Roeder

David 79, 432
Rogers
　Steve 163
Rosekind
　Mark 323
Rosell
　Sandy 351
Ross
　Eddie 241
RVSM 380, 381

S

Sabreliner 61, 383
SAGE 14, 57
San Diego 278, 320
São Paulo 334, 335, 336
SAR 179
Schornstheimer
　Bob 395
Schwinnaker
　Don 210
Schwoeble
　Bill 77
scud-running 20
Semi-Automatic Ground Environment 14
Seoul 302, 304, 305
sesquicentennial 412
Shaw
　Mark 67, 69, 85, 155
Shotgun 139
Slater
　Stanley 40

INDEX

Sondestromfjord 127, 129
Sondrestromfjord 149, 162
split S 49
Sprick 36
SSA 238
Stallings
 Ray 390
St. Andrews 124, 125
STOL 381
Stone
 Dick 252, 322
Sumwalt
 Robert 326
Super Cub 25
survival school 46, 47

T

T-29 13
T-33 27, 47, 48, 51, 63, 66, 67, 70, 85, 131, 154, 181, 192, 199, 202, 231, 351, 352, 358, 389, 414, 432
T-37 35, 36, 38
T-38 36, 39, 40, 41, 43, 49, 59, 65, 88, 193, 389, 414
T-41 31, 32
TAC 45, 61, 70
TACAN 147
Tamiami 73
Tampico 22
TAWS 417
TCAS 233, 295, 417
TDU-25 136
TDWR 253
Tehran 79, 338, 339

Texas A&M University 20
TF-102 48, 49, 50, 53, 86
Thornton
  Don 55
Thunderbirds 74, 117, 160
Tidewater Soaring Club 237
TMC 57
TOE 364
TOGA 337
Trent 362
TriStar 244, 245, 246, 247, 249, 250, 251, 259, 262, 266, 289
Truitt
  Rolland 77
Trusty
  Dennis 42
TU-95 86, 105, 107
Tweet 35, 36
TWEET 35
Tyndall 55, 59, 76, 127, 136, 167, 182, 186, 189, 195, 198
Tyndall AFB 55, 127, 136

U

UH-12C 226
Undergraduate Pilot Training 28
UPT 28, 31, 44, 48, 51
Uvalde 13, 18, 24, 119, 236, 238, 242, 352, 387, 388

V

V1 cut 26, 361
Vaile 41
  Rick 40

INDEX

Vestmannayer 103
Vientiane 303
VNAV 316
Voodoo 182, 198, 199

W

Ward
  Sam 49
Webb 395
  Gary 36
Weick
  Fred 24
Western
  Bob 62
William Tell 154, 156, 165, 174
Wilmington 61, 62, 63, 66, 220
Wilson
  Pat 257, 391
Winsett
  Gary 364
Woerth
  Duane 330
WSEM 75
WSO 199
Wygle
  Brien 230, 293, 294

Y

Yeager
  Chuck 171, 338, 355

Z

Zimmerman
 Vincent 369
Zombie 92

Photography Credits

Photos depicting US Air Force aircraft or equipment are work of a US Air Force Airman or employee, taken or made as part of that person's official duties, as a work of the US federal government; the image or file is in the public domain in the United States.

Photos in the "Flunt" chapter, such as "T-28 Climbing", "T-33," and "Don's Baron" were taken by Larry Pullen of Sugarland, TX.

Newsweek cover depicting Dave Roeder

Cloud-Ionosphere Discharge and Mother of Pearl Clouds by otherworldlyincantations.com

Photos depicting the author were taken with the author's camera by coercing innocent bystanders to snap the photos.

Author's Notes

I have attempted to explain the aviation terminology used in this book as part of the narrative. In the places where I have used insufficient detail to explain my story, I recommend the reader consult the following publications:

1. The Airmen Information Manual (AIM), glossary section https://www.faa.gov/air_traffic/publications/atpubs/pcg_html/glossary-a.html

2. The NATO Brevity Code, glossary section, available on the internet. Unfortunately, in addition to the terms that are commonly used by the USAF, this document contains codes that are useful only to other branches.

http://nato.radioscanner.ru/files/article140/brevity_words_app7e_.pdf

3. Various formation manuals. Several civilian organizations have published formation manuals. These generally follow Air Force terminology and procedures. A very comprehensive introduction to formation flying can be found at http://flyfast.org/sites/all/docs/FAST_FKG_2.0.pdf

A Final Thought

I hope you have enjoyed the stories about my flying career. Like them or not, please rate and/or comment on my book at Amazon. The web site www.aeromorphosis.com contains additional information that you might find interesting, such as additional stories, photos, and an email signup page. Feel free to correspond with me directly at don@aeromorphosis.com. I always enjoy visiting with fellow pilots and aviation enthusiasts.

don@aeromorphosis.com   www.aeromorphosis.com

www.ingramcontent.com/pod-product-compliance
Lightning Source LLC
Chambersburg PA
CBHW071812160426
43209CB00032B/1936/J